Buddha-Nature, Mind
and
The Problem of Gradualism in a Comparative Perspective on the Transmission and Reception of Buddhism in India and Tibet

Buddha-Nature, Mind
and
The Problem of Gradualism in a Comparative Perspective on the Transmission and Reception of Buddhism in India and Tibet

David Seyfort Ruegg

HERITAGE PUBLISHERS
New Delhi

Reprinted 2022 by
HERITAGE PUBLISHERS
19-A, Ansari Road, Daryaganj
New Delhi-110002
INDIA

In arrangement with SCHOOL OF ORIENTAL AND AFRICAN STUDIES

ISBN: 978-81-7026-176-6

Printed and bound in India

CONTENTS

Foreword

COMPARATIVE studies in religion and philosophy have over the years given rise to a number of questions and problems, and the very status and validity of the comparative method in these two fields have indeed often been the object of critical reflection and interrogation. This has been the case in particular where either totally different religious or historically independent philosophical traditions were the matter of comparison, even though the phenomenological method has of course proved to be productive in religious studies.[1]

Somewhat less problematical no doubt is religious and philosophical comparison within a single culture and closely related traditions. The specialist in Indian religion and philosophy for example has been accustomed to compare the Brāhmanical/Hindu, Jaina and Indian Buddhist traditions which – whatever their ultimate genetic relationships may be – have clearly followed distinct lines of development. Furthermore, within each of these three traditions, the Indianist has found it meaningful to undertake comparisons between separate currents: e.g., to name only some of the broadest, between Vaiṣṇavism and Śaivism, Śvetāmbara and Digambara, or Śrāvakayāna and Mahāyāna. Reference can be made in this connexion to two previous series of the Jordan Lectures, one by Louis Renou (*Religions of Ancient India*, 1953) and the other by Jan Gonda (*Viṣṇuism and Śivaism*, 1970). One form of comparison at least – a basically historical and textually oriented one – has thus been well-established among

[1] For recent discussions of the notion of comparative religion reference may be made to E. Sharpe, *Comparative religion: a history* (London, 1975); and F. Whaling, *Contemporary approaches to the study of religion*, i (Berlin–New York–Amsterdam, 1983), p. 165 ff. Concerning the comparison of Indian and Western philosophy, reference can still be made to S. Schayer, 'Indische Philosophie als Problem der Gegenwart' in: *Jahrbuch der Schopenhauer–Gesellschaft* 15 (Heidelberg, 1928), pp. 46–69, and D. H. H. Ingalls, *Journal of Oriental Research* (Madras) 22 (1954), pp. 1–11; see also recently W. Halbfass, *Indien und Europa* (Basel–Stuttgart, 1981). For the approach of a phenomenologist (and 'traditionalist'), see for example H. Corbin, *Philosophie iranienne et philosophie comparée* (Paris, 1985).

scholars of Indian religions and philosophies for more than a century and a half.

Extensive typological and structural studies in Indian religions and philosophies, or in the traditions of Buddhism, have on the other hand been relatively rare. Scholarly effort has hitherto been concentrated mainly on the necessary philological analysis of the texts, their pericopes and units of tradition, and on tracing historical developments and influences within India; in so doing, however, some practitioners of this historical-philological method have shown strangely little awareness of the presuppositions and pre-judgements with which they were operating, as if in the human sciences historical causality, development and influence were totally transparent and unproblematic things. Equally, the problems in intercultural transmission raised by the spread of Indian thought and civilization northwards and eastwards have attracted only modest attention. And even less work has been done on discovering comparable elements in the different Indian religious and philosophical traditions both within and outside India, i.e. on the task of identifying in terms of what has been termed family resemblances, in polythetic classification, the criss-crossing and sometimes overlapping strands that make up the traditions.[2] Yet, when we consider Buddhism in its various traditions in India, in China and in Tibet (where, in addition to strictly speaking Tibetan constituents, typologically Indic and Sinitic strands are to be identified beside Indian,

[2] The notion of family resemblance was made use of in philosophy by L. Wittgenstein in his *Philosophical investigations* (§ 67), and it has been the subject of further philosophical discussion since R. Bambrough, 'Universals and family resemblances', *Proceedings of the Aristotelian Society* 60 (1960–61), pp. 207–22 (reprinted in: G. Pitcher [ed.], *Wittgenstein, the Philosophical Investigations: A collection of critical essays* [New York, 1966], pp. 186–204). For comparative purposes in the anthropological study of descent and affinity, this notion has been employed, along with that of 'polythetic' as opposed to 'monothetic' classification, by R. Needham, e.g. in his 'Polythetic classification', *Man* 10 (1975), pp. 349–69. See also the same author's *Belief, language and experience* (Oxford, 1972) and *Against the tranquility of axioms* (Berkeley, 1983), pp. 36–65, with pp. 5–11 of the 'Advertisement' where Needham writes that 'the denotations of a verbal concept need express no essential idea that is common to all its applications' (p. 9). Traditional 'monothetic' classifications operate with the common-feature definition of a class, i.e. a class defined by the invariable presence of certain common characteristic attributes in each and every individual. By contrast, in a polythetic arrangement or chain no single feature is essential, or sufficient, for membership in the classification in which all the individuals do *not* share one single characteristic feature. I am indebted to Srinivasa Ayya Srinivasan for calling my attention to this work in social anthropology and for illuminating discussions of it.

Chinese and Central Asian components actually known historically to have been introduced from outside), the question may even arise as to whether the name 'Buddhism' denotes one single entity rather than a classification embracing (more or less polythetically) a very large number of strands held together by family resemblances. In their work Sinologues have been wont to focus above all on what is Chinese, and hence on discontinuities between Chinese and Indian Buddhism; and whereas some Tibetologists have emphasized continuities as well as differences between Indian and Tibetan Buddhism, others have preferred to underscore the discontinuities above all else.

In the following essays an attempt is made to investigate a pair of themes in Buddhist thought by considering, in historical and comparative outline, their treatment in some traditions of Indian and Tibetan Buddhism, while referring on occasion also to parallels in non-Buddhist Indian thought (Brahmanism and Jainism) and in Chinese Buddhism. The two themes are, schematically stated, 'nature' and 'nurture' in the twin realms of soteriology and gnoseology, a pair of topics that call for examination in terms of the notions of 'innatism', 'spontaneism' and 'simultaneism' as contrasted with graded acquisition and reinforcement through progressive cultivation. Connected themes are enstatic concentration (gnoseological rather than cataleptic) as against intellectual analysis, ethical and spiritual quietism in contrast to effort, and cataphaticism as opposed to apophaticism. Put in these terms, these notions are of course largely 'etic' ones of Western origin, and they require to be investigated and specified in the light of the rich 'emic' categories belonging to the traditions being considered. Since a full treatment of each of them in Indian and Tibetan thought could easily fill volumes, they can of course only be outlined in these essays. It perhaps needs to be explicitly noted also that, whereas the co-ordinate pair of theory (*darśana* = *lta ba, theôria*) and practice (*caryā* = *spyod pa, praxis*) underlies much of what is said in our Buddhist sources, praxis has perforce to be considered here more in terms of taxonomies or theories of practice than as spiritual experience and practice *per se*.[3] As for *paramārtha* and *saṃvṛti* – ultimate reality and the

[3] This specification is made explicit in response to a valuable methodological observation made by Alexander Piatigorsky.

surface level – which are also at the foundation of so much of what is at issue in our sources, they cannot be gone into separately for want of space.

The themes mentioned above will be considered in relation to the hermeneutics of the doctrine of the Buddha-nature – the *tathāgatagarbha* or germinal 'Essence' of the Tathāgata; to Emptiness of the heterogeneous (*gžan stoṅ* : **parabhāvaśūnyatā*) as opposed to Emptiness of own-nature (*raṅ stoṅ* : *svabhāvaśūnyatā*); to the contrast between 'simultaneist' (*cig c[h]ar* : *yugapad*) spontaneity and naturalness on the one side and on the other 'gradualist' (*rim gyis* : *krama*) reinforcement and cultivation – the tension in both theory and practice round which revolved, according to Tibetan sources, the 'Great Debate' of bSam yas that is reputed to have opposed the Indian *ācārya* Kamalaśīla and the Chinese *ho-shang* Mo-ho-yen (*hva šaṅ* Mahāyāna) at the court of the Tibetan ruler Khri Sroṅ lde btsan towards the end of the eighth century CE; to the notion of the *dkar po chig thub* as the unique and self-sufficient sovereign remedy which is effective against all the Ills of Saṃsāra, which gives rise immediately and all at once to Awakening – i.e. the direct 'face-to-face' encounter with, and recognitive identification (*ṅo 'phrod pa*) of, Mind (*sems* = *citta*) as it really is – and which is thus the specific 'remedy' that by itself 'cures' all conceptual constructions and discursivity of thinking that are at the root of Saṃsāra; and finally to the concepts subsumed under or associated with Quiet (*śamatha* = *ži gnas*) and Insight (*vipaśyanā* = *lhag mthoṅ*), which are thought of as making up a co-ordinated pair or an integrated syzygy.

According to the sources to be considered, the issues in the 'Great Debate' of bSam yas did not, it is true, necessarily hinge directly on the interpretation of the *tathāgatagarbha*-doctrine, which is in fact mentioned only occasionally in some of the relevant documents. And, conversely, the contrasts innate/acquired and cataphatic/apophatic in the hermeneutics of the *tathāgatagarbha* did not inevitably engage the oppositions simultaneousness/gradualness and ethical or intellectual quietism/effort. Nevertheless, the fact remains that the Indo-Tibetan problematics of *tathāgatagarbha*-hermeneutics and the issues addressed in the 'Great Debate' are evidently linked by a number of thematic strands that cross and intertwine, making up so to say lattices of ideas. And sometimes in the Tibetan exegetical traditions they have been collocated or treated in parallel.[4]

Now, in the entire spectrum of their applications, the terms *tathāgatagarbha*, *cig c(h)ar ba* and *rim gyis pa* do not appear to define a single, constant and unitary core-notion or essence. Rather, they correspond to contextually varying values grouped round these terms or *topoi*. In the case of *tathāgatagarbha*, this may well have to do with the fact that it is not a referring term for any entity (*bhāva*), but a metatheoretical expression or counter. As for the terms *cig char ba* and *rim gyis pa* – and also *dkar po chig thub* – they too do not designate invariant referents but seem rather to describe sets of features that vary from case to case; and they can be variously applied depending on their particular place in a given system of thought. Thus, while most schools recognize the *cig char ba* in some context, they may do so in differing ways and connexions, so that the specific application of this term and category can vary from school to school; nevertheless, the notions in question are bound together by a range of family resemblances.

An attempt is furthermore made here to show how, once the 'Great Debate' of bSam yas had become a partly dehistoricized *topos* in the Tibetans' later reconstruction of their (partly lost) early history, and in particular in their 'constitution of tradition', the expression 'teaching of the Hva šaṅ' has served, in the Tibetan historical and doctrinal texts, as a model or exemplar for a theory considered to have unduly stressed that form of quietism which

[4] The Buddha-nature (*saṅs rgyas kyi raṅ bźin*) and simultaneous Yoga-Bhāvanā (*theg pa chen po la cig char rnal 'byor du bsgom pa'i thabs*) are treated together for example in MS BN Pelliot tibétain 835. Cf. MS BL (IOL) Stein 693, ff. 15b, 27b–29b; Stein 710, f. 36b (*saṅs rgyas raṅ grub*) and f. 38a. See also Wang Hsi's *Cheng-li chüeh* in P. Demiéville, *Le concile de Lhasa* (Paris, 1952), pp. 107, 116, 118 and 151; and below, Chapter ii, pp. 73 and 86.

G. Tucci had at one time expressed the opinion that a substantial part of the Hva šaṅ Mahāyāna's ideas along with those of the Indian Siddhas were preserved not only in the Tibetan rDsogs chen school but also in the Jo naṅ pa school, whose doctrine was in large part based on the *tathāgatagarbha* theory; see G. Tucci and W. Heissig, *Die Religionen Tibets und der Mongolei* (Stuttgart, 1970), p. 27. Compare however our remarks in *Le traité du tathāgatagarbha de Bu ston. Rin chen grub* (Paris, 1973), p. 7 n. 1. This opinion was not repeated in the English version of Tucci's work, *The religions of Tibet* (London, 1980).

A kind of prefiguration
found in a number of Sūtras, for example in the Mahāyānist *Mahāparinirvāṇasūtra*
major source of the *tathāgatagarbha*-theory – which is itself described as a medicine or remedy.

excludes ethical and intellectual effort or that form of understanding that focuses non-analytically on the Empty alone, in contravention of the Buddhist principle that Quiet (*śamatha*) and Insight (*vipaśyanā*) – like means (*upāya*) and discriminative understanding (*prajñā*) – are co-ordinate and have to be cultivated together either in alternation or in unison as a fully integrated syzygy (*yuganaddha*). In this way, in Tibetan philosophical discourse, the figure of the Hva šaṅ Mahāyāna and his teaching have come to fulfil a practically emblematic function, one that may in fact be somewhat different from the position actually occupied by the historical *ho-shang* Mo-ho-yen. The following study will then be concerned as much with the impact and significance of the 'Great Debate' of bSam yas for the Tibetan tradition – in other words its *Wirkungsgeschichte* – as with the question of what actually happened at the discussions in which the *ho-shang* Mo-ho-yen was involved toward the end of the eighth century in Tibet.

A fundamental problem at issue is, very briefly stated, the relation between the Fruit (*phala* = *'bras bu*) – i.e. ultimate and perfect Awakening (*anuttarasamyaksambodhi*) in buddhahood –, the spiritual Ground (*gži*) – known as the *tathāgatagarbha* or Buddha-nature – and the Path (*mārga* = *lam*) in all its stages. (To a certain degree, this is also the problem of the relation between *paramārtha* and *saṃvṛti*, or between *nirvāṇa* and *saṃsāra* which is usually described in the Mahāyāna as one of non-duality.) Now, to the extent that non-duality and non-difference are being focused on, the Fruit of buddhahood is stated to be Awakened to immediately, that is, without any mediating process consisting in the practiser's utilization of means (*upāya*); and such direct comprehension could thus be described as a face-to-face encounter with and recognitive identification of Mind (*sems ṅo 'phrod pa*). Yet over-emphasis on such immediacy – implying as it would a telescoping together of Ground and Fruit – runs the risk of making redundant the Path with its virtues and perfections (*pāramitā* = *phar phyin*) – and especially the first four of them that lead to the *prajñāpāramitā* – and it would then represent less a theory of non-duality than one of monistic identity between Ground and Fruit (i.e. a theory not accepted in any simple form in Mahāyāna Buddhism). In some Buddhist traditions, the complex problem of the relation (or the description of the relation) between ultimate Awakening and means – viz. the virtues of generosity, etc. – has been treated in terms of the dedicatory transmutation (*pariṇāmanā* = *yoṅs su bsṅo ba*) of these virtues into Awakening (*bodhi*); interestingly, however, this question of *pariṇāmanā* was scarcely thematized in the documents relating to the 'Great Debate' of bSam yas.[5]

In discussing the simultaneous/gradual polarity in Buddhist thought, especially on the Sūtra-level of the Pāramitāyāna, it is essential to be quite clear as to whether it is the Fruit or the Path that is in question. Now, that the realization of the Fruit at the very end of the practice of the Path is instantaneous (and in some sense 'simultaneous') is generally recognized, and this was therefore hardly the issue. It is accordingly the status of the Path – alongside the difficult problem of the 'homology' of Ground and Fruit and the 'proleptic anticipation' of the latter in the former – that is the problem being addressed.

The question further arises as to whether, given its positive and cataphatic character, the *tathāgatagarbha* theory was a syncretism, or a symbiotic accommodation, with the *ātman*-doctrine of Brāhmanical thought – that is, in effect, a crypto-Brāhmanical 'soul'-theory in Buddhism. Or was it perhaps conceived as inclusivistic of this *ātman*-doctrine in the sense of Paul Hacker's 'inclusivism', i.e. as incorporating this 'soul'-theory in a subordinate position? Or, again, is it an authentic Buddhist treatment of a theme – and a religious and philosophic problem – which recurs in various forms throughout the history of Indian thought? A related question arises

[5] It is true that Sa skya Paṇḍi ta has referred to *pariṇāmanā* in proximity to some references he made to the (*dkar po*) *chig thub*, i.e. to a spiritual factor, said to have been assumed by the Hva šaṅ Mahāyāna during the 'Great Debate' of bSam yas, that is supposed to operate as the unique and self-sufficient factor making possible the immediate and 'simultaneous' achievement of Awakening. See for example his *sDom gsum rab dbye*, ff. 34a and 38b, and his *sKyes bu dam pa rnams la spriṅ ba'i yi ge*, f. 5b. However, in these places *pariṇāmanā* is not treated as either a bridge between, or as a factor permitting a leap from, the conditioned level of activity and impurity to the unconditioned level. And Sa skya Paṇḍi ta is evidently criticizing the treatment of *pariṇāmanā* as a *supplement* to the *chig thub*, that is, as supporting a factor that was supposed by its proponents to be already totally effective and altogether self-sufficient in achieving Awakening. On *pariṇāmanā* in connexion with the elimination of *nimitta* and *upalambha* and with reference to the *cig char*/*rim gyis* opposition, see also MS BN Pelliot tibétain 116 (125–6) and Pelliot tibétain 823, *verso*.

with respect to the theory of the Emptiness of the hetero (*gžan stoṅ*) in contradistinction to that of the Emptiness of own-nature (*raṅ stoṅ*) associated with Prajñāpāramitā and Madhyamaka thought. Are these two opposed theories of *śūnyatā* to be placed on exactly the same level and accordingly to be treated as incompatible and mutually exclusive? Or are they complementary in the sense that they somehow supplement each other? Or, again, are they perhaps simply incommensurable (somewhat in the sense that this term currently has in the history of science)?

Opposed – and hence apparently irreconcilable – strands of thought are indeed to be found in our sources. But it would seem that more consideration, and probably more weight, have to be given to the possibility that the strands in question are forms of thought (and techniques) existing as polarities in tension between which the Buddhist traditions have from early times felt the need to strike a balance, rather than necessarily contradictory doctrines (and incompatible techniques) which could be harmonized only artificially and superficially, by some stratagem such as 'inclusivism'.

Some aspects of the proto-history of the opposition between 'simultaneist innatism' – expressed in mystical or cataphatic terms – on the one side and analytical, and gradualist, cultivation – expressed in terms of intellection or apophaticism – on the other side have been recently addressed by Lambert Schmithausen, who has distinguished between 'positive-mystical' and 'negative-intellectualist' conceptions of liberation and Awakening in earlier Buddhist canonical sources.[6] Similarly, in a recent publication by Paul Griffiths, the analysis of Buddhist meditation is based on an antithesis between the mystical-enstatic and the intellectual-analytical,[7] with the Attainment of Cessation (*nirodhasamāpatti*) even being compared with cataleptic trance.[8]

[6] See L. Schmithausen, 'On some aspects of descriptions or theories of 'liberating insight' and 'enlightenment' in Early Buddhism', in: K. Bruhn and A. Wezler (eds.), *Studien zum Jainismus und Buddhismus: Gedenkschrift für Ludwig Alsdorf* (Wiesbaden, 1981), pp. 199–250, especially p. 214 ff. To these two trends Schmithausen (p. 218 f.) has added the 'Saṃjñāvedayitanirodha-Liberation theory' in which the progressive *anupūrvavihāra* pattern covers nine successive stages beginning with the first Dhyāna and continuing through a stage where notions and feelings come to a stop.

[7] P. J. Griffiths, *On being mindless: Buddhist meditation and the mind-body problem* (La Salle, 1986).

[8] Griffiths, *op. cit.*, p. 11, describes the *nirodhasamāpatti*-theory as 'even more radical in its rejection of mental activity than are the dominant Western models for the understanding

The question thus again arises as to how these currents found in Sūtra-Buddhism, in fundamental classical Śāstras and in later Indian and Tibetan sources in fact relate to each other. Are they to be regarded as altogether heterogeneous and antithetical in the sense of being incompatible and mutually exclusive? And was the attempt to reconcile and harmonize the 'positive-mystical' with the 'negative-intellectualist', as found already in some earlier texts, 'inclusivistic' in Hacker's sense, as has been suggested by Schmithausen?[9] Or are they rather strands making up the whole fabric of Buddhist theory and practice, and standing in a structural relation of complementarity, with emphasis being placed sometimes on the one and sometimes on the other, whereas the two are in actuality considered to be required to supplement, and to reinforce, each other?

When analysing the textual pericopes and units of tradition identifiable in the literature of Buddhism, it will be useful to examine them not only in terms of historical stratification and chronological accretion of earlier and later textual matter, and of possible attempts made subsequently to reconcile and harmonize incompatible elements, but also in terms of a synchronic and structural co-ordination, motivated by considerations of a philosophical or meditative kind, of distinct but still complementary

of catalepsy'. See also Schmithausen, *op. cit.*, p. 223. However, Buddhist tradition seems usually to have regarded that form of exclusively concentrative enstasis that amounts to catalepsy as characteristic not of the supramundane (*lokottara*) *bhāvanā* of the Samāpattis but of the mundane (*laukika*) *bhāvanāmarga* alone. On this often neglected distinction see Chapter iv below.

[9] Schmithausen, *op. cit.*, pp. 223 and 230. Schmithausen has defined Hacker's 'inclusivism' as 'a method of intellectual debate in which the competing doctrine, or essential elements of it, are admitted but relegated to a subordinate position, or given a suitable reinterpretation, and which aims not so much at reconciliation but at prevailing over the other doctrine or its propounders' (p. 223). And he adds that this 'inclusivistic' tendency 'is especially conspicuous in a few texts belonging to the '"negative-intellectual" current' (p. 223).

The question arises in thi

trends continue two genetically different traditions – one a rigoristic, ascetic and suppressive tradition attested e.g. in connexion with the Buddhist Samāpattis and Vimokṣas, but nevertheless of non-Buddhist origin, and the other the authentic Buddhist meditation in which insight plays a major part, and which is characteristic of Buddhist mindfulness, the Dhyānas and the realization of the four *satyas*. See J. Bronkhorst, *The two traditions of meditation in Ancient India* (Stuttgart, 1986). Bronkhorst's treatment of the relevant material is not infrequently based on unexplicated or unexamined (and anything but self-evident) presuppositions about 'contradictions' in the traditions. (See e.g. the review by S. Collins, *Journal of the Royal Asiatic Society*, 1987, pp. 373–5.)

(or, perhaps, incommensurable) currents. In other words, we may be faced here not just with historically heterogeneous and logically incompatible elements artificially, or even forcibly, brought together in the course of diachronic stratification reflected in text-historical layers, but also by currents in synchronic tension and structural contrast.

Not only for Kamalaśīla but also for his Sūtra and Śāstra sources the synergistic co-ordination of *śamatha* and *vipaśyanā* in a syzygy is no more a mere artifice, or a case of inclusivistic subordination, than is the co-ordination of salvific means (*upāya*) and discriminative knowledge (*prajñā*), of Compassion (*karuṇā*) and Emptiness (*śūnyatā*), etc. In many classical periods of the Buddhist tradition it is indeed precisely this co-ordination of polarities that constitutes the specific character of theory and practice.

The relation between a positive or mystical current and a negative or analytical one – for example a cataphatic approach and positive theory and an apophatic approach and negative theory concerning insight and Awakening – or between the Emptiness of the heterogeneous (*gžan stoṅ*) and the Emptiness of own-nature (*raṅ stoṅ*) theories of *śūnyatā* and the *tathāgatagarbha* can provide the comparativist with interesting and methodologically instructive cases of opposed theories and approaches existing in tension. Certain Buddhist traditions have regarded the first pair – attested respectively in the 'scholastic corpus' (*rigs tshogs*) and the 'hymnic corpus' (*bstod tshogs*) both ascribed to the same Nāgārjuna – as complementary (or, perhaps, as incommensurable in the sense mentioned above). But other traditions have subordinated one theory to the other, regarding the subordinate one as intentional (*ābhiprāyika*) and as representing only a provisional sense in need of further interpretation (*neyārtha*) and the superordinate theory as corresponding accordingly to the definitive and ultimately intended sense (*nītārtha*) in the Buddha's teaching. And although the latter pair – viz. Emptiness of own-nature as expressed in the 'Second Cycle' of the Buddha's teaching and Emptiness of the heterogeneous as ostensibly taught in parts of the 'Third Cycle' – has frequently been regarded as antithetical and contradictory – with the one being interpreted as *nītārtha* and the other as *neyārtha* – it may be possible within the frame of systematic Buddhist hermeneutics to think in terms of a complementarity (or incommensurability) between two theories belonging to distinct universes of religious-philosophical discourse rather than in terms of a contradiction between theories competing on the same level. At all events, a theory such as that of the *tathāgatagarbha* in the 'Third Cycle' clearly cannot be simply, reductionistically or 'inclusivistically' identified with the classical Prajñāpāramitā or Madhyamaka notion of *śūnyatā* as expressed in the 'Second Cycle'. Nonetheless, at least some hermeneuticians – for example those of the Tibetan dGe lugs pa school – have been prepared to let them stand side by side as valid teachings that are both definitive in sense (*nītārtha*), rather than treat the one as definitive and the other as intentional and in need of being further interpreted in a sense other than the obvious and provisional surface meaning, as has been done in other hermeneutical traditions.

To return now to the pair of *śamatha* and *vipaśyanā*, and to the concentrative and enstatic current on the one side and the analytical and observational current on the other side, as soteriological methods on the Path of Awakening they can be not as mutually exclusive and contradictory, but as complementary and as equally necessary for the achievement of Awakening. If one current is emphasized at the expense of the other, there can indeed emerge an unbridgeable gap between them in philosophical theory and also in the theory of spiritual practice. But cultivated as co-ordinate components of the Path, they not only reinforce each other but they are both seen in theory and practice to be necessary in order to achieve their full effect.

With regard to the gradual/sudden (or subitist) polarity as it is known in sinological studies, it may well be that the circumstance that it 'assumed its particular importance in the Chinese Buddhist tradition suggests that it resonated with, or gave form to, a similar pre-existent polarity within Chinese thought',[10] and even that it is

[10] P. Gregory (ed.), *Sudden and gradual* (Honolulu, 1987), p. 1.

a 'peculiarly sinitic mode of approaching the enlightening experience'.[11] The materials gathered in these essays nevertheless document the fact that the gradual/simultaneous polarity – *krama/yugapad* in Sanskrit and *rim gyis/cig char* in Tibetan – is neither uniquely and exclusively nor pre-eminently Chinese, and that it is in fact very well attested as a polar contrast or tension, and sometimes also as a conflict, in the Indian Buddhist traditions too. That the cultural and intellectual matrices and networks of concepts in which this polarity has found expression differ appreciably between India and China is of course no less clear, so that it is no doubt legitimate to speak of distinct Indian and Chinese developments (and also of Indic and Sinitic models in the Buddhism of Tibet). Meaningful comparison can perhaps be most fruitfully pursued in terms of typologies, structures and lattices of family resemblances.

As for the historical relation between Ch'an/Zen and the teachings of the Indian Siddhas, R. A. Stein and L. Gómez have noted that it is very unlikely that Ch'an could have derived from or been directly influenced by Indian Vajrayāna or Siddha schools;[12] and to assume that the former originates from the latter would no doubt involve an historically unwarranted 'soft methodology' (to borrow an expression used in another connexion by Gómez[13]). Nevertheless, *mutatis mutandis*, the typological parallels and family resemblances do seem clear enough for the comparativist to have to address them very seriously.[14]

The extent to which *mahāmudrā*[15] is to be seen as 'gradualist' or 'simultaneist' was moreover an important subject of reflection and discussion in Tibet. And Sa skya Paṇḍi ta for one considered what

[11] Tu Wei-ming, 'Afterword: Thinking of "enlightenment" religiously', in: P. Gregory (ed.), *op. cit.*, p. 448.

[12] R. A. Stein, 'Illumination subite ou saisie simultanée: Note sur la terminologie chinoise et tibétaine', *Revue de l'histoire des religions* 179 (1971), pp. 5–6, who concludes: 'Si on se décidait à retenir les analogies [entre le Tch'an et le tantrisme indien ou la Mahāmudrā], on devrait sans doute songer à des développements parallèles'; and L. Gómez, 'Purifying gold', in: P. Gregory (ed.), *op. cit.*, p. 70.

[13] L. Gómez, *op. cit.*, p. 139, n. 14.

[14] And the possibility of the existence of links between the Vajrayāna and some trends in at least later Ch'an (if only in Tibet) cannot be totally excluded *a priori* either. See below, Chapter iii, pp. 122, 131–2, 137.

[15] Globally described as 'gradualist' by L. Gómez, *op. cit.*, p. 143, n. 41. But this description would not fit well the current of the Tibetan Mahāmudrā tradition represented by Žaṅ Tshal pa for example (see Chapter iii).

he termed 'Neo-Mahāmudrā' (*da lta'i phyag rgya chen po*) to have continued ideas of the Hva šaṅ Mahāyāna. Whether Sa skya Paṇḍi ta conceived of this continuation only in terms of direct genetic and historical dependence or also in terms of typological similarity is perhaps not quite certain, as is the question whether he would have himself made such a conceptual distinction. At all events he writes that the 'Neo-Mahāmudrā' he was criticizing was based on texts left behind in Tibet by the Hva šaṅ.[16] Nevertheless, that the Hva šaṅ's 'simultaneist' teaching was not unprecedented in the history of Buddhist thought is amply demonstrated by a study of the Indian documents including Kamalaśīla's *Bhāvanākramas* where much earlier canonical discussions of the point are cited. And the link between 'Neo-Mahāmudrā' and the teachings of the Hva šaṅ Mahāyāna posited by Sa skya Paṇḍi ta could then be due to a typological relationship, without a direct historical dependence having necessarily to be assumed by the historian and comparativist to exist between them.[17]

*

The essays in this book are based on the Jordan Lectures in Comparative Religion delivered at the School of Oriental and

[16] See Sa skya Paṇḍi ta, *sDom gsum rab dbye* (sDe dge ed.), f. 26a. On texts concealed by the Hva šaṅ before his banishment from Tibet, and on the motif of the boot he left behind, see the 'Alternative Tradition' of the *sBa bžed* (ed. mGon po rgyal mtshan, Beijing, 1982, p. 75), apparently used by Sa skya Paṇḍi ta also in his *Thub pa'i dgoṅs gsal* (sDe dge ed.), f. 50a. The boot the Hva šaṅ is said to have left behind in Tibet has sometimes been interpreted as a token of the future revival there of his teaching. Cf. below, Chapters ii and iii.

In the case of the 'Neo-Mahāmudrā' as well as of what he terms 'Chinese-style rDzogs chen' (*rgya nag lugs kyi rdzogs chen*), Sa skya Paṇḍi ta writes in his *sDom gsum rab dbye* (f. 25b) that the notions *yas 'bab* and *cig char ba*, and the notions *mas 'dzegs* and *rim gyis pa* are equivalent, there being no distinction in point of fact.

[17] In an article entitled 'Sa skya pandita's account of the bSam yas Debate: History as polemic', *Journal of the International Association of Buddhist Studies* 5 (1982), pp. 89–99, Roger Jackson has tried to show that Sa skya Paṇḍi ta's treatment of the Debate and the *dkar po chig thub* problem was 'simply a case of polemical anachronism' motivated by 'virulent opposition to the White Panacea and other *mahāmudrā* teachings' which he wished to 'discredit' (p. 96). Recently, in an article in the *Journal of the International Association of Buddhist Studies* 10/2 (1987), pp. 27–68, M. Broido has taken up this line of argument and sought to explain Sa skya Paṇḍi ta's critique as inspired by 'personal animosity (p. 30) against Phag mo gru pa, and as 'invective' (p. 45). Treating Sa skya Paṇḍi ta's critique in such a way as to reduce it to mere distortion, polemic and invective however results in trivializing the very real, and meaningful, problems being seriously addressed by him – problems that had a long history in Buddhism even before he took

African Studies, University of London in March 1987. In view of both the lecture-form at their origin and the limitations of space available, they do not lay claim to being comprehensive treatments of the themes with which they deal. As already noted, a full-scale history of these themes could easily fill several volumes. The reader will not therefore find here an exhaustive discussion of either the primary or secondary sources. It is hoped, nevertheless, that this study will make it possible for the reader to form an idea both of the historical, philosophical and religious significance of the subjects treated and of the major hermeneutical and comparative problems that surround their interpretation. In the notes appended to the essays the reader will find references to many of the main primary sources and to further discussions and bibliographical material in the secondary sources (to the extent that these unfortunately so often inaccessible materials have been available). These essays will have fulfilled their purpose if they succeed in focusing attention on a number of salient points in Buddhism and in indicating approaches that may be of value in the analysis and interpretation of the complex themes and vexed questions that have been broached.

For rendering classical Chinese terms and the names of Chinese Buddhist masters the Wade-Giles system has been employed. The names of places still existing have however been rendered according to the *pinyin* system currently in use in China (for example Dunhuang instead of Tun-huang).

them up. It has also to be borne in mind that Sa skya Paṇḍi ta's account of the issues raised in the 'Great Debate' of bSam yas is parallelled not only by the accounts found in the *sBa bžed*, which he cites, but also by material included in the History attributed to the rDzogs chen master Ñaṅ ral (see Chapter ii below). As for Broido's assertion (p. 42) that Sa skya Paṇḍi ta charged the proponents of the *dkar po chig thub* and related doctrines with being no Buddhists at all, the passage he quotes (in his note 67) as evidence from the *Thub pa'i dgoṅs gsal* (f. 50b2) does not demonstrate this point. In the text cited, *phyi rabs pa* is simply the opposite of *sṅa rabs pa* 'earlier'. And although it is true that Sa skya Paṇḍi ta has described the opposed doctrines he rejects in the *Thub pa'i dgoṅs gsal*, f. 50b2 ff., as neither Śrāvakayāna nor Mahāyāna and hence as not being the teaching of the Buddha (see f. 48b4), there is surely an important difference between characterizing and then rejecting a doctrine as non-Buddhist in the course of a reasoned argument about matters of fundamental importance and denouncing the holder of this doctrine as being no Buddhist at all. In its turn the description *phyi rabs pa* has to be understood in the context of what Sa skya Paṇḍi ta terms 'Neo-Mahāmudrā', in contradistinction to what he considers to be the old, and authentic, Mahāmudrā that belongs to the Tantric division of Buddhism, and which he has by no means rejected (see Chapter iii below).

The author wishes to thank the Centre of Religion and Philosophy and the authorities of the School of Oriental and African Studies, University of London, for the opportunity to present these papers, and the participants in the seminars for their observations and criticisms which helped to clarify many a point.

I

The Buddhist Notion of an Immanent Absolute as a Problem in Comparative Religious and Philosophical Hermeneutics

BECAUSE of its philosophical and religious significance in the fields of soteriology and gnoseology the Mahāyānist theory of the *tathāgatagarbha* occupies a crucial position in Buddhist thought, and indeed in Indian thought as a whole. No doubt the number of Indian Buddhist sources devoted to this theory is relatively limited: they are chiefly the *Tathāgatagarbhasūtra* together with very considerable portions of other Sūtras such as the *Śrīmālā*, the Mahāyānist *Mahāparinirvāṇa*, and some sections of the *Laṅkāvatāra* and the *Ghanavyūha*; several Tantric texts; and the long first chapter of the *Ratnagotravibhāga* with its very extensive commentary which quotes a number of Sūtras dealing with the subject that are now otherwise unavailable in their original Indian versions. The majority of the other Sūtras and Indian Śāstras of the Mahāyāna either allude only incidentally to the *tathāgatagarbha*, sometimes even with a critical intent, or they do not explicitly refer to it at all, as is the case also with the Śrāvakayānist literature. And, so far as we know, it is chiefly in the Buddhism of Central Asia (Khotan, Tibet and Mongolia) and East Asia that the problem of the *tathāgatagarbha* assumed the proportions of a controversial topic, and that it has as such remained until the present day the object of numerous discussions and sometimes even of polemics. However, the foundations of these Central and East Asian developments were clearly present in India, as a careful study of the extensive materials available readily demonstrates. In particular, the hermeneutical problems posed by the theory of the *tathāgatagarbha* are by no means unknown to the Sūtras and earliest Śāstras on the subject.[1]

In virtue of both their extent and their contents, the Sūtras treating the *tathāgatagarbha* – or other systematically related doctrines such as the natural luminosity (*prakṛtiprabhāsvaratā*) of Mind (*citta*) and the spiritual Germ existent by nature (*prakṛtistha-gotra*)[2] – are amongst the most important of the Mahāyāna. And the *Ratnagotravibhāga*, a work traditionally included among the treatises ascribed to Maitreya, is unquestionably one of the basic Śāstras of the Mahāyāna; its subtitle *Mahāyānottaratantraśāstra* indeed underscores the fact that it is a text summarizing what was considered the final and ultimate teaching of the Mahāyāna. The idea that the doctrine of the *tathāgatagarbha* and Buddha-nature is one of the supreme teachings of the Mahāyāna is explicitly stated besides in the *Mahāparinirvāṇasūtra*.[3]

Mahāyānist doctrine is mainly concerned with the Path (*mārga*) of the Bodhisattva and supreme and perfect Awakening (*bodhi*), that is, the state of a *buddha*. Now the term *tathāgatagarbha* is used to denote the 'buddhomorphic' Base or Support for practice of

[1] On Buddhist Sūtra-hermeneutics see É. Lamotte, 'La critique d'interprétation dans le bouddhisme', in *Annuaire de l'Institut de Philologie et d'Histoire Orientales et Slaves* (Mélanges Grégoire, Brussels), 9 (1949), pp. 341–61, and also the same author's 'La critique d'authenticité dans le bouddhisme', in *India antiqua* (Festschrift J. Ph. Vogel, Leiden, 1947), pp. 213–22; R. Thurman, 'Buddhist hermeneutics', *Journal of the American Academy of Religion* 46 (1978), pp. 19–39; and *Tsong Khapa's Speech of Gold* (Princeton, 1984); D. Seyfort Ruegg, 'Purport, implicature and presupposition: Sanskrit *abhiprāya* and Tibetan *dgoṅs pa / dgoṅs gži* as hermeneutical concepts', *Journal of Indian Philosophy* 13 (1985), pp. 309–25, and 16 (1988), pp. 1–4.

Concerning in particular the hermeneutical questions arising in connexion with the *tathāgatagarbha* teaching, see D. Seyfort Ruegg, *La théorie du tathāgatagarbha et du gotra* (Paris, 1969), and *Le traité du tathāgatagarbha de Bu·ston Rin·chen·grub* (Paris, 1973), pp. 27f., 49f., 73f., 114n., 122–3, 134. On Tantric hermeneutics, with which this paper will not be directly concerned, much interesting work has recently been done by M. Broido; see e.g. *Journal of the Tibet Society* 2 (1982), p. 5ff., and *Journal of Indian Philosophy* 12 (1984), p. 1ff.

[2] On the meanings of *gotra*, see D. Seyfort Ruegg, *Bulletin of the School of Oriental and African Studies* xxxix (1976), pp. 341–63, as well as *La théorie du tathāgatagarbha et du gotra*.

[3] *Mahāparinirvāṇasūtra* (Tibetan translation of the Mahāyānist version from Sanskrit), f. 195a6, and Colophon, f. 222b. Here and below, references are to the lHa sa edition of the Tibetan bKa' 'gyur. (For an English translation of a (Sino-)Japanese version of this Sūtra, see Kosho Yamamoto, *The Mahayana Mahaparinirvana-Sūtra* [Karin Buddhist Series 5], Tokyo, 1973–1975.)

the Path, and hence the motivating 'cause' (*hetu:dhātu*) for attainment of the Fruit (*phala*) of buddhahood. Even when the texts do not use the term *tathāgatagarbha* to designate this factor making it possible for all living beings ultimately to attain liberation and buddhahood, the importance of the theme of the *tathāgatagarbha* is therefore basic to the soteriology and gnoseology of the Mahāyāna.

To designate this same factor, certain texts use in addition the terms (*tathāgata*)*dhātu*, *prakṛtistha-gotra* and *prakṛtiprabhāsvara-citta*, words that have a longer history in the development of Buddhist thought. The at least partial systematic equivalence of these terms from the points of view of soteriology and gnoseology is set out in several of the scriptural sources for the *tathāgatagarbha* doctrine.

The Soteriological and Metaphysical Status of the *Tathagatagarbha* as a Problem in Exegesis and Hermeneutics

If the fundamental rôle played by the notion of the 'Embryo-Essence' (*garbha*), or Germ, and by the spiritual 'Element' (*dhātu*) of the *tathāgata* is accordingly clear, the metaphysical and soteriological status of the *tathāgatagarbha*, *tathāgatadhātu* and *gotra* is somewhat less so. While the *prakṛtistha-gotra* as the Support (*ādhāra*) for practice of the Path is evidently situated on the 'causal' level – i.e. that of the sentient being in Saṃsāra – and while the *tathāgatagarbha* is said to exist in all sentient beings without exception, the *tathāgatadhātu* on the other hand is present not only on this level of ordinary sentient beings but also, evidently, on the level of buddhahood itself. This difference makes it impossible to regard the *tathāgatagarbha* and *tathāgatadhātu* as simply identical in all doctrinal contexts.

The *tathāgatagarbha* is characterized as permanent (*nitya*), immutable (*dhruva*), blissful (*sukha*), and eternal (*śāśvata*), and sometimes we are even told that it is *ātman*. These are epithets that one would expect to relate to the Absolute – indeed, *prima facie*, to a substantial Absolute.

The parallelism between the *tathāgatagarbha* (or its equivalents) and the Vedāntic *ātman* is quite striking and it might even be thought at first sight that a crypto-Vedāntic tendency has here come to the surface in Buddhism. The *Laṅkāvatārasūtra* accordingly calls attention to the danger of simply equating the Buddhist teaching on the *tathāgatagarbha* with the *ātmavāda* of the Tīrthikas; and it clearly distinguishes between the Buddha's doctrine of the Embryo-Essence of the *tathāgata* and the heterodox doctrine of a permanent and substantial universal Self.[4]

In evaluating the interrelation of the theory of the *tathāgatagarbha* with the *ātmavāda*, everything depends on just what the Buddhist and Brāhmanical philosophers mean by the word *ātman*. For the Buddhists and Brahmanists evidently do not always intend exactly the same thing when they use this word. Moreover, even within Buddhist usage, there is a difference between the use of the word *ātman* in a positive (or *svamata*) context, as an epithet of a factor such as the *tathāgatagarbha*, and its employment in a negative or polemical (i.e. *paramata*) context to designate an eternal entity rejected in Buddhist thought. It must be observed furthermore that the Buddhist critique of the *ātman* is generally directed against the notion of an unchangeable substantial entity; and it has been remarked by scholars that the earlier Buddhists seem not to refer to the Upanisadic *ātman/brahman*,[5] and that the majority of the later Buddhists also practically ignore

[4] *Laṅkāvatārasūtra* (ed. B. Nanjio), ii, pp. 77–79. In the introductory paragraph of Ch. vi of the *Laṅkāvatārasūtra* (p. 220.3), *ātman* nevertheless appears in exactly the same context in which the expression *tathāgatagarbha-ālayavijñāna* appears in the sequel in the same Sūtra.

[5] On this point H. Nakamura, 'The Vedānta philosophy as was revealed in Buddhist scriptures', in *Pañcāmṛtam* (Śāradīya Jñāna Mahotsava 3, Śrī Lāl Bahādur Śāstrī Rāṣṭrīya Saṃskṛta Vidyā Pīṭha, Delhi, 2024 [= 1968], pp. 6, 8–12), was somewhat less categorical than P. Horsch, 'Buddhismus und Upaniṣaden', in *Pratidānam* (Festschrift F. B. J. Kuiper, The Hague, 1967), pp. 462–77, who considered that there are no references to the Upaniṣadic *ātman / brahman* in the earlier Buddhist literature. And in his *History of early Vedānta philosophy*, I (Delhi, 1983), Nakamura has expressed the opinion that the concept of Brahmā and other Upaniṣadic ideas are to be found scattered throughout the early Buddhist scriptures (pp. 135–9). K. R. Norman, 'A note on *attā* in the *Alagaddūpama-sutta*' in *Studies in Indian philosophy* (Memorial volume in honour of Pandit Sukhlaji Sanghvi, L.D. Series 84, Ahmedabad, 1981), pp. 19–21, finds an echo of the Upaniṣadic *ātman* in the world-*ātman* concept of the Majjhimanikāya (I, pp. 130–42) (on which see, however, P. Horsch, *loc. cit.*, p. 467). But it is very difficult indeed to say how specific to the Upaniṣads the *ātman*-concept mentioned in this Sutta in fact was. A recent study on the *ātman*-problem especially in the Theravāda tradition is S. Collins, *Selfless persons* (Cambridge, 1982).

the Advaita-Vedānta of Śaṃkārācārya.[6] The question therefore arises as to the extent to which the Buddhist critique of the *ātmavāda* is applicable to the Vedāntic *ātman/brahman*, at least in its philosophically elaborated versions.[7]

The Buddhist texts themselves have much of interest to say on the subject of parallels between Buddhist and Brahmanical thought. One important Sūtra, the Mahāyānist *Mahāparinirvāṇasūtra*, alludes to the problem of the interrelation of the Buddhist and Brahmanical notions of the *ātman* and absolute reality in the following passage:

> The six [Tīrthika-]masters asked: 'Gautama, if the self (*ātman*) does not exist, who will do good and evil?' – Bhagavat replied: 'If what is called "self" does [it], can one say [of this "self", as the Tīrthikas do] that it is "permanent" (*nitya*)? And if it is permanent, does it sometimes do good and sometimes evil? If there is a moment when it does both good and evil, will it be said that the self is "infinite"? If it is the self that acts, why does it do something evil? If it is the self that acts, and if [this self] is knowledge, how is it that doubt arises in a being about the non-existence of the self? Hence, as concerns the Tīrthika doctrine, the self certainly does not exist.'[8]

[6] The *Advaita*-Vedānta seems to be mentioned for the first time in Buddhist literature by Kamalaśīla in his Pañjikā on Śāntarakṣita's *Tattvasaṃgraha* (328 f. dealing with the Aupaniṣadikas). Bhāskara is mentioned, together with a certain 'Bhagavant' (= Śaṃkara-Bhagavatpāda?), by Advayavajra, *Tattvaratnāvalī* (p. 19).

On the earlier Vedānta see Bhāvaviveka, *Madhyamakahṛdayakārikās* ch. viii (cf. iii.288f.). To what extent the Buddhists before Bhāvaviveka were really familiar with the Vedānta in its Upaniṣadic sources is problematical. On a passage of the *Ta-chih-tu-lun* ascribed to Nāgārjuna – and supposed by É. Lamotte to refer to Upaniṣadic ideas (see *Traité de la Grande Vertu de Sagesse*, II [Louvain, 1949], pp. 738 and 747) – see K. Bhattacharya, *L'ātman-brahman dans le bouddhisme ancien* (Paris, 1973), pp. 133–5. On the *Daśabhūmivibhāṣāśāstra*. also ascribed to Nāgārjuna, and on works attributed to Āryadeva, see H. Nakamura, *History of early Vedānta philosophy*, I, pp. 158, 165. And on Aśvaghoṣa, the *Mahāvibhāṣāśāstra* and Harivarman's *Tattva/Satyasiddhi*, see Nakamura, *op. cit.*, p. 141f.

[7] A recent study on this difficult question is K. Bhattacharya, *L'ātman-brahman dans le bouddhisme ancien*. See also the same scholar's article on *brahman* in Buddhist literature in *Sri Venkateswara Univ. Oriental Journal* (Tirupati), 18 (1975), pp. 1–8.

[8] *Mahāparinirvāṇasūtra*, Tibetan version translated from the Chinese, vol. kha, f. 221a of the lHa sa ed. (quoted in Bu ston's *mDzes rgyan*, f. 26b–27a, and translated in D. Seyfort Ruegg, *Le traité du tathāgatagarbha de Bu·ston Rin·chen grub* [Paris, 1973] pp. 123–4).

The Sūtra then explains:

> 'What is called "self" is the *tathāgata*. Why is this so? The [Buddha-]Body (*sku*) being infinite is free from the blemish of doubt, and it neither acts nor grasps, so that it is said to be "permanent". In virtue of non-production and non-cessation (*anutpāda, anirodha*) it is said to be "blissful" (*sukha*). In virtue of the absence of the impurities of *kleśa* it is said to be "very pure" (*pariśuddha, viśuddha*). In virtue of the absence of ten marks, it is said to be "Empty" (*śūnya*). Consequently, the *tathāgata* is permanent, blissful, self, very pure, Empty and without marks. – The Tīrthikas [then] said: "If the *tathāgata* is Empty because he/it is permanent, blissful, self, very pure, and without marks, this is indeed so! And knowing that the *dharma* taught by Gautama is also not Empty (*stoṅ pa ma yin pa*), we accept and retain it." Many Tīrthikas then took to religion in the Teaching of the Buddha with their minds full of faith.'[9]

In another passage the *Mahāparinirvāṇasūtra* represents the Tīrthikas who behold the radiance of the Buddha as thinking the following:

> 'If only Gautama did not teach a nihilistic view (*uccheda-dṛṣṭi*), we would accept instruction and the discipline (*śīla*) from him.' – [The Buddha thereupon observes:] 'I then knew the thoughts of these wandering ascetics (*parivrājakas*) ... I said to them: "Why do you think that I teach a nihilistic view?"' – The wandering ascetics answered: 'Gautama, in all the Śūtras you have said that there is no self in all living beings. If you thus say that no self exists, how can that not be a nihilistic view? If no self exists, who will bind himself by discipline and who will infringe it? – Bhagavat replied: 'I have not said that no self exists in all living beings. If I have

[9] *Ibid.* Bu ston, *mDzes rgyan*, f. 27a, considered that this statement is, however, intentional (*dgoṅs pa can* = *ābhiprāyika*), the motive (*dgos pa* = *prayojana*) being to introduce Tīrthikas to the Buddha's teaching (by *avatāraṇābhisaṃdhi*) and the intentional foundation (*dgoṅs gźi*) being the Emptiness of *dharmas* having discursive development (*prapañca*) in *tathatā*, which is free from *prapañca* relating to the dichotomously conceptualized binary pair Empty/not Empty (*stoṅ mi stoṅ gi spros pa*) (the negative here being a case of *paryudāsa*-type negation). On the terms *dgoṅs pa can*, *dgoṅs gźi* and *dgos pa*, see below.

always said that the Buddha-nature (*saṅs rgyas kyi raṅ bžin*) exists in all living beings, is this very Buddha-nature then not self? Thus I do not teach a nihilistic theory. If, because one does not see the Buddha-nature of all sentient beings, one asserts the not permanent, the not self, the not blissful, and the not very pure, it is said that one teaches nihilism.' Then, after the ascetics had heard the explanation that this Buddha-nature is self, they all produced the thought (*citta*) directed toward supreme and perfect Awakening (*anuttara-samyaksambodhi*). And having at that moment entered religious life (*pravraj-*), they exerted themselves on the path of Awakening (*bodhimārga*).'[10]

But the Sūtra nevertheless continues:

> This Buddha-nature is not in reality *ātman*, and it is for the sake of sentient beings that a self is spoken of. Whereas in virtue of the existence of causes and conditions the Tathā-gata h
> there is no self. Though he has spoken thus, this was no untruth either. It is because of the existence of causes and conditions that it is said that the self is not-self. Whereas self exists in reality, it is with a view to the world of living beings (*loka*) that it has been said that there is no self. But that was no untruth. The Buddha-nature is not-self (*bdag med de*); and if the Tathāgata has spoken of 'self', this is because a designation has been employed (*btags pa yin pa'i phyir*).[11]

Elsewhere the same Sūtra explains:

> If what is called 'self' were an eternally permanent (*kūṭa-sthanitya*) *dharma*, there would be no freedom from suffering (*duḥkha*). And if what is called 'self' did not exist, pure

[10] *Mahāparinirvāṇasūtra*, Tibetan version translated from the Chinese, vol. kha, f. 137b–138a (quoted in Bu ston's *mDzes rgyan*, f. 22a–23a, and translated in *Traité*, pp. 113–14).

[11] *Ibid.* In this case Bu ston, *mDzes rgyan*, f. 23a, has explained that designating the *tathāgatagarbha*, which is not self, as self is a case of *pratipakṣābhisaṃdhi*, i.e. that this teaching was intended as a counteragent against the contempt the Tīrthikas may feel for the Dharma (because they take it to be nihilistic).

> religious conduct (*brahmacarya*) would be of no avail ... It is to be known that the Buddha-nature is the Middle Way (*madhyamā pratipat*) altogether free from the two extremes (*antadvaya*) ... Non-duality is reality:[12] by nature self and not-self are without duality (*gñis su med pa*). The Lord Buddha has thus affirmed that the meaning of the *tathāgatagarbha* is unfathomable ... In the *Prajñāpāramitā-Sūtra* also I have already taught that self and not-self are without duality by characteristic.[13]

Furthermore it is explained:

> When one sees that all is Empty, failure to see the non-Empty will not be called the Middle Way. When one sees all up to [the limit of] non-self, failure to see the self will not be called the Middle Way. What is called 'Middle Way' is Buddha-nature.[14]

In these passages the *Mahāparinirvāṇasūtra* is evidently making use of paradoxical and antiphrastic expressions to emphasize the difficulty of understanding – the unfathomability – of absolute reality, and also, perhaps, to show that the sense of a given statement depends on the pragmatic situations in which it is uttered and on exactly what is meant by the terms used in it. It is, moreover, to be remembered that any statement carries along with it and evokes, in the discursus of linguistic usage, a counter-statement. Thus, while the Sūtra certainly does not seek to defend any heterodox theory of the *ātman*, it still does not reject out of hand an absolute which may, at least provisionally and conventionally, be designated by the name '*ātman*', etc.

The commentary on the *Ratnagotravibhāga* sums up the problem by saying:

> It is to be understood that attainment of the perfection of supreme-self (*paramātma-pāramitā*) is the fruit of cultivating

[12] *yaṅ dag pa ñid* (*samyaktva* ?).

[13] *Mahāparinirvāṇasūtra*, Tibetan version translated from the Chinese, vol. ka, f. 186a–188b (quoted in Bu ston's *mDzes rgyan*, fol. 24a–b, and translated in *Traité*, pp. 117–18).

[14] *Mahāparinirvāṇasūtra*, Tibetan version translated from the Chinese, vol. kha, f. 130a–b (quoted in Bu ston's *mDzes rgyan*, f. 26a, and translated in *Traité*, p. 121).

the perfection of discriminative understanding (*prajñāpāramitā*), as the reverse (*viparyaya*) of attachment to the postulation of the non-existent self of the heterodox, who see a self in the five Groups as objects of appropriation.[15] For all the heterodox have imagined as self a thing consisting of matter (*rūpa*) and the other [*skandhas*], [but] which does not have this [self] as its nature; and this thing as grasped by them is always not-self (*anātman*) by reason of the [very] fact that it does not conform to the characteristic of self (*ātmalakṣaṇa*).[16] But the Tathāgata has attained the supreme limit of the non-substantiality of all things (*sarvadharmanairātmya*) by means of exact gnosis; and this non-substantiality as seen by him is always considered as self because it conforms to the proper characteristic of not being self (*anātmalakṣaṇa*). For [here] non-substantiality (*nairātmya*) is held to be self in the manner of 'that which is fixed in the mode of non-fixation'.[17]

From the viewpoint of the Buddhist, then, the situation is that the Tīrthikas' conception of *ātman* does not, and cannot, really correspond to their own definition of the *ātman*; and for this reason it is unacceptable.[18] Hence it is first said in the passage quoted above that the self – i.e. the self of the speculative *ātmavāda* (to which the *ātman* of the *Mahāparinirvāṇasūtra* and the other comparable Buddhist scriptures only appears to correspond) – does not exist.[19] But this does not imply that the reality

[15] *Ratnagotravibhāga*-Commentary i.36, p. 31.10–12: *pañcasûpādānaskandheṣv ātmadarśinām anyatīr hyānām asadātmagrāhābhirativiparyayeṇa prajñāpāramitābhāvanāyāḥ paramātmapāramitādhigamaḥ phalaṃ draṣṭavyam*. On the 'showing' (*paridīpana*) of *lokottaradhamas* by the counteragent (*pratipakṣa*) of *laukikadharmas*, see also *Ratnagotravibhāga*-Commentary i. 154–5 (p. 76.19).

[16] i.e. to the postulated definition of an *ātman*.

[17] The *Ratnagotravibhāga-Commentary* i. 36 reads here (p. 31.13–16): *tathāgataḥ punar yathābhūtajñānena sarvadharmanairātmyaparapāramiprāptaḥ / tac câsya nairātmyam anātmalakṣaṇena yathādarśanam avisaṃvāditvāt sarvakālam ātmâbhipreto nairātmyam evâtmêti kṛtvā / yathôktaṃ sthito 'sthānayogenêti /* – Cf. *Mahāyānasūtrālaṃkārabhāṣya* ix. 23 on *paramātman*.
Cf. *Aṣṭasāhasrikā Prajñāpāramitā* i, p. 8, for the application of the antiphrastic statement *susthito 'sthānayogena*.

[18] See also *Mahāyānasūtrālaṃkārabhāṣya* vi. 2. Cf. Āryadeva, *Catuḥśataka* x. 3ab (quoted in Candrakīrti's *Prasannapadā* ix. 12, *avataraṇikā*): *yas tavâtmā mamânātmā tenâtmâniyamān na saḥ* / 'Y lf f
ries phyir).'

[19] See above, p. 21.

sometimes referred to in the Sūtra by the name *ātman* does not exist; for in this case the term is used to designate absolute reality in such a manner that theory and definition coincide. Hence it is next said that the self does indeed exist in reality, even though one is no doubt obliged to reject the concept of a self so long as one has in mind the speculative *ātmavāda* of the Tīrthikas. But, again, a one-sided affirmation of a supposedly 'true' absolute as the referent of the term *ātman* would be no more finally correct than the negation of an *ātman*. In short, for the Buddhist, the principle of the Middle Way always remains fully operative, and he therefore eschews both the eternalist and the nihilist views.

Exegetical and Hermeneutical Approaches: Some Methodological Considerations

Obliged as they thus were by these apparent parallels clearly to differentiate between the *tathāgatagarbha* – and the Buddhist notions of absolute reality informed by certain inseparable and constitutive factors – on the one side and on the other side an eternal and unchanging entity like the *ātman* or *brahman*, the Buddhist philosophers had available two hermeneutical possibilities, either of which would permit them to remain faithful to their fundamental principle of the non-substantiality (*nairātmya*) of the individual (*pudgala*) – as accepted by practically the whole of the Buddhist tradition[20] – and the non-substantiality of the factors of existence (*dharma*) – as elaborated in the Mahāyāna.

I

One solution to this hermeneutical problem was based on the idea of a teaching given by the Buddha that is not final and definitive, but which is 'intentional' (*ābhiprāyika*) and non-definitive since its meaning requires to be elicited by explication and further

[20] The Vātsīputrīyas are an (at least apparent) exception.

interpretation (*neyārtha*).[21] It consists in supposing that a teaching concerning the presence of the *tathāgatagarbha* in all living beings is really an expedient device motivated by the Buddha's wish to attract persons clinging to the idea of a Self and thus to introduce them to his teaching, which will then free them from this clinging; or again by the Buddha's wish to eliminate in his disciples such ethical and cognitive obstacles to the cultivation of the path of spiritual liberation as a feeling of depression on the part of those who have little confidence in their ability to attain buddhahood,[22] or a feeling of superiority on the part of those who might look down on others less capable than themselves, or an inability to distinguish between the real and unreal according to the Middle Way. These motives have been expressly mentioned in the Sūtra literature as well as in the *Ratnagotravibhāga*.[23] And on the basis of the passage of the *Laṅkāvatārasūtra* (ii, p. 78) relating to the intentional and non-definitive nature of the *tathāgatagarbha* doctrine, Candrakīrti[24] and some of his Tibetan followers – e.g. Sa skya Paṇḍi ta[25] and Bu ston[26] – have emphasized the intentional (*dgoṅs pa can* = *ābhiprāyika*) and non-definitive character of a teaching requiring further interpretation in another sense (*draṅ don* = *neyārtha*). For such a teaching refers on the literal surface-level to an *ātman*-like spiritual principle such as the *tathāgatagarbha*; but it is considered to have ultimately in

[21] On these two terms and concepts in Sūtra hermeneutics, see the literature quoted above in n. 1. It should be emphasized that here the term 'intentional' is being used as a technical equivalent in English for Sanskrit *ābhiprāyika*, an adjectival derivative from *abhiprāya* 'intention; purport' by means of the suffix *-ika-* denoting 'belonging to'. See the present writer's article on the terms *abhiprāya* = *dgoṅs pa* and *dgoṅs gži* in the *Journal of Indian Philosophy*, 13 (1985), pp. 309–25.

[22] According to Harivarman's *Tattva/Satyasiddhiśāstra* (ch. xxx), the Buddha has taught original purity of Mind as an expedient because indolent persons, on hearing that Mind is originally impure, would think that they will be unable to remove its impure nature, and they would therefore not strive to produce the pure Mind. See S. Katsumata, 'Concerning various views of human nature', *Tōyō University Asian Studies* 1 (Tōkyō, 1961), pp. 38–39.

[23] *Ratnagotravibhāga* i. 156–7. Cf. Bu ston, *mDzes rgyan*, f. 19a–25a (translated in *Traité*, pp. 105 ff.).

[24] See *Madhyamakāvatāra* vi. 95 (edited by L. de La Vallée Poussin, p. 198.14–15) with reference to the teaching mentioned in the *Laṅkāvatārasūtra*, ch. ii, that the *tathāgatagarbha* possessing all thirty-two *lakṣaṇas* of a *buddha* exists in *sattvas* 'sentient beings'.

[25] See Kun dga' rgyal mtshan, *sDom gsum rab dbye*, f. 9a.

[26] See Bu ston's *mDzes rgyan*, *passim*.

view as its 'intentional ground' (*dgoṅs gži*) the theory of *nairātmya*, *śūnyatā* and *bhūtakoṭi*[27] as generally understood in the Mahāyāna. As will be seen below, the author of the *Tarkajvālā* evidently also had a similar view of the purport of the *tathāgatagarbha* doctrine.

This concept of intentionality is far from being a merely *ad hoc* hermeneutical device of some commentators, and it has behind it a long history in Indian semantics and semiotics. Already in Patañjali's *Mahābhāṣya*, *vivakṣā* 'intention to express' appears as a factor that can determine the use of a word-form. This *vivakṣā* may be either ordinary and 'mundane' (*laukikī vivakṣā*), which means that it corresponds with ordinary linguistic usage as covered by the usual rules of grammar; or it can on the other hand depend on the intention that a speaker has in a given set of circumstances and context (*prāyoktrī vivakṣā*).[28] When used independently, an expression is determined by the speaker's intention to express; but if an expression is conditioned by external circumstances also it is said to be dependent.[29] The later Sanskrit grammarians then extended the scope of this principle of intention. Jinendrabuddhi, the commentator on the *Kāśikā*, states that the determining factor in word-formation may be not only the existence of a corresponding object referred to but also the speaker's intention to express.[30] Śaraṇadeva (twelfth century) also considers word-formation to be dependent on *vivakṣā*.[31] We furthermore read in a *paribhāṣāsūtra* of the *Cāndravyākaraṇa* (no. 68): 'The determination of the desired [word form] results from pervasion by an intention to express (*vivakṣāvyāpter iṣṭāvasāyaḥ*).' Hence, according to this developed doctrine, it is the

[27] See *Laṅkāvatārasūtra* ii, p. 78.6–7, and vi, p. 223.3–4. On the concepts of *dgoṅs gži* and *draṅ don* see D. Seyfort Ruegg, *Journal of Indian Philosophy*, 13 (1985), pp. 309–25, and 15 (1987), pp. 1–4.

[28] Patañjali, *Mahābhāṣya* V. i. 16, which explains: *laukikī vivakṣā yatra prāyasya sampratyayaḥ / prāya iti loko vyapadiśyate*. Here *loka* = *prāya* is the general, as opposed to the individual in *prāyoktrī vivakṣā*.

[29] Cf. *Mahābhāṣya* I. ii. 59: *tad yadā svātantryeṇa vivakṣā tadā bahuvacanaṃ bhaviṣyati, yadā pāratantryeṇa tadaikavacanadvivacane bhaviṣyataḥ //* (comment on Pāṇini I. ii. 59 *asmado dvayoś ca*). Cf. *Mahābhāṣya* III. i. 87 (p. 67.12–13).

[30] *Nyāsa* on *Kāśikā* I. i. 16: *na hîha śabdaśāstre vastunaḥ sattaiva śabdasaṃskārasya pradhānam kāraṇam / kiṃ tarhi / vivakṣā ca /*.

[31] *Durghaṭavṛtti* on II. ii. 8: *vivakṣādhīnā śabdavyutpattiḥ*. Cf. on I. iii. 36.

speaker's intention to express that is decisive in the domain of word-formation; and the criterion of *vivakṣā* can also serve the purpose of justifying an unusual individual word-form (in the case of *prāyoktrī vivakṣā*) or frequently met word forms that are, nevertheless, not covered by the usual rules of grammar (in the case of *laukikī vivakṣā*).[32]

As for the Buddhist logicians' theory, it has beeen summed up by Dharmakīrti who states that *vivakṣā* is the cause linking word and meaning, and that linguistic convention (*saṃketa*) has the function of revealing this intention.[33]

The concept of significative intention later came to occupy a perhaps even more important place from our present point of view in the Indian theories of aesthetics and poetics (*alaṃkāra-śāstra*). There the secondary semantic function (*gauṇavṛtti*) based on transfer of meaning (*upacāra*) or metonymy – i.e. *lakṣaṇā* 'indication' – is at least partly governed by the concept of a speaker's motive (*prayojana*) when uttering a sentence. For example, if in a sentence the primary denotation (*abhidhā*) of a word gives no intelligible and satisfactory meaning, it may be supposed that its use in that sentence is figurative or 'indicational' (*lākṣaṇika*). Nevertheless, in terms of this doctrine, the assumption of *lakṣaṇā* is no mere arbitrary procedure because the following conditions must operate: (i) the primary meaning of a word – the *mukhyārtha* conveyed by denotation (*abhidhā*) – must show incompatibility (*anupapatti*) with the intended purport of the sentence in which it is found, so that the former is as it was

[32] Cf. L. Renou, *Terminologie grammaticale du sanskrit*, s.v. *vivakṣā*. See also Helārāja on *Vākyapadīya* III. iii (*sambandha*°). 1 concerning the *prayoktur abhiprāyaḥ* 'intention of the user [of speech]', which is one of the three things conveyed by the use of words, together with the *ātmīyaṃ rūpam* of the word (Bhartṛhari's *svarūpa*) and the *arthaḥ phalasādhanaḥ* (Bhartṛhari's *bāhyo 'rthaḥ*). Bhartṛhari himself (III. iii. 1a) speaks of the *jñānaṃ prayoktuḥ*. Helārāja observes that the relation between word and the speaker's intention is one of effect and cause (*kāryakāraṇabhāva*, rather than the *vācyavācakabhāva* which obtains between *artha* and *śabda*).

[33] *Pramāṇavārttika* i. 327ab: *vivakṣā niyame hetuḥ saṃketas tatprakāśanaḥ*. The auto-commentary explains: *vivakṣayā hi śabdo 'rthe niyamyate, na svabhāvataḥ, tasya kvacid apratibandhena sarvatra tulyatvāt / yatrâpi pratibandhas tadabhidhānaniyamābhāvāt / sarvaśabdaiḥ karaṇānāṃ abhidhānaprasaṅgāt / tasmād vivakṣāprakāśanāyâbhiprāyanivedanalakṣaṇaḥ saṃketaḥ kriyate /* (cf. ii. 16). In i. 65 Dharmakīrti contrasts the idea that words (*vācaḥ*) are dependent on *vivakṣā* with the idea that they are dependent on a thing (*vastuvaśa*).

cancelled by the latter (*mukhyārthabādha*);[34] (ii) then either the secondary meaning (*gauṇārtha*) expressed by a word retains only a remote semantic connexion with the primary meaning and significative power of the word and is sanctioned rather by established and recognized linguistic convention (*rūḍhi*); [35] or the secondary meaning of the word is practically dissociated from the primary meaning, in which case it will be conditioned by the specific motive (*prayojana*) the speaker has when uttering the sentence in which the word occurs.[36] In his *Locana* on the *Dhvanyāloka* (i.1 and i.4) of Ānandavardhana (ninth century), Abhinavagupta (tenth-eleventh century) has enumerated cancellation of the primary meaning (*mukhyārthabādha*), cause (*nimitta*) and motive (*prayojana*) as the three 'seeds' of meaning-transfer (*upacāra*).

To quote an often-mentioned example of such a motivated utterance: according to many classical Indian poeticians and semiologists, the words *gaṅgāyāṃ ghoṣaḥ* – meaning literally 'the herdsmen's station *in* the Ganges [river] – is a case of *prayojanavatī lakṣaṇā* or motivated indication because the use of the unexpected and semantically anomalous expression *gaṅgāyām* 'in the Ganges' – instead of, e.g., *gaṅgātīre* 'on the banks of the Ganges' or some other similar expression – has the purpose of conveying the presence in this herdsmen's station of a high degree of coolness, purity and holiness (*śītalatvapavitatvasevyatva*), i.e. the very qualities which characterize the Ganges and which are thus transferred to this herdsmen's station by means of this particular 'indicational' turn of phrase.[37]

The concept of *prayojana* came, finally, to play a fundamental rôle in Indian semiology in the doctrine of poetic suggestion (*vyañjanā*) or resonance (*dhvani*), i.e. that factor considered by

[34] According to some sources, the incompatibility consists in *tātparyānupapatti*, i.e. in incompatibility with the true purport of the sentence with regard to the speaker's intention. See e.g. Viśanātha Nyāyapañcānana, *Siddhāntamuktāvalī* 82; Dharmarājādhvarīndra, *Vedāntaparibhāṣā*, § iv. 30.

[35] *tadyogaḥ*; *mukhyārthasambandha* or *śakyasambandha*; also *nimitta*. See Abhinavagupta, *Locana* (Kashi Sanskrit Series ed., 1940) i. 1 (p. 30) and i. 4 (p. 59).

[36] Cf. Mammaṭa (second half of the eleventh century), *Kāvyaprakāśa* ii. 9; Viśvanātha (fourteenth century?), *Sāhityadarpana* ii. 5–7. On these and related points see e.g. K. Kunjunni Raja, *Indian theories of meaning* (Adyar, 1969).

[37] See Abhinavagupta, *Locana* i. 4 (p. 60).

many authorities to constitute a third semantic function additional to, and distinct from, both primary denotation (*abhidhā*) and secondary indication (*lakṣaṇā*). Indeed, in his famous commentary on the *Dhvanyāloka*, Abhinavagupta has stated that this suggestive function of words belongs to the domain of *prayojana*.[38]

It is of the greatest interest to observe that practically the same semiological concept and criteria have been applied in Buddhist hermeneutics to identify and define a scriptural statement that is intentional (*ābhiprāyika*) and in need of interpretative elicitation in a sense other than the obvious surface one (*neyārtha*) since it is non-definitive within the frame of a given philosophical system. Thus, before a scriptural passage can be characterized as being *ābhiprāyika* and *neyārtha*, its meaning must be shown to be cancelled by another teaching the meaning of which is, in a particular doctrinal system, recognized as final and definitive (*nītārtha*) and non-*ābhiprāyika*. In addition, it must refer indirectly, by a kind of philosophical-systematic 'implicature',[39] to a certain 'deep meaning' which has not been directly conveyed to the addressed disciple by the statement in question but which is final and definitive. And, thirdly, the use of a non-definitive statement requiring further interpretative elicitation in another sense (*neyārtha*) must be conditioned by a definable and legitimate motive (*prayojana*) of the speaker – in the case of a Sūtra the Buddha himself who, in virtue of his expertness in means (*upāyakauśalya*), employs an *ābhiprāyika* and *neyārtha* statement as a device (*upāya*) in order to benefit his listener.[40]

[38] Abhinavagupta, *Locana* i. 17: *dhvananaṃ prayojanaviṣayam* (p. 148 f.). Cf. i. 4 (p. 60–61) and iii. 33 (p. 441–2).

[39] For this use of the term 'implicature', see the present writer's article in *Journal of Indian Philosophy*, 13 (1985), pp. 313 and 316 f.

[40] The hermeneutical status of the Buddha's teaching would thus differ significantly from that of the Vedic *śruti*, inasmuch as the latter is considered by the Mīmāṃsakas to be authorless (*apauruṣeya*). In his *Svavṛtti* on the *Pramāṇavārttika* i (Svārthānumānapariccheda) 325, Dharmakīrti – followed by Karṇakagomin and Manorathanandin – observes that, according to this assumption of Jaimini's Mīmāṃsā school, there could be no *vivakṣā* (linking *śabda* with *artha*), no *saṃketa* and no *abhiprāya* – in other words no authorial intention – for the Veda.

In Buddhist hermeneutics as traditionally practised, there can be no question of radically relativizing the intended purport of a canonical utterance or text (so-called semantic autonomy) and banishing the idea of authorial intention (so-called authorial irrelevance)

The Tibetan hermeneuticists have accordingly identified three characteristic factors that define a scriptural statement as intentional (*dgoṅs pa can* = *ābhiprāyika*) in the sense that it is of non-definitive meaning and, hence, in need of further interpretative elicitation in another sense (*draṅ ba'i don* or *bkri ba' i don* = *neyārtha*): (i) the motive (*dgos pa* = *prayojana*) impelling the speaker (i.e. the Buddha) to give the teaching in question; (ii) the 'intentional ground' or intended 'deep meaning' (*dgoṅs gži*) not conveyed (to the addressee) on the surface-level of the teaching in question, but only as it were by philosophical-systematic implicature and presupposition; and (iii) an incompatibility between the *ābhiprāyika* 'surface' teaching that is *neyārtha* and the actually intended non-*ābhiprāyika* 'deep meaning' that is *nītārtha*. This last factor, known as *dṅos la gnod byed* or incompatibility with the primary meaning, is clearly very close to the poeticians' and semiologists' *mukhyārtha-bādha* 'cancellation of primary meaning'. And the first of the above-mentioned three factors, the motive, is equally close to the poeticians' and semiologists' *prayojana*. As for the second factor, the *dgoṅs gži* (**abhipreta-vastu*), it is parallel to (though probably not derived from or immediately reducible to) the concept of *vyaṅgya*, i.e. the meaning that is conveyed by the suggestive function of a word according to the *dhvani* theory of Indian poetics (which was itself apparently modelled on that of *sphoṭa*).[41]

Let us now return to our scriptural statements that accept *ātman*, or that present the *tathāgatagarbha* and Buddha-nature as permanent, immutable, blissful, *ātman*, etc. In order to show that

in favour of an interpretation, or 'reading', gained against the background of the reader's (or listener's) prejudgement or preknowledge. Buddhist hermeneutical theory, although it most certainly takes into account the pragmatic situation and the performative and perlocutionary aspects of linguistic communication, differs accordingly from much contemporary writing on the subject of literary interpretation and the hermeneutic circle. For criticisms of these recent trends in hermeneutics, see E. Betti, *Teoria generale della interpretazione* (Milan, 1955), and *Die Hermeneutik als allgemeine Methodik der Geisteswissenschaften*² (Tübingen, 1972); E. D. Hirsch, *Validity in interpretation* (New Haven, 1967) and *Aims of interpretation* (Chicago, 1976).

[41] For the *dgoṅs gži* see above, n. 27. And for some applications of this theory in Tibetan Sūtra hermeneutics, see *Le traité du tathāgatagarbha de Bu·ston Rin·chen·grub*, pp. 83–119, and *La théorie du tathāgatagarbha et du gotra*, pp. 158, 166, 199 n., 208, 212, 221 f., 399.

they are intentional (*ābhiprāyika*) and non-definitive because their meaning requires explication and further interpretation (*neyārtha*), it will be necessary to establish three things: (i) that they are cancelled by the teaching of the non-substantiality of the *pudgala* and the *dharmas*, which is recognized in the Mahāyāna to be final and definitive; (ii) that the non-definitive 'surface meaning' relates intentionally – i.e. by systematic 'implicature' – to a 'deep meaning', *viz.* the *bhūṭakoṭi* and *śūnyatā* or *dharmanairātmya*;[42] and (iii) that the use of the intentionally motivated statement proceeds from certain identifiable and legitimate motives such as the above-mentioned wish on the Buddha's part to attract and instruct those clinging to a Self (*ātmagrāha*), to encourage those who have little confidence in their own spiritual capabilities, and to eliminate pride based on the idea that one is superior to the irreligious and 'damned' *icchantikas* constitutionally
least temporarily) to attain liberation.

The parallelism between the semantic theory of suggestion (*vyañjanā*) and poetical resonance (*dhvani*) on the one hand and the Buddhist hermeneutician's theory of *ābhiprāyika* and *neyārtha* teaching on the other is, therefore, striking. They seem to have been fully elaborated about the same time, for the aesthetic theory of *vyañjanā* and *dhvani* was developed chiefly by Ānandavardhana and his commentator Abhinavagupta from the ninth to the eleventh century, whilst the Buddhist theory appears in well worked out form by the time of Ratnākaraśānti in the beginning of the eleventh century. The basic principles of this Buddhist hermeneutical theory however appear much earlier in the works of Candrakīrti (seventh century);[43] and its germs are indeed traceable in such works as the *Abhidharmasamuccaya* of Asaṅga (fourth century).

In Asaṅga's *Mahāyānasaṃgraha* in particular, mention is made of the Buddha's *avatāraṇābhisaṃdhi* (Tib. *gžug pa la ldem por dgoṅs pa*), that is, of that kind of allusive intention by means of which the Buddha is held by the Buddhist hermeneuticians to introduce certain non-Buddhists to the Śrāvakayāna through surface-level

[42] See *Laṅkāvatārasūtra* ii, p. 78; and vi, p. 223.

[43] In addition to Candrakīrti's *Madhyamakāvatāra* vi. 95 (already cited above), see *ibid.*, vi. 97; and his *Prasannapadā* i, pp. 41–43, and xv. 11, p. 276.

(*saṃvṛti*) reference to a personal entity (*pudgala*), such a provisional teaching being in accord with the inclinations of these still immature addressees.[44] And in his *Madhyamakakārikās* Nāgārjuna has observed that the Buddha sometimes made use of the designation (*prajñapita*) '*ātman*' and sometimes taught (*deśita*) *anātman* – in the manner so to say of the first two positions of a tetralemma (*catuṣkoṭi*) – whilst on other occasions he taught that there is neither *ātman* nor *anātman* (xviii.6). According to Candrakīrti's *Prasannapadā* these three forms of teaching are meant to accord with the mental inclinations (*āśaya*) of distinct and progressively more advanced types of disciples (*hīnamadhyotkṛṣṭa-vineyajana*). The form of teaching based on a tetralemma is regarded by Nāgārjuna as an *anuśāsana* (xviii.8), that is, according to Candrakīrti, as a progressive and graded teaching (*anupūrvyā śāsanam*) adapted in each stage to different degrees of addressees to be trained (*vineyajana*) by the Buddha.[45]

Although only further detailed investigation can perhaps determine whether the literary or the philosophical application of these semiological and hermeneutical principles is older, the fact remains that virtually the same notions have found employment in both areas. This parallelism underscores once again the fundamental importance for the history of Indian thought of its exegetical and hermeneutical methodology based on analysis of language and meaning, as distinct from particular doctrines which of course vary considerably from school to school. These methods employed by the Indian thinkers appear, then, as a unifying thread behind the very great diversity of philosophical schools and even religions.

[44] Asaṅga, *Mahāyānasaṃgraha* § 2.31 with Vasubandhu's *Bhāṣya* (D, f. 154b), and *Asvabhāva's *Upanibandhana* (D, f. 233b) which interprets the allusion to a *pudgala* in terms of an *upapāduka sattva*.

The references to *avatāraṇābhisaṃdhi* as a means of reducing the addressed disciple's terror (*uttrāsa*) in the *Mahāyānasūtrālaṃkāra* (xii. 16) and *Bhāṣya* – as well as in Sthiramati's *Vṛttibhāṣya* (D, f. 240b) and *Asvabhāva's *Ṭīkā* (D, f. 107a) – concern exclusively the Śrāvaka's introduction to the Mahāyāna by the provisional teaching bearing on the existence of *rūpa*, etc., and not the introduction of the 'outsider' by provisional allusions to a *pudgala* (or *ātman*). On *abhisaṃdhi* and related terms, see D. Seyfort Ruegg in: C. Caillat *et al.* (ed.), *Formes dialectales dans les littératures indo-âryennes* (Paris, 1989), p. 299 ff.

[45] Cf. *Kāśyapaparivarta* § 57; Nāgārjuna, *Ratnāvalī* ii. 3–4; and Āryadeva, *Catuḥśataka* xiv. 21 with Candrakīrti's comment which mentions a tetralemma based on the *ātman* notion. See the analysis in D. Seyfort Ruegg, *Journal of Indian Philosophy* 5 (1977), pp. 7–9.

It is clear, however, that so powerful a hermeneutical instrument as the idea of an intentionally motivated 'surface' teaching of provisional or non-definitive meaning requiring interpretation in a sense other than the obvious surface one, and opposed to a 'deep' teaching of final and definitive meaning, had to be handled with care and restraint – and no doubt also as sparingly as possible – in order not to be tainted with arbitrariness and disregard for a canonical corpus. Moreover, it is plain that the mere existence of a motive behind a teaching cannot *alone* suffice to justify the conclusion that it is 'intentional' (*ābhiprāyika*) in the technical sense in question, in other words that it is of provisional or non-definitive value; for any teaching at all is motivated to the extent that its author has in view an intended meaning when he communicates it. This is indeed the reason the hermeneuticians have insisted that the other two above-mentioned conditions should also be satisfied.

II

An alternative solution to the problem raised by the status of the *tathāgatagarbha* and the theory of the absolute in the canonical texts dealing with it is suggested, however, by a careful analysis of the doctrine of the Sūtras and Śāstras expounding this doctrine with a view to determining its precise position in relation to the doctrine of non-substantiality (*nairātmya*) and Emptiness (*śūnyatā*), which is generally accepted in the Mahāyāna.

If we examine the form of the *tathāgatagarbha* doctrine that the *Laṅkāvatrārasūtra* has described as comparable (at least *prima facie*) with the *ātmavāda* of the Tīrthikas, we in fact notice that it does not correspond exactly with the *tathāgatagarbha* teaching that has usually been set out in the *Tathāgatagarbhasūtra* and elsewhere, but rather with the idea that in all sentient beings there exists a spiritual principle already having the specific characteristics (*lakṣaṇa*) of perfect buddhahood, i.e. with an idea that is very similar indeed to the *ātmavāda*.[46] Thus, according to the *Laṅkāvatārasūtra*, it is this idea that all *sattvas* are *already in the full sense buddhas* that is to be questioned. But the theory of an Embryo-Essence of the

[46] See *Laṅkāvatārasūtra* ii, p. 77.15–78.1.

tathāgata usually taught in the majority of the Sūtras as well as in the *Ratnagotravibhāga* is hardly reducible to this latter idea, which the Buddhist would have to treat as either metaphorical or intentional when it appears in a scriptural text.[47]

Moreover, the doctrine of *śūnyatā* is not repudiated either by the *Ratnagotravibhāga* (see i.156) and its Commentary or by the principal scriptural sources dealing with the *tathāgatagarbha* and the doctrines related to it. On the contrary, certain passages of the Commentary on the *Ratnagotravibhāga* and of the *Śrīmālāsūtra* it quotes[48] even support a certain kind of assimilation of the *tathāgatagarbha* with *śūnyatā* (though in these passages the question of the precise meaning of *śūnyatā* remains open).[49] Furthermore, the Commentary on the *Ratnagotravibhāga* effectively disposes of the notion that *śūnyatā* could be either an entity to which to cling or the destruction of a previously existing entity. Now the *tathāgatagarbha* has been presented in these sources in a way corresponding to this definition of Emptiness (*Ratnagotravibhāga* i.154–5 and i.12), so that some commentators consider the *tathāgatagarbha* doctrine to be in fact a restatement of the *śūnyatā* doctrine.[50]

An analysis of the *tathāgatagarbha* theory in addition reveals that, if absolute reality on the so-called causal (*gži*) level – *viz.* the *tathāgatagarbha* – or on the resultant (*phala* = *'bras bu*) level –

[47] It is to be noted that this latter form of the *tathāgatagarbha* teaching, which is on the face of it comparable with the *ātmavāda*, seems to be less frequently met with. See for example *Mahābherīsūtra*, f. 181b, quoted in Bu ston's *mDzes rgyan*, fol. 6a (translated in *Traité*, p. 79). But contrast e.g. *Mahāparinirvāṇasūtra*, kha, f. 134b, quoted in *mDzes rgyan*, f. 18a (translated in *Traité*, p. 103). In this connexion, the doctrines of the Tibetan Jo naṅ pa school, and the related doctrines of other schools, pose a problem that will have to be treated separately.

[48] *Ratnagotravibhāga*-Commentary i. 154–5, quoting the *Śrīmālādevīsiṃhanādasūtra*, fol. 445a.

[49] See also *Laṅkāvatārasūtra* ii, p. 79.8–9, and vi, p. 223.3–4, already cited. The *gžan stoṅ* of the Jo naṅ pa and similar schools, as opposed to the *raṅ stoṅ*, needs to be considered in this connexion.

[50] See *Ratnagotravibhāga* i. 160 along with several of the Tibetan commentaries. On the hermeneutical tradition that assimilates the *tathāgatagarbha* and *śūnyatā* theories, and which is represented for example by the Tibetan dGe lugs pas, see *Théorie du tathāgatagarbha et du gotra*, p. 402 f.

viz. the *dharmadhātu*, buddhahood, etc. – has been described cataphatically by the positive terms 'permanent', 'immutable', 'blissful', etc., it is not because this reality is regarded as some kind of permanent substantial entity endowed with these attributes as inhering properties, but rather because the *paramārtha* is so characterized in order to distinguish it from the *saṃvṛti* level that is properly characterized by the *saṃskṛtalakṣaṇas* of impermanent, painful, etc. It is therefore thought by some interpreters that, when applied to the unconditioned, this positive *definition through inversion* of what is specific to the conditioned does not imply the existence of the *paramārtha* as a permanent substantial entity established 'in truth', i.e. hypostatically (*bden par grub pa*). Inasmuch as such a definition uses terms in a descriptive and systematic context without, however, applying them to a thing regarded as an entity having self-existence (*svabhāva*), it is perhaps what might be called metatheoretical; that is, it does not refer to some objective, first-order entity. And, as noticed above, in the context of the description of Buddha-nature as *ātman*, our texts have themselves spoken of a designation (*prajñapti*).

The positive description of absolute reality found in certain Buddhist texts proceeds, in addition, from what might be termed its *gnoseological constitution*. For these 'qualities' (*dharma*, *guṇa*) are thought of not as separable properties inhering in an entity as their substratum, but rather as inseparable (*avinirbhāga*) and as therefore constituting, or *informing*, absolute reality on the level of gnoseology.[51]

In terms of this interpretation – and irrespective of whether its wording is held to be explicit and literal (*sgra ji bžin pa* = *yathāruta-*) or not – the *tathagatagarbha* teaching is considered by many authorities to be of certain and definitive meaning (*nītārtha*). That is, according to the alternative interpretation being discussed here which has been favoured for example by the Tibetan Prāsaṅgikas of the dGe lugs pa school, because the doctrine of the *tathāgatagarbha* relates in the last analysis to *śūnyatā* and *nairātmya* it must be of definitive meaning (*nītārtha*); for following the definition provided by the *Akṣayamatinirdeśasūtra*, a Sūtra in which *śūnyatā*,

[51] This gnoseological aspect has been of fundamental importance for the Jo naṅ pa and related schools in Tibet.

ānimitta, *apraṇihita*, *anabhisaṃskāra*, etc., are taught is *nītārtha*.[52] And here, in the frame of this Sūtra's definition, the question whether the teaching is expressed literally and explicitly need not arise. Therefore, in this hermeneutical system at least, the term *nītārtha* will mean 'of definitive meaning' or 'of certain meaning' (Tibetan *ṅes pa'i don*), rather than 'of explicit meaning' (a usage that is appropriate in the hermeneutical system of the Vijñānavādins – who follow the *Saṃdhinirmocanasūtra* – and also of the Yogācāra-Mādhyamikas).

The version of the *tathāgatagarbha* doctrine found in the *Tathāgatagarbhasūtra* and other Sūtras of the same category can, moreover, probably even be regarded as being in addition of explicit meaning. For what these texts have spoken of is the presence of an Embryo-Essence (*garbha*) or Germ of the *tathāgata* in the conscious stream of all sentient beings. On the other hand, in its presently available form at least, the version of the teaching mentioned in the *Laṅkāvatārasūtra* according to which the *tathāgatagarbha* incarnate in sentient beings is endowed with the thirty-two perfectly developed characteristics of the *buddha* (p. 77) raises very considerable problems for Buddhist thought. And even though this version of the *tathāgatagarbha* doctrine is stated to refer to *śūnyata*, *ānimitta*, *apraṇihita*, etc., such a purport has presumably to be taken here as the intentional ground (*dgoṅs gźi*) or 'deep meaning' of an intentional (*dgoṅs pa can* = *ābhiprāyika*) statement having as its motive (*dgos pa* = *prayojana*) the Buddha's wish to eliminate the terror that immature people (*bāla*) feel for selflessness and non-substantiality (*nairātmyasaṃtrāsa*), in other words their fear of Emptiness.[53]

Now, as is well known, Śaṃkarācārya has sometimes been accused by his Brāhmanical opponents of being a Buddhist in disguise. In the present context what is of special interest is the at

[52] See Candrakīrti's quotation of the Sanskrit text of the *Akṣayamatinirdeśasūtra* in his *Prasannapadā* i, p. 43. Compare also the *Samādhirājasūtra* vii. 5, also quoted in *Prasannapadā* i, p. 44.

[53] See *Laṅkāvatārasūtra* ii, p. 78. Cf. *Le traité du tathāgatagarbha de Bu·ston Rin·chen·grub*, Introduction, pp. 32–33, 57 f.; and *La théorie du tathāgatagarbha et du gotra*, pp. 313 ff., 393, 403.

least partial parallelism between the Buddhist's positive description of absolute reality both by means of attributes that are the reverse of those properly applicable to the relative level and by means of characterization through inseparable constitutive qualities on one side, and on the other Śaṃkara's treatment of *satya* 'truth', *jñāna* 'knowledge' and *ananta* 'infinite' as constitutive qualities of *brahman*. According to his Bhāṣ *paniṣad*, *satya*, *jñāna* and *ananta* are in fact distinctive characteristics proper only to *brahman*, which they thus differentiate from all else. Hence these essential characteristics are not mere attributes inhering in *brahman* as one member of a class; for *brahman* – the real – is unique. These epithets therefore define its uniqueness by delimiting (: *niyantṛtva*) it from all that it is not, i.e. the unreal.[54] Despite very important differences in the philosophical background and problematics between Śaṃkara and the Buddhist philosophers in question, the similarity in the procedures and methods used to define ultimate reality is thus remarkable.

The suggestion that certain Buddhist and Brāhmanical notions of the absolute have some points of contact is therefore not unworthy of consideration. Indeed, we have already encountered some passages where the *Mahāparinirvāṇasūtra* represents the Tīrthikas as readily assenting to that particular formulation of the Buddha's teaching in which the existence of the Buddha-nature or *tathāgatagarbha* is emphasized. And elsewhere the same Sūtra goes so far as to say that Brāhmaṇa Tīrthikas have borrowed some of the Buddha's teachings and incorporated them in their own scriptures.[55] If he may be supposed to have been influenced, however indirectly, by earlier Buddhist thinking on the problem of the *paramārtha*, Śaṃkara could be a case in point.

In a remarkable passage the *Laṅkāvatārasūtra* moreover points to a certain equivalence between various names and notions of the

[54] It has been suggested by M. Biardeau that this theory of the *Taittirīyopaniṣadbhāṣya* represents a final stage in the development of Śaṃkara's thought, following on his apophaticism; see *Indo-Iranian Journal* 3 (1959), p. 100 (cf. *Journal asiatique* 1957, p. 371 f.). But P. Hacker has placed this *Bhāṣya* in the middle period of Śaṃkara's philosophical development; see *Wiener Zeitschrift für die Kunde Süd und Ostasiens* 12–13 (1968), pp. 129–30, 135, 147. Cf. also G. Maximilien, *Wiener Zeitschrift für die Kunde Südasiens* 19 (1975), p. 117 f.

[55] See Bu ston, *mDzes rgyan*, f. 22a–b (translated in *Traité* p. 113–14) and f. 27a (translated in *Traité*, p. 123–4).

supreme, which is called by some *svayambhū*, *buddha*, *brahman* (or: *brahmā*?), *viṣṇu*, *īśvara*, etc., and by others *śūnyatā*, *tathatā*, *bhūtakoṭi*, *dharmadhātu*, *nirvāṇa*, *advaya*, etc.[56] And the great Svātantrika-Mādhyamika authority Bhāvaviveka (sixth century) remarks in the chapter of his *Madhyamakahṛdayakārikās* devoted to an exposition of reality (*de kho na ñid* = *tattva*) that the great Bodhisattvas Ārya-Avalokiteśvara, Ārya-Maitreya and others revere the supreme *brahman* (neuter) under the apparently paradoxical mode of non-reverence (*anupāsanayoga*).[57] The commentary on the *Madhyamakahṛdayakārikās*, the *Tarkajvālā*, in its section dealing with the Vedānta, adds that the absolute is *brahman* (or *brahmā*?) because it is essentially *nirvāṇa* (*mya ṅan las 'das pa'i bdag ñid*).[58]

In the section of the *Tarkajvālā* devoted to Śrāvakayāna teachings it is nevertheless pointed out that the all-pervasiveness of the *tathāgatagarbha* and also the Vijñānavādin's *ādānavijñāna* (= *ālayavijñāna*) has been taught for the sake of certain persons who have not freed themselves from the dogmatic postulation of a self (*ātmagrāha*).[59] It may be that the author of this commentary (just like his later Prāsaṅgika counterpart Candrakīrti) himself regarded the *tathāgatagarbha* doctrine as intentional and non-definitive.[60] It is furthermore remarked in the *Tarkajvālā* that the proposition that the *tathāgata* has not entered into Nirvāṇa and that he is not 'extinguished' (*źi ba* = *śānta*) – an idea found in the *Mahāparinirvāṇasūtra* – would be incompatible with the fundamental principles of Buddhist thought (the *dharmoddānas*).[61]

In reply to the suggestion that, in view of parallels between them, the *nairātmya* of the Buddhist is really similar to the Vedantic *ātman*, it is moreover explained in the sections of the

56 *Laṅkāvatārasūtra* iii, p. 192–3.

57 Bhāvaviveka, *Madhyamakahṛdayakārikā* iii. 290: *āryāvalokiteśāryamaitreyādyāś ca sūrayaḥ / anupāsanayogena munayo yad upāsate //*. See also *Tarkajvālā* iii, 289 f. (P. f. 140a) (cf. *Indo-Iranian Journal* 5 [1961–2], p. 273).

58 *Tarkajvālā* viii, f. 286b5 (Peking ed.). Cf. *Indo-Iranian Journal* 2 (1958), pp. 177 and 188. The 'small fault' (*alpāparādha*) of the Aupaniṣadikas has been referred to by Śāntarakṣita in his *Tattvasaṃgraha* (330).

59 *Tarkajvālā* iv, f. 169a8.

60 Cf. *Théorie du tathāgatagarbha et du gotra*, pp. 35, 403–405.

61 *Tarkajvālā* iv, f. 169b1.

Madhyamakahṛdayakārikās and *Tarkajvālā* dealing with the Vedānta that this is not so. For *nairātmya* is precisely the absence of the self-nature characteristic of the Vedantic *ātman*. Nor could that which is *anātman* be at the same time *ātman* because of the incompatibility (*virodha*) of the two. And no comparison may be drawn with, for example, horse-nature that is at the same time not cow-nature (*ba laṅ gi ño bo ma yin pa*), that is, with a case of implicative and presuppositional (*paryudāsa*) negation rather than of the non-implicative and presuppositionless *prasajya*-negation involved in *nairātmya*. Accordingly, this *bhāva-niḥsvabhāvatā* could never be an *ātman* that is either a creator-agent (*byed pa po* = *kartṛ*, as in the theistic systems) or an enjoyer-agent (*za ba po* = *bhoktṛ*, as in the Sāṃkhya), these entities being as unreal as the proverbial son of a barren woman. In so far as a cognitive object without self-nature is made the object of thought, it might perhaps be conceived of e.g. as single and unique; but this will be a mere mental construction, which is the source of imputation (*samāropa*).[62]

It is clear, then, that the authors of the basic Mahāyāna-Śāstras were no more ready to admit any form of substantialism on the level of the unconditioned than they were on that of the conditioned: the Mahāyānist *pudgalanairātmya* and *dharmanairātmya* make this quite impossible.

Moreover, for the canonical texts teaching the *tathāgatagarbha* and Buddha-nature, the Middle Way eschewing both eternalism and nihilism remained valid. And the affirmation of an absolute or *ātman* opposed to *anātman* or *nairātmya* in a dichotomously conceptualized binary pair (*vikalpa*) based on discursive proliferation (*prapañca*) would, therefore, be no more acceptable than the purely nihilistic position of a dogmatic denial of the absolute.

Therefore, contrary to what has sometimes been suggested – and despite the undeniable parallels noted above between the problems treated and the methods used on the Buddhist and Brahmanical sides – the *tathāgatagarbha* theory, as well as the theory of the *paramārtha* with which it is connected, can not

[62] *Tarkajvālā* viii, f. 305a–b.

constitute an 'absolute monism that is more Brahmanical than Buddhist'.[63] Not only is this Buddhist theory not reducible to an *ātmavāda* – i.e. a theory positing a permanent and substantial *ātman* – but the non-duality (*advaya*) to which the Buddhist texts refer is not simply identical with the Vedāntic *advaita*. In fact, in the perspective of the theory of the non-differentiation of *tathatā* and *dharmadhātu*, there is non-duality (*advaya*) of the *dhātu* of the *sattva* and the *dhātu* of the *tathāgata*, just as, according to the Madhyamaka, there is non-duality of *saṃsāra* and *nirvāṇa*, or cf the impure (*samalā*) and the pure (*nirmalā*) *tathatā*. But the sources do not thereby posit the substantial existence of some kind of spiritual entity apart from which nothing would be real, in the sense of the monistic Advaita-Vedānta. (It is true that in the history of Buddhist thought we occasionally meet an ontological and more or less substantialist interpretation of absolute reality, and also of the *tathāgatagarbha*, for example in the tradition of the 'Void of the heterogeneous' (*gžan stoṅ*) taught in the Tibetan Jo naṅ pa school and some of its Indian sources. But it should be noted that the Jo naṅ pa theory was inspired to a great extent by the Tantric notion of the immanence of buddhahood, and in particular by the Kālacakra system; and the Jo naṅ pas would appear to have extrapolated when they applied to the original *tathāgatagarbha* doctrine certain concepts of this Tantric system. This point is in need of further investigation.)

To sum up, in Buddhist Mahāyānist thought we find both a *via negationis*, in which reality is represented negatively and ap-

[63] See É. Lamotte *L'enseignement de Vimalakīrti* (Louvain, 1962), p. 56. Comparable views have been expressed by E. Frauwallner, in *Beiträge zur indischen Philologie und Altertumskunde* (Festschrift W. Schubring, Hamburg, 1951), p. 155 (= *Kleine Schriften*, p. 644) and *Anthropologie religieuse, Supplements to Numen*, Vol. II (Leiden, 1955), p. 129 (= *Kleine Schriften*, p. 699); and by H. Nakamura, *History of early Vedānta philosophy*, i (Delhi, 1983), pp. 153–7, and 182 (cf. p. 136).

Such interpretations of the *tathāgatagarbha* and related doctrines would appear not only to have largely overlooked the fundamental questions of systematic exegesis and hermeneutics referred to above, but also to depend on a theory of language and communication in which non-referring or metalinguistic (and sometimes metatheoretical) expressions – i.e. 'counters' or 'chiffres' such as *tathāgatagarbha* and *ātman* as encountered in the texts quoted above – are treated as if they must necessarily designate substantial referents of an object-language. Such interpretations thus seem to derive not merely from historical-philological method, but also from a pronouncedly positivistic view of the world (and of language).

proached *apophatically*, and a *via eminentiae*, in which it is represented positively and approached *cataphatically*. The former approach is no doubt characteristic of the vast majority of Buddhist texts of both the earlier and later periods. But the latter approach is to be found both in the earliest texts (where we find allusions for example to an *amataṃ padaṃ* and to *nibbāna* as *nicca*, *dhuva*, etc.[64]) and in the Mahāyāna. In neither of these cases would it however seem justified to assume the survival of some 'pre-canonical Buddhism' radically different from the canonical forms.[65] The problem is surely more one of philosophy, hermeneutics, and linguistic description than of historical survivals.

Equally important, it would be quite incorrect to represent Buddhism as invariably asserting the non-existence of self and making a dogma of *nairātmya* and *śūnyatā*. While it is of course true that the known schools of Buddhism (with the apparent exception of the Vātsīputrīya Pudgalavādins) rejected the current speculative theories concerning a substantial self, an authoritative Sūtra has nevertheless warned that the dogmatic view of Emptiness (*śūnyatādṛṣṭi*) is even more dangerous than the individualist dogma (*pudgaladṛṣṭi*). And it is explained that *śūnyatā* is in fact release from all speculative views founded on discursive development of the dichotomously constructed conceptual opposition self/non-self, etc.[66] For the Middle Way lies precisely 'between'

[64] See for example *Itivuttaka* II. ii. 6 (§ 43, p. 37): *atthi ... ajātaṃ abhūtaṃ akataṃ asaṅkhataṃ. no ce taṃ ... abhavissa ajātaṃ ... asaṅkhataṃ, nayidha jātassa ... saṅkhatassa nissaraṇaṃ paññāyetha. ...*

āhāranettippabhavaṃ nâlaṃ tad abhinanditum /
tassa nissaraṇaṃ santaṃ atakkāvacaraṃ dhuvaṃ //
ajātaṃ asamuppannaṃ asokaṃ virajaṃ padaṃ /
nirodho dukkhadhammānaṃ saṅkhārūpasamo sukho //

ti; and *Itivuttaka* III. ii. 2 (§ 51, p. 46) and III. iii. 4 (§ 73, p. 62): *kāyena amataṃ dhātuṃ phassayitvā nirupadhiṃ / ... deseti sammāsambuddho asokaṃ virajaṃ padaṃ // ti*. Compare also *Suttanipāta* 204; *Theragāthā* 521 and 947, *Dhammapada* 114; Aṅguttaranikāya II 247; III 356; Majjhimanikāya I 436–7; Saṃyuttanikāya IV 373; *Paṭisambhidāmagga* I 13, 15, 70; and *Saddanīti* (ed. H. Smith), p. 70.

[65] See for example the present writer's remarks in *The study of Indian and Tibetan thought* (Leiden, 1967), pp. 9–13, 37–38.

[66] *Kāśyapaparivarta* §§ 55–57, 64–65. See also Nāgārjuna, *Mūlamadhyamakakārikā* xiii. 8; and *Ratnagotravibhāga*-Commentary i. 32–33 (p. 28.5–13).

the extremes included in any such binary pair.[67] As between the respective faults of the eternalist dogma and the nihilist dogma, then, all the schools of Buddhism would wish to say is probably that the nihilistic one may, in practice, be even more dangerous than its opposite because it makes spiritual effort impossible. But this clearly does not amount to a dogmatic positing of eternalism or the *ātmavāda*.

What is of paramount importance in the last analysis is perhaps not so much whether absolute reality is to be described positively or negatively, as whether the theory adopted actually avoids representing this reality either as the nihilistic destruction of some (pre-existing) entity or as a real void to which one might cling dogmatically. This is because the Middle Way consists, as has been seen, precisely in the cessation of all dichotomous conceptual constructions (*vikalpa*) concerning a self as opposed to a non-self, etc. Hence it has been possible for the Mahāyāna Buddhist on occasion to make use even of the terms *nitya*, *ātman*, etc., in order to indicate, through characterization by inversion, or to point to absolute reality, while at the same time rejecting any view which posits an *ātman* as an eternal entity.

The Cognitive Status of the *Tathāgatagarbha* and the Absolute

If from the soteriological point of view the *tathāgatagarbha* theory somehow implies the immanence of the absolute – or, inasmuch as the *tathāgatagarbha* is 'still' obscured by adventitious impurities (*āgantukamala*), at least its proleptical presence – in all beings in Saṃsāra, the question arises as to how a practiser is to realize it cognitively. For our sources not only state that absolute reality is beyond the range of ratiocinative thinking (*atarkya*) and free from the four extreme positions of discursive thinking (*catuṣkoṭi*) and that it cannot therefore be expressed verbally (*avācya*, *anabhilāpya*), but they also affirm that it is discursively inconceivable (*acintya*) and even unknowable (*ajñeya*). In other words, if

[67] In *Samādhirājasūtra* ix. 27 it is even stated that the wise person does not take a stand in a middle *position* either. On the rejection of the last two positions of the 'tetralemma' (*catuṣkoṭi*), see D. Seyfort Ruegg, *Journal of Indian Philosophy* 5 (1977), pp. 1–71.

paramārtha is unthinkable, is not absolute reality in its function of Base or Support of spiritual practice (*pratipatter ādhāraḥ*) – that is, the *prakṛtistha-gotra* or *tathāgatagarbha* – cognitively inaccessible also? And in this case are we not confronted with a curious, and indeed somewhat paradoxical, situation in which an absolute that is (at least proleptically) immanent in all sentient beings from the soteriological point of view would, nevertheless, be cognitively transcendent?

Concerning the gnoseological status of the *tathāgatagarbha*, one point seems to be clear. If the texts affirm that the *paramārtha* is ineffable, this means that discursive language cannot grasp its very nature; for such language is inextricably bound up with pragmatic and discursive usage (*vyavahāra*) and the dichotomizing conceptual construction (*vikalpa*) inherent in discursive proliferation (*prapañca*). And if these texts add that the *paramārtha* is unthinkable, this no doubt signifies that it cannot be the object of such conceptual thinking. But does it then follow that the *paramārtha* cannot be comprehended (*adhigam-*, etc.) by any form of knowledge, and that conceptual thinking and language can never point to it, by anticipation as it were (as in *udbhāvanā-aṃvṛti*)? Though the sources indeed speak frequently enough of comprehension (*adhigama*) of the absolute and state that it is to be known directly and introspectively (*pratyātmavedanīya*, etc.), the replies which the fundamental works on the *tathāgatagarbha* theory have given to these questions are unfortunately perhaps not quite as explicit as one might wish. And as a result later commentators are sometimes in disagreement about the exact gnoseological status of the *paramārtha* as well as of the *tathāgatagarbha*.

One group of thinkers has held that the *tathāgatagarbha* is in fact cognitively inaccessible and quite transcendent: not only is it beyond language (*sgra* = *śabda*) and discursive construction (*rtog pa* = *kalpanā*), but it cannot even be the object of a cognitive judgement (*žen pa'i yul*).[68] This school can of course found its thesis on the *Ratnagotravibhāga*,[69] and on its commentary which

[68] See 'Gos lo tsā ba gŽon nu dpal, *Deb ther sṅon po*, cha, f. 10b (Roerich, p. 349).
[69] *Ratnagotravibhāga* i. 9 and 153.

quotes a number of scriptures to this effect.[70] The *Śrīmālāsūtra* in particular states that the Mind which is very pure by nature is hard to comprehend; it is only accessible to Bodhisattvas endowed with the great *dharma*, and not to Pratyekabuddhas and Śrāvakas who only approach it through confidence or 'faith' (*śraddhā*) in the *tathāgata*.[71]

Another group of thinkers has on the contrary come to the conclusion that the *paramārtha* is accessible to the practiser, at least to a certain degree, even on the earlier stages of the path. This school also considers that it is even possible to indicate – to point to – it by words.[72] This is indeed what the Sūtras and Śāstras are concerned with doing. For their interpretation these commentators can also find authority in the systematic exegesis of the scriptures which make the *paramārtha* immanent not only soteriologically but also gnoseologically.

This problem of the transcendence as against the immance of the absolute is closely connected with the idea of confidence or 'faith' (*śraddhā*).

The *Ratnagotravibhāga*, following Sūtras quoted in its commentary, has indeed stated that the *paramārtha* can only be cognitively approached (*anu-gam-*) through faith.[73] And the commentary sums the matter up by saying that *dharmatā* is the object of neither deliberative thinking (*na cintayitavyā*) nor dichotomizing conceptual construction (*na vikalpayitavyā*), and that it can therefore be the object only of convinced adhesion (*adhimoktavyā*).[74]

Convinced adhesion (*adhimukti, adhimokṣa*) figures in fact as one cause of the purification of the *tathāgatadhātu* from the

[70] *Ratnagotravibhāga*-Commentary i. 12, 25 and 153.

[71] *Śrīmālāsūtra*, f. 450a, quoted in the *Ratnagotravibhāga*-Commentary i. 25 (p. 22.1–4).

[72] E. H. Johnston in his edition of the *Ratnagotravibhāga*-Commentary i. 12 (p. 12–14) – a quotation from the *Śrīmālāsūtra* – reads *sūcyate* 'is indicated, pointed to'. L. Schmithausen has proposed altering this reading to *ity ucyate* (*Weiner Zeitschrift für die Kunde Südasiens* 15 [1971], p. 137). The term *sūcyate* is found again in *Ratnagotravibhāga*-Commentary i. 93, where it is applied to the *caturākāraguṇaniṣpattyasambhinnalakṣaṇo nirvāṇadhātuḥ*; and in i. 1, in connexion with the seven-fold *adhigamārtha*.

[73] *Ratnagotravibhāga*-Commentary i. 153 and i. 1; compare also v. 9.

[74] *Ratnagotravibhāga*-Commentary i. 153 (*avataraṇikā*).

adventitious impurities that obscure it;[75] it leads to the attainment of reality, and it is the antidote against the *icchantika*'s hostile resistance (*pratigha*) to the *dharma* of the Mahāyāna.[76] And if a person is so to speak committed (*adhimucya*) to the immutability of the *dharma*, he does not experience fatigue with regard to the *dharma*.[77]

The circumstance that absolute reality can be cognitively approached (*anu-gam-*, *ā-gam-*) through faith[78] holds true, according to the sources,[79] not only for the worldling (*pṛthagjana*), but also for the Śrāvaka and Pratyekabuddha, who can comprehend the inconceivable (*acintya*) fact of both the naturally pure Mind (*prakṛtipariśuddhacitta*) – i.e. the *tathāgatagarbha* – and its state of defilement (*upakliṣṭatā*) only through faith (*śraddhā*).[80] And it also holds true for the 'young' Bodhisattva newly started on his course (*navayānasamprasthita*); for such a young Bodhisattva is not yet able to know the *tathāgatagarbha* as absolute *śūnyatā* because his mind is distracted from Emptiness (*śūnyatāvikṣipta*) by reason of the fact that he mistakenly takes it either to be the destruction of a previously existing entity or to be some negative entity to which to cling.[81]

It is for these reasons that the transcendence of absolute reality and of the *tathāgatagarbha* which can only be comprehended through faith has been maintained by the Tibetan commentators rṄog Blo ldan šes rab (1059–1109), the pupil of the Kashmiri scholar Sajjana, and by gTsaṅ nag pa (twelfth century), and then later by Bu ston (1290–1364) (who in any event assimilated the *tathāgatagarbha* directly with the *dharmakāya* on the resultant level of the Fruit, i.e. with the *buddha*-level).

But other interpreters, especially those of the dGe lugs pa school, have laid the emphasis elsewhere. They have preferred to

[75] *Op. cit.*, i. 36. [76] Cf. *op. cit.*, i. 12.

[77] *Op. cit.*, i. 68, quoting the *Sāgaramatiparipṛcchā*.

[78] *Op. cit.*, i. 153; cf. v. 9. [79] Cf. *op. cit.*, i. 1 and 25.

[80] *Śrīmālāsūtra*, f. 450a, quoted in *Ratnagotravibhāga*-Commentary i. 25. Cf. f. 445a, quoted in *Ratnagotravibhāga*-Commentary i. 154–5.

[81] *Ratnagotravibhāga*-Commentary, *avataraṇikā* to i. 154–5; and the *Śrīmālāsūtra* quoted thereafter.

It may be recalled here that these texts too support the assimilation of the *tathāgatagarbha* to *śūnyatā*: *tathāgatagarbhajñānam eva tathāgatānāṃ śūnyatājñānam* (*Śrīmālāsūtra*, f. 445a) and *tathāgatagarbhaśūnyatārthanaya* (*Ratnagotravbhāga*-Commentary i. 154–5 *avataraṇikā*, p. 75.17). Compare pp. 33 and 36 above.

regard faith above all as a necessary preliminary that is required to calm and clarify the mind (cf. *cittaprasāda*) so that one may be able to understand the *paramārtha*. This shift in emphasis regarding the gnoseological status of the *paramārtha* and the rôle of faith is due to several reasons, some of which evidently proceed from systematic exegesis. In the first place, these interpreters observe that *śraddhā* – to the extent that it is based on a communication received from outside in the form of an instruction from a teacher or a text – is necessarily bound up with language, and hence with *vikalpa* and *prapañca*. (This is a principle emphasised also by the Buddhist epistemologists.) Now it is, as we have seen, axiomatic with all the schools that the ultimate comprehension of absolute reality must be direct and immediate, and that it is attained finally through non-conceptual gnosis (*jñāna* = *ye śes*); and it is therefore plain that faith could never be considered the direct and immediate instrument of the ultimate comprehension of the *paramārtha*. Hence, without in any way minimizing the transcendental absoluteness of ultimate reality, the advocates of this interpretation stress a certain immanence of the *paramārtha*. And, needless to say, faith understood as receptive calmness and clarity of spirit (*prasāda*) remains highly prized by these thinkers also. It is, moreover, to be noted that the passage of the *Ratnagotravibhāga*-Commentary (i. 153) quoted above does not really stand against this interpretation; for in it the opposition is not between faith and direct non-conceptual gnosis, but between faith and ratiocincative or discursive knowledge.[82] The implication, then, is that the *paramārtha* may indeed have to be approached in the first instance through faith – that is, with receptive clarity of mind – but this certainly does not deny that its actual comprehension ultimately takes place through non-conceptual gnosis.

In the second place, these interpreters differ from certain other Buddhist schools in maintaining that not only the Nobles (*ārya*) belonging to the Vehicles of the Bodhisattva but also Nobles of the other two *yānas* – the Ārya-Śrāvakas and Pratyekabuddhas – have also to be able to comprehend the non-substantiality of the *dharmas* as well as of the individual (*pudgala*). Thus, according to them, the difference between the advanced adepts of the three

[82] Cf. *Ratnagotravibhāga*-Commentary i. 12.

yānas in this matter rests in the precise mode of their comprehension of *śūnyatā*, which is fuller in the case of the Ārya-Bodhisattva than in the case of the Ārya-Śrāvaka and Pratyekabuddha.[83] Following this interpretation, the references in Sūtra (the *Śrīmālāsūtra*, etc.) and Śāstra (the *Ratnagotravibhāga* and its Commentary) to the essential rôle of faith in understanding the *paramārtha* have therefore to do with the fact that only the Bodhisattva endowed with the sharpest faculties (*tīkṣṇendriya*) is able to understand it in all its aspects exclusively through his transcending discriminative knowledge (*prajñā*) without first having to have recourse to faith. Consequently, faith may properly be said to be a characteristic feature of the other two ways, that of the Śrāvaka and that of the Pratyekabuddha. In sum, although the object of the Śrāvaka's and the Pratyekabuddha's understanding – *nairātmya* and *śūnyatā* – is the same as the Bodhisattva's, the mode of their comprehension is not as full and all-embracing, and their understanding in this sense is only partial.[84]

It thus appears that these thinkers have drawn what we might call the systematic consequences of the gnoseological implications of the *tathāgatagarbha* theory by combining it with the theory of the One Vehicle (*ekayāna*). In fact, apart from its classificatory or taxonomic function (and an occasional polemical rôle), the doctrine of the *yānas* has a very clearly marked gnoseological content in Mahāyānist thought. It is very difficult if not impossible to reconcile the theory of the three ultimately distinct Vehicles of the Śrāvaka, Pratyekabuddha and Bodhisattva, only the last of which would lead to buddhahood, with the theory of the *tathāgatagarbha*, which affirms that the germinal capacity for buddahood is present in all sentient beings without exception,

[83] Cf. D. Seyfort Ruegg, *The literature of the Madhyamaka school of philosophy in India* (Wiesbaden, 1981), p. 7 n. 16 and p. 74; *La théorie du tathāgatagarbha et du gotra*, pp. 171, 231 f., 239, 309 f. See also É. Lamotte, *Le traité de la Grande Vertu de Sagesse*, IV (Louvain, 1976), p. 2135 f.

[84] A rather different view of the rôle of faith in the *tathāgatagarbha* literature has been put forward by S.-B. Park, *Buddhist faith and sudden enlightenment* (Albany, 1983). There, in his interpretation of the *Ta ch'eng ch'i hsin lun* ascribed to Aśvaghoṣa, he opposes what he terms 'patriarchal faith' (Chinese *tsu hsin*, implying 'I am buddha') to 'doctrinal faith' (Chinese *chiao hsin*, implying 'I can become buddha').

and which can therefore be thought to imply that they are all destined sooner or later to become *buddhas*. But the *ekayāna* theory, which holds that all vehicles ultimately converge in a single course leading to buddhahood, is quite in harmony with, and complementary to, the theory of the *tathāgatagarbha*.[85]

BUDDHA-NATURE AND *PARAMĀTMAN* IN A COMPARATIVE PERSPECTIVE

If we now consider the Buddha-nature or *tathāgatagarbha* and the Buddhist *paramātman* in a comparative perspective, in the light of the complex relationship seen in the transmitted texts of the *Mahāparinirvāṇasūtra*[86] between the *ātman* idea of the Brahman Tīrthikas and these Buddhist theories – and, indeed, between the Brāhman Parivrājakas and the Buddha – several explanatory models suggest themselves.

Are we perhaps confronted here with a quite straightforward example of historical influence exercised by Brahmanism on Buddhism? And, if this be the case, do we find here a case of 'just use' – i.e., something comparable to the *usus iustus* or *chrêsis* of non-Christian ideas in early Christianity discussed by Paul Hacker[87] – whereby Buddhists might have sought thoroughly to transform and reorient for their own needs an idea originally, and fundamentally, foreign to them? Or was this an attempt on the part of the Buddhists to take over and incorporate, in the specific sense of Hacker's inclusivism,[88] a Brahmanical idea with only superficial modification, subordinating it merely in a formal way to Buddhism and, perhaps, seeking at the same time to conceal their debt to a Brahmanical concept? Or, again, do we have here

[85] On the gnoseological implications of the *ekayāna* doctrine, see *La théorie du tathāgatagarbha et du gotra*, especially pp. 177–243.

[86] See above, pp. 21–24.

[87] See P. Hacker, *Kleine Schriften* (Wiesbaden, 1978), pp. 338 ff., 798 ff. On Buddhism and *chrêsis*, see *op. cit.*, p. 351.

[88] See P. Hacker, *op. cit.*, Index *s.v.* Inklusivismus; and his article 'Inklusivismus' in G. Oberhammer (ed.), *Inklusivismus* (Vienna, 1983), pp. 11–28. As examples of inclusivism in Buddhism – which Hacker further characterizes as 'inclusivism of strength' – Hacker cites the Buddhist notion of *tapas* and Brahmā (p. 23 ff.). It should be made clear that Hacker has not himself mentioned the Buddhist *tathāgatagarbha* or *paramātman* theories as examples of either inclusivism or *chrêsis*.

a Buddhist effort to find a perhaps syncretistic accommodation with Brahmanism? Or, on the contrary, might a fundamental religious and philosophical problem – one that is common, *mutatis mutandis*, to so many schools of Indian thought – be coming here to the surface from a common Indian religious and philosophical ground while taking on a specifically Buddhist stamp? (These alternative hypotheses are not all mutually exclusive, and more than one process could conceivably have been involved in the development of the Buddhist theories in question.) A full and detailed study of the Mahāyānist *Mahāparinirvāṇasūtra* and all the related texts will be required to enable us to decide which of these alternatives is (or are) applicable in each individual case.

One thing seems at all events clear: the antithesis *anātman/ātman* cannot, in the present context, be used as a criterion for distinguishing between the Buddhist and the Brahmanical Tīrthika.

Against the first alternative – the hypothesis in its general form of a Buddhist borrowing from Brahmanical thought as entertained for example by E. Frauwallner, É. Lamotte and H. Nakamura[89] – arguments have been advanced above based not only on the fundamentally important place occupied in Mahāyānist thought by these theories and their relation to certain concepts found in the old Buddhist canon – e.g. the natural luminosity of Mind, the notion of a spiritual Germ and that of a stable, permanent and immortal state (*pada*)[90] – but also on the distinctive and specific way that these theories have been taught and explicated in the relevant Buddhist Sūtras and Śāstras which makes any simple identification between them most difficult and problematic. In these circumstances, then, it will not do to treat them as foreign imports at some point in the history of Buddhism under the overwhelming influence of Hinduism and/or Brahmanical philosophy. The problem of the natural luminosity of Mind, the 'buddhomorphic' Ground of Awakening and the relation between it and buddahood as the Fruit of Awakening is in fact too deeply embedded in Buddhist thought, and it is too significant religiously and philosophically,

[89] See above, n. 63. [90] See above, p. 43.

for such an explanation to be wholly satisfactory. And the same considerations militate equally against the 'just use' version of the hypothesis of historical borrowing by Buddhists from Brahmanism. As for the version of this hypothesis based on religio-philosophical inclusivism, although (in agreement with Hacker's model) a resemblance – or, rather, parallelism – exists between the *ātman* of Brahmanical thought and the *tathāgatagarbha* and *paramātman* theory of the Buddhists, and although the superiority of the latter to the former is asserted or assumed by the Buddhists, the fact remains that (contrary to Hacker's model) they are not normally identified by the Sūtras and Śāstras that teach them; whereas the difference between the two is not only noted but is considered fundamental by these same sources.

Concerning the second main hypothesis of a Buddhist accommodation with Brahmanical thought, it is important to observe that such a view of the matter is not unknown to the Buddhist tradition. But its applicability will depend on precisely what is to be understood by accommodation, and also on what status is assigned to the relevant theories in Buddhist systematic hermeneutics. The accommodation model is compatible with the view mentioned above found in important sections of the Buddhist tradition according to which, in the Buddha's allusions to an *ātman* or *pudgala*, there is involved a certain *avatāraṇābhisaṃdhi*, that is, an 'allusive intention of introduction' effecting the attraction (*ākarṣaṇa*), by means of a provisional and 'intentional' (*ābhiprāyika*) teaching, of persons attached to the idea of a permanent *ātman*, who are thus not yet ready to receive the Buddha's ultimate and definitive teaching of non-substantiality (*nairātmya*) since it inspires terror (*saṃtrāsa*) in them.[91] According to this view, the intentional teaching in question will be considered as *neyārtha* and, consequently, as not giving expression to the Buddha's definitive (*nītārtha*) doctrine.

In such a form of accommodation with the Brahmanical *ātman*, there is no question of a syncretism between Buddhism and

[91] See above, p. 38.

Brahmanism if by syncretism we understand a merging of the two.[92]

The problem posed by the theories of the Buddha-nature, the 'buddhomorphic' Ground of Awakening and the *paramātman* cannot, however, be evacuated by simply treating the Sūtras teaching them as 'intentional' and *neyārtha*. For, as seen above, such teachings are too well-documented and philosophically rooted in several strata of Buddhist thought. They are indeed treated by a considerable part of the Buddhist hermeneutical tradition as non-intentional and *nītārtha*, for they are explicated in such a manner as to be consonant with the definitive teachings of *nairātmya* and *śūnyatā* according to the criterion established by the *Akṣayamatinirdeśasūtra* and the *Samādhirājasūtra*.[93] And, above all, they have been set out in a specifically Buddhist manner. Hence, following this view too, there is neither inclusivism nor syncretism, and also no conclusive evidence of *usus iustus*.

In sum, in its older texts as well as in more recent ones, the Buddhist canon contains references to what can be regarded as an absolute on the level of Ground or Fruit. These references can be neither interpreted away nor overlooked; and it would be as misleading to assign them an exclusively precanonical or protocanonical status as it would be to regard them as exclusively late and non-canonical. In the Mahāyāna these ideas have found clear expression in the theories of the Buddha-nature and *tathāgatagarbha* as the buddhomorphic Ground of buddhahood expounded in the *tathāgatagarbha*-Sūtras and the related Śāstras such as the *Ratnagotravibhāga* (ch. i), the *Mahāyānasūtrālaṃkāra* (ch. ix) and the *Abhisamayālaṃkāra* (ch. i), and also in the Tantras.

Moreover, a positive theory and a cataphatic approach both to this Ground and to buddhahood are well documented in the history of Buddhist thought beside the predominant apophatic theory. Sometimes these two doctrines appear as complementary, or indeed as incommensurable, theories. (This is the case in particular when they are developed into the theory of Emptiness

[92] For a discussion of syncretism in the Buddhist context see H. Bechert, *Buddhism in Ceylon and studies on religious syncretism in Buddhist countries* (Göttingen, 1978), p. 19 ff.; compare also W. Heissig and H. J. Klimkeit (eds.), *Synkretismus in den Religionen Zentralasiens* (Wiesbaden, 1987).

[93] See above, pp. 37–38.

of own-nature [*raṅ stoṅ*] and Emptiness of the heterogeneous [*gžan stoṅ*].) More often, the one is considered to be of provisional meaning requiring elicitation in another sense (*neyārtha*) and to be hierarchically subordinate to the other, which is definitive and of certain value (*nītārtha*). (This interpretation is also available when the *raṅ stoṅ* and *gžan stoṅ* theories are regarded as antithetical.)

Finally, and most importantly, the *tathāgatagarbha* and *paramātman* theories in Buddhism, together with the procedure of characterization of the absolute by inversion in relation to the relative, [94] may be seen as intended to neutralize and cancel both *ātmavāda* and *anātmavāda* in so far as they represent a binary pair of conceptually antithetical positions that the Buddhist Middle Way is to transcend. Thus, at a certain stage in Buddhist thought, these theories serve as a sort of metatheory that founds a metalinguistic description of the absolute – which is itself inexpressible within the binary structure of discursive thinking (*vikalpa*) and the four positions of the tetralemma (*catuṣkoṭi*), and hence in a language presupposing positive and negative entities.[95]

In the light of the available evidence, then, it appears difficult to maintain that, far from denying the Upaniṣadic *ātman*, the Buddha only denied what was mistakenly believed to be the *ātman*, and that the *Mahāyānasūtrālaṃkara* and the *Ratnagotravibhāga*-Commentary have continued in the line of the Upaniṣadic *ātman* doctrine, as has been argued by Kamaleswar Bhattacharya in his nevertheless challenging and well-documented book on *ātman-brahman* in Buddhism.[96] It may be the case that the Buddha and the older Buddhist texts did not negate the *ātman* in due propositional form, and that such a negation belongs to later sources only. But to conclude that the old Buddhist tradition was in basic agreement with the Upaniṣadic *ātman* doctrine is quite another matter, especially when it is anything but certain that this older tradition was even familiar with the Upaniṣads.[97] The overwhelming weight of the Buddhist tradition clearly does not support this conclusion. And its acceptance would not only imply

[94] See above, pp. 24–25. [95] See above, pp. 41, 44f., 48.

[96] Bhattacharya, *L'ātman-brahman dans le bouddhisme ancien*, pp. 3, 69–70, 137–8.

[97] See above, p. 20.

that the majority of Buddhists have misunderstood the Buddha's teaching but overlooks the highly important distinctions between the *ātman* and the Buddhist *tathāgatagarbha* and *paramātman* made in the Buddhist Sūtras and Śāstras treating the latter.

The theories in question accordingly seem to be no less deeply rooted and motivated in Buddhist thought than is the *ātman* theory in other forms of Indian thought. But rather than either an identity or a convergence of the *tathāgatagarbha* doctrine with the Brāhmanical *ātmavāda* we have here a distinct theory that stands in a highly interesting tension with the *ātmavāda*. We have also found the Buddhists sometimes sharing a common stock of philosophical and exegetical methods with the Brahmanical schools. But these methods are variously applied on each side. Historically they are sometimes even attested for the first time in Buddhist texts, without it however being possible to prove that they actually originated there.[98] Be this as it may, the Buddhists have concluded that the Brahmanist Tīrthikas' doctrine of the *ātman* (as they understood it) was both radically incoherent in itself[99] and incompatible with the Buddha's intention.

Thus we seem to have distinct, and unconflatable, theories and treatments of problems which are deeply embedded in Indian thought. They emerge from a common ground or substratum of religious and philosophical thinking but remain in a relation of tension.

When referring to a common ground or substratum, it should then be clear that it is not being suggested here that Buddhist thought may be assimilated or reduced to another system called Brahmanism or (in the narrower sense) Hinduism. What we call Indian Buddhism is the creation of Indians, and very often of Brahmans, in the context of Indian civilization; but it is a distinct creation beside Upaniṣadic and later Vedāntic thought. When considering the Brāhmanical *ātman* and the Buddhist theories in question, the common ground and the differences have equally to be kept clearly in mind.

[98] See above, pp. 31, 33–34. [99] See above, p. 25.

II

The Great Debate between 'Gradualists' and 'Simultaneists' in eighth-century Tibet

Introduction

FOR THE Tibetologist and historian of Buddhism, and equally for the specialist in comparative religion and intercultural studies, the remarkable encounter that took place in Tibet in the second part of the eighth century between the traditions of a non-scholastic, 'spontaneist' and more or less quietist Dhyāna (Ch'an) Buddhism – represented by several Chinese and Korean Ho-shangs and in particular by their best-known protagonist in Tibet, the Ho-shang Mo-ho-yen[100] – and the scholastically highly developed and monastically organized Yogācāra-Mādhyamika tradition of India – represented by Śāntarakṣita and his disciple Kamalaśīla – is a subject of very considerable interest.

This encounter of two traditions and the ensuing confrontation between its representatives have often been described as a Sino-Indian or Indo-Chinese controversy, debate or council. And the debate has been referred to by scholars as the Council of lHa sa (Demiéville), the Council of bSam yas (Tucci) and, more

[100] On the name Mo-ho-yen, as well as on the epithet *ho-shang* (Tib. *hva šaṅ*) derived from Skt. *upādhyāya* 'master', see P. Demiéville, *Le concile de Lhasa* (Paris, 1952), pp. 9 ff.

It should be recalled that other Ho-shangs such as Me 'go/mgo and Kim (Ch. Chin, below, n. 116) had preceded Mo-ho-yen in Tibet. See e.g. *sBa bžed*, ed. mGon po rgyal mtshan (Beijing, 1982) (=G), pp. 6–10, 65, 67–68; ed. R. A. Stein (Paris, 1961) (*Žabs btags ma* version =S), pp. 4–6, 8–10, 55, 57; dPa' bo gTsug lag phreṅ ba, *mKhas pa'i dga' ston*, ja, ff. 115a5, 116a4. The *Chos 'byuṅ* by Ne'u Paṇḍi ta, the *sNon gyi gtam Me tog phreṅ ba*, ed. T. Tsepal Taikhang, *Rare Tibetan historical and literary texts from the library of Tsepon W. D. Shakabpa*, I (New Delhi, 1974), f. 15a (p. 87), indeed mentions their presence already at the time of King Sroṅ btsan sgam po in the seventh century; and Bu ston (*Chos 'byuṅ*, f. 124b6) gives the name Ma hā de va tshe, while the *Deb ther dmar po* (f. 16b = p. 35) gives the name Ma hā de ba. Cf. P. Demiéville, *Concile*, p. 11, n. 4, on the Hva šaṅ Mahādeva at the time of Sroṅ btsan sgam po.

recently, the Council of Tibet (Demiéville and Ueyama). It should be noted at the outset that in the strict ecclesiastical sense this confrontation was not, however, a council, nor was it even a synod. The Tibetan historical sources have most often represented it as a debate (*rtsod pa*) in the form of an investigative discussion (*gšags*) between two parties that took place, in quite classical Indian and Buddhist style, with the Tibetan ruler acting as witness and arbiter (*dpaṅ po* = *sākṣin*). In the Chinese texts from Dunhuang, the discussion between the Ho-shang Mo-ho-yen (Tib. Hva šaṅ Mahāyāna or Mahā yan) and his interlocutors is presented mainly in the form of a series of polemical questions put to Mo-ho-yen with his replies.[101] In the Tibetan Dunhuang documents (and in the *bSam gtan mig sgron*),[102] Mahāyāna's teachings take the form of aphorisms or logia.

At the beginning of the discussion between Kamalaśīla and Mo-ho-yen as described in Tibetan sources, the Chinese Master asks whether, being senior in residence, he will be required either to put questions or to answer them. Kamalaśīla replies that he should discuss in accordance with his true thinking (*dgoṅs pa ltar šags thob cig*, *sBa bžed*, S, p. 57; see also Ñaṅ ral, *Chos 'byuṅ Me tog sñiṅ po*, ed. R. O. Meisezahl, f. 430a2), or that he should formulate his thesis (*pratijñā*) in accordance with his true thinking (*dgoṅs pa ltar dam bca' žog cig*, *sBa bžed*, G, p. 68), or that he should discuss his intended theory (*dgoṅs pa'i lta ba la šags thob cig*, dPa' bo gTsug lag phreṅ ba, *mKhas pa'i dga' ston*, f. 116b7). According to a passage of Wang Hsi's *Cheng-li chüeh*, Mo-ho-yen requested a discussion with the 'Brahman monk' (f. 128a), but Mo-ho-yen is later shown describing himself as unfit for debate because of his advanced years and asking the King to put an end to the controversy (f. 143a). Indeed, what he was obliged in the

[101] See Demiéville, *Concile*. The source of the questions put to Mo-ho-yen according to Wang Hsi's *Cheng-li chüeh* is the so-called 'Brahman monk' (*Concile*, pp. 39–40), presumably Kamalaśīla.

The question and answer form of discussion was evidently used also in cases where there appears to have been no debate, for example in T'an-k'uang's 'Dialogues' translated by W. Pachow, *A study of the twenty-two dialogues of Mahāyāna Buddhism* (Taipei, 1979), and in Hung-jen's 'Discourse' translated by W. Pachow, *Chinese Buddhism* (Washington, 1980), pp. 35–53. For T'an-k'uang and his rôle in connexion with the problems posed by the 'Great Debate', see below, p. 128.

[102] See below, p. 66.

discussions to state, following the Sūtras, was, he says, conceived only as an answer to the questions put to him; it was not the true system of his Dhyāna, which is ineffable (ff. 153a–155a).

In connexion with this encounter Demiéville once wrote: 'En matière d'histoire tibétaine ... il faut se méfier des méfiances hâtives'.[103] In the case of what will be referred to here as the Great Debate, and of the complex issues occupying the 'Gradualists' and 'Simultaneists' in their encounter, the sources need to be studied with great attentiveness and care using every instrument that philological, historical, religious, philosophical and hermeneutical analysis can place in our hands. Our sources often differ as to details, and sometimes they diverge on more important matters too. Some of them are contemporary with the events related, or they at least reproduce accounts ultimately going back to these events. Other sources are on the contrary later, they certainly contain interpretations and some distortions, and they may partake of what has been called the 'invention of tradition'.[104] They are all of course the product of intellectual and historical processes that need to be identified and reconstructed. It would probably be illusory, however, to think that from any of these sources we can now retrieve a definitive factual version of events exactly as they happened. But to say this is not to espouse historical scepticism or agnosticism. For it is of the greatest interest to investigate the accounts of these formative events in the history of Tibetan civilization and thought provided by Tibetan sources, and especially by the histories written before the middle of the fourteenth century, and to discover how their views of the Great Debate relate to Buddhist religious and

[103] *Concile*, p. 18.

[104] *The invention of tradition* is the title of a book of essays, edited by E. Hobsbawm and T. Ranger (Cambridge, 1983), dealing with rather different situations in modern England, Scotland, Wales, continental Europe, India and Africa; and the use of the expression here should not be understood as implying an identification with such situations. For the bSam yas monastic cantre, one might compare also the concept of '*Lieux de mémoire*', the title of a collection of essays edited by P. Nora (Paris, 1986).

On the constitution of tradition in the case of Ch'an Buddhism in the Sung period – after a break in the clan and school traditions of the T'ang – see H. Schmidt-Glintzer, *Die Identität der buddhistischen Schulen und die Kompilation buddhistischer Universalgeschichten in China* (Munich, 1982), p. 27 ff.

philosophical history.[105] This is what will be essayed in the following, and an attempt will be made to see what light these views throw on religious and philosophical currents in Tibet and in Buddhism. In this way we shall be able to see how Tibetan Buddhists received and reacted to two important and distinct traditions within Buddhism and to the Chinese and Indian masters who were the transmitters of these traditions.

Although the accounts we find in the extant versions of the *sBa bžed*, in the *Chos 'byuṅ Me tog sñiṅ po* of Ñaṅ Ñi ma 'od zer, in Bu ston's *Chos 'byuṅ*, and in the *mKhas pa'i dga' ston* of dPa' bo gTsug lag phreṅ ba differ in several respects, what happened seems in broad outline to have been the following according to the Tibetan sources.

In the third quarter of the eighth century, during the reign of Khri Sroṅ lde btsan, (*rg. c.* 755–794?),[106] one of the foremost Buddhist masters of the time, Śāntarakṣita, was invited to Tibet with a view to establishing Buddhism on a firm and lasting institutional and philosophical basis. Śāntarakṣita was responsible for the ordination of the first Tibetan monks according to the rite of the Mūlasarvāstivāda Vinaya (perhaps in 779) and for the foundation (in perhaps 787 or in 775–779) of bSam yas, the first monastic centre to be established in central Tibet. In the course of his work in spreading the Buddhist Dharma and establishing the Tibetan Saṃgha, Śāntarakṣita encountered influential Buddhist masters of Chinese origin who were known in Tibet by the generic name *hva šaṅ* derived from the Chinese word *ho-shang* (Skt. *upādhyāya*). Around the teachers of both Chinese and Indian origin who were active in propagating Buddhism there then gathered a number of Tibetan monk-disciples and lay followers. And as a consequence of this teaching activity flowing from both

[105] Extracts relevant to the Great Debate from the *sBa bžed* (*Žabs btags ma* version) and dPa' bo gTsug lag phreṅ ba's *mKhas pa'i dga' ston*, as well as from Bu ston's *Chos 'byuṅ* and some later sources, have been assembled by G. W. Houston, *Sources for a history of the bSam yas debate* (St. Augustin, 1980).

[106] Many contemporary Tibetan historians however place the birth of Khri Sroṅ lde btsan, or his accession to the throne, in the year 790, and his death in 858 (or 848). See for example Tshe tan žabs druṅ, *bsTan rtsis kun las btus pa* (mTsho sṅon Printing House, 1982).

the Chinese and Indian Buddhist traditions (not to speak of important Central Asian influences) there came to the fore certain differences between the doctrinal and monastic traditions of Śāntarakṣita's school and the apparently less organized meditative and teaching traditions of the Ho-shangs that were linked in particular with Ch'an (Dhyāna) Buddhism. Then, owing apparently to an accident, Śāntarakṣita died in Tibet. And his disciple Kamalaśīla, evidently already renowned in India, was invited, probably in accordance with his master's recommendation to the King, to continue Śāntarakṣita's work in Tibet.

It was probably in the 780s or early 790s that the tension between the two Buddhist currents of thought mentioned above reached a critical point. According to a number of Tibetan historical sources, a full-scale debate was then arranged between the party led by Kamalaśīla, the successor of the Ācārya-Bodhisattva Śāntarakṣita, and the Hva šaṅ Mahāyāna. It is said to have taken place under the supervision of the ruler Khri Sroṅ lde btsan himself at the Byaṅ chub gliṅ temple of the bSam yas monastic centre. In this debate as reported by our sources, Kamalaśīla appears as the leading figure of the Indo-Tibetan school, which was placed to the monarch's left in the debate. And the Hva šaṅ Mahāyāna figures as both the protagonist and main spokesman of a Sino-Tibetan school, which was placed to the monarch's right.

As Tibetan supporters of Kamalaśīla's school special mention is made of Ye šes dbaṅ po – a leading monk from the influential sBa family identified with sBa gSal snaṅ or sBa Ratna, who was appointed chief monk (*riṅ lugs* = *chos dpon*) by Khri Sroṅ lde btsan – and 'Ba'/sBa dPal dbyaṅs – another monk evidently connected with the same family, who was named chief monk when Ye šes dbaṅ po retired after meeting with certain difficulties.[107] Mention is also made of sBa Saṅ ši (ta). A certain Vairocana – who despite his name may have been a Tibetan – is also named as a follower of this school.[108]

[107] Religious from the dBa'(s)/sBa and Myaṅ families were already associated with, or were disciples of, Śāntarakṣita according to the Turkestan (Ša cu) document published by F. W. Thomas, *Tibetan texts and documents*, II (London, 1951), p. 85.

[108] These names are found in the lists of the *sad mi mi bdun*, who were to form the first Tibetan Saṃgha at bSam yas. See the discussion in G. Tucci, *Minor Tibetan texts*, II (Rome, 1958), p. 12 ff. (On a Vairocana who wrote in Sanskrit, and who was presumably an Indian, see V. V. Gokhale, *Annals of the Bhandarkar Oriental Research Institute*, Diamond Jubilee Volume [1977], pp. 635–43.)

On the other side, as supporters of the Hva šaṅ Mahāyāna and/or opponents of Ye šes dbaṅ po, special reference is made to a triad of disciples – a certain mÑa' Bi ma or sÑa Bye ma (perhaps a Vimala[mitra]?),[109] Myaṅ Ša mi (who is known to our sources also as the associate of another, earlier Ho-shang)[110] and an unnamed master from the rṄog family[111] – as well as to Co rMa rma[112] and the Bhadanta Laṅ ka.[113] Khri Sroṅ lde btsan's 'Bro consort ('Bro bza) and his maternal aunt (*sru*) are also mentioned as supporters of the Hva šaṅ Mahāyāna.[114] And as an opponent of Ye šes dbaṅ po mention is made in particular of Myaṅ/Ñaṅ Tiṅ ṅe 'dzin bzaṅ po, who was apparently the associate of an earlier Ho-shang too.[115]

It is noteworthy that Kamalaśīla figures here as only one of the principal debaters on the side opposed to the Hva šaṅ Mahāyāna,

[109] See *sBa bžed*, G, pp. 65 and 68 (sÑa Bye ma), and S, p. 55 (mÑa Bi ma); Ñaṅ ral Ñi ma 'od zer, *Chos 'byuṅ Me tog sñiṅ po*, ed. R. O. Meisezahl (St. Augustin, 1985), ff. 426b3 and 429b3 (Ña Bi ma); dPa' bo gTsug lag phreṅ ba, *mKhas pa'i dga' ston*, ja, ff. 115a5 and 116b4 (sÑags Bye ma la). Cf. Demiéville, *Concile*, p. 41.

The *rus*-name here may be equivalent to gÑags (as in the case of gÑags Jñāna-Kumāra, the disciple of Vimala), in which case the Bi ma/Bye ma in question would of course be a Tibetan, rather than the Indian Vimala(mitra).

[110] See *sBa bžed*, G. pp. 65 and 67; S, pp. 55.1 and 57.11; *mKhas pa'i dga' ston*, ja, f. 115a4 and 116b4; Ñaṅ Ñi ma 'od zer, *Chos 'byuṅ Me tog sñiṅ po*, f. 429b3 together with f. 426b3.

On Ša mi see also G. Tucci, *Minor Buddhist texts*, II, pp. 9–10. A certain Myaṅ gŠa (?) mi go cha has been mentioned in connexion with the Bodhisattva (i.e. Śāntarakṣita) in the document published by F. W. Thomas, *op. cit.*, p. 85. This document also mentions another member of the Myaṅ family in the same context.

[111] For rṄog Rin po che, compare Demiéville, *Concile*, p. 33.

[112] In the *mKhas pa'i dga' ston*, ja, f. 118b7, Co rMa rma is described as the *gzims mal pa* or chamberlain (cf. f. 120b6) (cf. Tucci, *Minor Buddhists texts*, II, p. 38, and *Preliminary report on two scientific expeditions in Nepal* [Rome, 1956], p. 89). Compare *Chos 'byuṅ Me tog sñiṅ po*, f. 429al.

[113] The Bhadanta Laṅka is not mentioned in the *Chos 'byuṅ Me tog sñiṅ po* (f. 429a), which mentions Co ma (?) only.

[114] On these two see Demiéville, *Concile*, pp. 25, 33.

[115] See *sBa bžed*, G, p. 63–64; S, p. 54; and *mKhas pa'i dga' ston*, ja, f. 114b4; *Chos 'byuṅ Me tog sñiṅ po*, f. 425'al (=Ms B, f. 237a7).

The *Chos 'byuṅ Me tog sñiṅ po* also refers to his being a disciple of Vimalamitra (f. 472a4) and to his exile and murder (?) (f. 473a; Ms B, f. 258a) at the time of King Glaṇ dar ma. This source in addition mentions his connexion with dBu ru (f. 472a4). On Tiṅ ṅe 'dzin and the Myaṅ. see also the inscription of the dBu ru Žva'i lha khaṅ in H. E. Richardson, *A corpus of early Tibetan inscriptions* (London, 1985), pp. 43 ff. Cf. Tucci, *Minor Buddhist texts*, II, p. 52 f.; below, p. 75.

and that in this capacity mention is made also of Ye šes dbaṅ po (in the unsupplemented version of the *sBa bžed* and in the 'Alternative Tradition' quoted in the same text) and of 'Ba' dPal dbyaṅs (in the unsupplemented version of the *sBa bžed*) and/or (sBa) Saṅ ši (ta) (in the supplemented version of the *sBa bžed*).[116] Indeed, Kamalaśīla – who had reportedly only recently arrived in Tibet – was presumably still unable to speak Tibetan fluently. But this circumstance would of course neither prove that he was not directly involved in the Great Debate nor that he was not present at it.[117] According to the Tibetan historical texts under consideration, the Great Debate ended with the Hva šaṅ's conceding defeat and the Tibetan monarch's decree that his teachings should no longer be propagated in Tibet. Several sources also record that it was further decreed that Nāgārjuna's theory (*lta ba*) should be accepted,[118] while in the domain of practice (*spyod pa*) the Six Perfections should be kept to.[119]

In view of the weighty Tibetan participation in the Great Debate on Kamalaśīla's side and also of the close association of Tibetans with the Hva šaṅ Mahāyāna – whose teachings cannot,

[116] This Saṅ ši (ta) has sometimes been identified with (sBa) dPal dbyaṅs, but the question of his identity is far from clear. See Tucci, *Minor Buddhist texts*, II, pp. 11–12, 22, 24; P. Demiéville, in M. Soymié (ed.), *Contributions aux études sur Touen-houang* (Geneva-Paris, 1979), pp. 4–7 (referring also to H. Obata).

The *sBa bžed* (S, p. 5) mentions a rGya phrug gar mkhan Saṅ ši. And a Saṅ ši is mentioned also in connexion with sBa gSal snaṅ (G, p. 10 ~ S, p. 9); he seems to have been linked with Kim Hva šaṅ (S, p. 10; cf. G, p. 7). Kim – Chinese Chin Ho-shang – was the name of a Korean Ch'an master, Musang (Ch. Wu-hsiang, 694–762) who taught in Sichuan (Chengdu). Cf. S. Yanagida, in W. Lai and L. Lancaster (eds.), *Early Ch'an in China and Tibet* (Berkeley, 1983), pp. 18, 193; P. Demiéville, in Jao Tsong-yi and P. Demiéville, *Peintures monochromes de Dunhuang* (Paris, 1978), p. 47, and in M. Soymié (ed.), *op. cit.*, pp. 4–5, 7, 11–12 (referring also to Z. Yamaguchi). – Wu-chu (Tib. Bu chu, 717–774), who is known to the rDzogs chen tradition (*bSam gtan mig sgron*), was in contact with Wu-hsiang/Musang in Chengdu (Demiéville, *Contributions*, p. 5); but there were significant differences in their views (p. 7).

[117] On the question of the language(s) in which the discussions and debates were held, their number, and of the participants in them, see P. Demiéville, *T'oung-Pao* 56 (1970), p. 42; Y. Imaeda, *Journal asiatique* 1975, p. 129.

[118] See *sBa bžed*, S, p. 62.6 (the specific reference to Nāgārjuna is not in the other version); Bu ston, *Chos 'byuṅ*, f. 129b5; *mKhas pa'i dga' ston*, ja, f. 119a2; Ñaṅ Ñi ma 'od zer, *Chos 'byuṅ Me tog sñiṅ po*, f. 435b5.

[119] The accounts of the Great Debate differ to a greater or lesser extent in the various sources, and there seems to have taken place a conflation with earlier discussion(s) in which a certain Me mgo (?) (rather than Mo-ho-yen) was the leading Ho-shang.

moreover, be exclusively identified with any specific known Chinese school of Ch'an and may reflect a version peculiar to Central Asia notwithstanding elements in common with the Northern, Southern and Pao-t'ang Schools – it may then be more accurate to speak not (as has often been done) of a clash in Tibet between Indian and Chinese Buddhism and of an ensuing Sino-Indian debate or council, but rather of the encounter, tension and confrontation between certain Indo-Tibetan and Sino-Tibetan traditions. (This question of the description of the traditions facing each other will be discussed in Chap. iii.)

At issue in this encounter, and in the ensuing Great Debate, were the doctrine of the 'Gradualists' (*rim gyis pa*) known as gradual engagement (*rim gyis 'jug pa*) – and also as the *(br)tse(n) mun/min (pa)* (Chinese *chien men [p'ai]*) – of Kamalaśīla and his Tibetan followers and the teaching of the 'Instantaneists' or 'Simultaneists' (*cig c[h]ar ba*) otherwise known as simultaneous engagement (*[g]cig c[h]ar gyis 'jug pa*) – and also as the *(s)ton mun/min (pa)* (Chinese *tun men [p'ai]*) – of the Ho-shang Mo-ho-yen and his Tibetan followers.[120]

I. On Some Earlier Tibetan Historical Sources on the Great Debate

For long the best known Tibetan historical source on the Great Debate was no doubt Bu ston's *Chos 'byuṅ* (f. 128a–129b). In 1935 E. Obermiller – who had already published in 1932 an English translation of the relevant section of Bu ston's history – called attention also to what he supposed to be one of Bu ston's main sources on the subject, the third *Bhāvanākrama* by Kamalaśīla.[121] This work indeed contains many passages that are perti-

[120] See *sBa bžed*, S, p. 54; Ne'u Paṇḍi ta, *Chos 'byuṅ*, f. 22a1; Bu ston, *Chos 'byuṅ*, f. 129b; Dalai Lama V, *Bod kyi deb ther dpyid kyi rgyal mo'i glu dbyaṅs*, f. 39b (=p. 89); Thu'u bkvan Blo bzaṅ chos kyi ñi ma, *Grub mtha' šel gyi me loṅ*, rGya nag chapter, f. 10 ff. (with the transcriptions *tun men/min* and *tsi'an men/tsi yan min*).

For some pseudo-etymological explanations, based on Tibetan, of the originally Chinese expressions, see *sBa bžed*, G, p. 64 and S, p. 54.12–13; dPa' bo gTsug lag phreṅ ba, *mKhas pa'i dga' ston*, ja, f. 115a; and Ñaṅ Ñi ma 'od zer, *Chos 'byuṅ Me tog sñiṅ po*, f. 426b.

[121] E. Obermiller, *Journal of the Greater India Society* 2 (1935), pp. 1–11. See also Obermiller's posthumously published facsimile edition of the third *Bhāvanākrama* (Moscow, 1963).

nent to the Great Debate with Mo-ho-yen; but none of Kamalaśīla's three *Bhāvanākramas* actually mentions Mo-ho-yen. And based as it is largely on quotations from Sūtras, Kamalaśīla's treatment of the progressive stages of meditative realization (*bhāvanā* = *bsgom pa*) involving, beside Quieting of mind (*śamatha* = *ži gnas*), the fundamental factors of exact analytic investigation (*bhūtapratyavekṣā* = *yaṅ dag pa'i so sor rtog pa*) and its culmination in analysis of the factors of existence (*dharmapravicaya* = *chos šin tu rnam par 'byed pa*) or discriminative knowledge produced from meditative realization (*bhāvanāmayī prajñā* = *bsgom pa las byuṅ ba'i šes rab*), and then finally in Insight (*vipaśyanā* = *lhag mthoṅ*), refers specifically neither to any particular debate or to any individual opponent. Kamalaśīla's three treatises are accordingly relevant to Buddhist philosophical theory and practice in general.

As for the historical existence of Kamalaśīla and his master Śāntarakṣita, it is of course very well established by their extant works available in Sanskrit or in Tibetan translations in the bsTan 'gyur as well as by many references in original Tibetan historical and philosophical works. The historical existence of the Hoshang Mo-ho-yen/Hva šaṅ Mahāyāna (or Mahā yan) and of the debate(s) in which he took part in Tibet – the two matters left somewhat unclear in Tibetan bsTan 'gyur as well as in the Sanskrit sources – has, despite some hesitations and obscurities in the Tibetan traditions, been demonstrated by Wang Hsi's *Tun-wu ta-cheng cheng-li chüeh* or 'Ratification of the true principles of the Great Vehicle of Sudden Awakening' preserved in two Chinese manuscripts from Dunhuang (*Pelliot 4646* and *Stein 2672*) which has been translated into French and commented on by Demiéville in his *Le concile de Lhasa* and 'Deux documents de Touen-houang sur le Dhyāna chinois'.[122] In addition to Wang Hsi's Preface, the *Cheng-li chüeh* comprises three 'Memorials' two of which consist

[122] In: *Essays on the history of Buddhism presented to Professor Zenryu Tsukamoto* (Kyōto, 1961), pp. 1–27.

Pelliot tibétain 823 contains a Tibetan version of a part of Wang Hsi's *Cheng-li chüeh*; cf. Y. Imaeda, *Journal asiatique* 1975, p. 127 ff. For further parallels between the Chinese sources and Tibetan manuscripts from Tun-huang, see L. Gómez, 'The direct and gradual approaches of the Zen master Mahāyāna: Fragments of the teachings of Mo-ho-yen' in: R. Gimello and P. Gregory, *Studies in Ch'an and Hua-yen* (Honolulu, 1983), p. 106 ff.

mainly of a number of questions put to Mo-ho-yen together with his replies. On the Tibetan side corroboration is forthcoming from the Tibetan Dunhuang documents, a number of which have been recently analysed by L. Gómez in his 'The direct and gradual approaches of Zen Master Mahāyāna: Fragments of the teachings of Mo-ho-yen'.[123]

Modern scholarly study of the Tibetan Dunhuang sources on Dhyāna and Ch'an was inaugurated in 1939 when Marcelle Lalou published MS BN Pelliot tibétain 996.[124] This document contains the lineage of a certain Tibetan Dhyāna master named Tshig tsa Nam (m)k(h)a'i sñiṅ po which includes a Dhyāna teacher named A rtan hyver, who travelled from India to Kučā, and two Chinese masters.[125] The same Dunhuang text also contains a summary of the teachings of another important early Dhyāna master, sPug Ye šes dbyaṅs.[126] Subsequently, and especially over the past decade and a half, there has been a veritable flood of articles on the Dunhuang documents pertaining to the history of Ch'an, and on the Ho-shang Mo-ho-yen. The extensive recent Japanese literature on the subject was inaugurated in 1968 by Ueyama Daishun, who has since been joined by many other scholars; this literature has been surveyed in a recent publication by D. Ueyama.[127] Some of the relevant Western and Japanese secondary literature has also been considered by L. Gómez.[128]

[123] See n. 122.

[124] M. Lalou, 'Document tibétain sur l'expansion du Dhyāna chinois', *Journal asiatique* 1939, pp. 505–23.

[125] Cf. *bSam gtan mig sgron* or *rNal 'byor mig gi bsam gtan* (see below, n. 129), f. 90b3; Tucci, *Minor Buddhist texts*, II, p. 21; R. Kimura, *Journal asiatique* 1981, p. 187.

[126] Cf. R. Kimura, *Journal asiatique* 1981, p. 183 ff.

[127] D. Ueyama, 'The study of Tibetan Ch'an manuscripts recovered from Tun-huang: a review of the field and its prospects' in: W. Lai and L. Lancaster, *op. cit.*, pp. 327–49. See also P. Demiéville, 'Récents travaux sur Touen-houang', *T'oung Pao* 56 (1970), pp. 1–95, and 'L'introduction au Tibet du bouddhisme sinisé d'après les manuscrits de Touen-houang' in M. Soymié, *Contributions aux études sur Touen-houang*, pp. 1–15, together with G. Mala and R. Kimura, 'Additif' in: M. Soymié (ed.), *Nouvelles contributions aux études de Touen-houang* (Geneva, 1981), pp. 321–7; G. Mala, 'Empreinte du Tch'an chez les mystiques tibétains' in: *Le Tch'an (Zen): racines et floraisons* (Hermès 4, Nouvelle série, Paris, 1985), pp. 387–424.

[128] L. Gómez, 'Indian materials on the doctrine of Sudden Enlightenment' in: W. Lai and L. Lancaster (eds.), *op. cit.*, pp. 393–434; and 'The direct and gradual approaches of the Zen master Mahāyāna' in: R. Gimello and P. Gregory (eds.), *op. cit.*, pp. 69–167.

Another major source for the Dhyāna tradition in Tibet, as well as for the Mahāyoga and Atiyoga or rDzogs chen, is the *bSam gtan mig sgron* or *rNal 'byor mig gi bsam gtan*. This text is ascribed to the rDzogs chen master gNubs chen Saṅs rgyas ye śes, who is reputed to have lived in the eighth or ninth century.[129] What is of importance in the present context is the fact that this text contains a chapter on the Gradualist's Tsen min/men – i.e. the *rim gyis pa* or *rim [gyis] 'jug pa* – which is in turn connected with those Sūtras communicated to persons of inferior faculties (*dbaṅ po tha śal*, f. 31b) whose meaning moreover requires to be elicited in another sense (*draṅ ba don : neyārtha*, f. 12a), and which is further described as a method that is as it were misleading (*rim gyis sbyoṅ ba bslu 'drid 'dra*, f. 25b). The next chapter concerns the more advanced 'Simultaneist' sTon mun – i.e. the *cig car ba* or *cig car 'jug pa* – which is connected with the final and definitive sense (*ṅes don* = *nītārtha*, f. 25b), that is, the real intended sense (*yaṅ dag dgoṅs pa'i don*, f. 25b).[130] This work contains a veritable mine of

[129] *bSam gtan mig sgron*, or *rNal 'byor mig gi bsam gtan*, published in 1974 in Leh by S. W. Tashigangpa in his Smanrtsis Shesrig Spendzod, vol. 74. The date of this text as we have it is not altogether free from doubt.

Its reputed author, gNubs (chen) Saṅs rgyas ye śes, is usually stated to have lived at the time of Padmasambhava, and to have been a pupil of Vimalamitra and even Śrīsiṃha towards the end of the eighth century. In his *gSaṅ sṅags sṅa 'gyur la bod du rtsod pa sṅa phyir byuṅ ba rnams kyi lan du brjod pa, ṅes don 'brug sgra* (ed. Sanje Dorji, *Collected writings of Sog-bzlog-pa Blo-gros-rgyal-mtshan*, Volume I, New Delhi, 1975), f. 9a–b, Sog bzlog pa (b. 1552/3) has rejected the opinion (apparently maintained by 'Bri khuṅ dPal 'dzin) that sNub (*sic*) ban Saṅs rgyas ye śes was a contemporary of King dPal 'khor btsan – the son of gNam lde 'od sruṅs, son of Glaṅ dar ma, and supposedly the last of the old Central Tibetan line of kings – which would have put him no earlier than the end of the ninth century. The *bSam gtan mig sgron* cites (f. 91b) a *bDen gñis 'jug pa*, but this is not the work by Atiśa included in the dBu ma section of the bsTan 'gyur. This text knows the Ch'an succession of seven masters (*bdun brgyud*) beginning with 'Darmodhāra' (Bodhi-Dharma) and culminating in Mahāyāna (Mo-ho-yen) (f. 8a), as well as the story of the sandal/boot of 'Darmotāra' (f. 12b) (see below, pp. 73, 87–88) but it is uncertain how firm a basis these references can provide for the dating of the text. Very significant, however, is the reference to absolute, non-presuppositional and non-implicative, negation (*med par dgag pa* = *prasajyapratiṣedha*, f. 37a) and, in a note is small letters, to *sādhyasama* (? *sgrub bya mthun pa*, f. 73b); these concepts became common in Tibetan philosophical literature starting in the eleventh century. 'Gos gŽon nu dpal refers to the *bSam gtan mig gi sgron ma* being studied in the eleventh century (*Deb ther sṅon po*, ga, f. 17a5; Roerich, p. 137).

[130] For the need of superior faculties (*dbaṅ po rnon po*) to understand the Hva śaṅ's teaching, and for the function of the ultimate and definitive sense (*ṅes don* as opposed to *draṅ don*) in this teaching, see Ñaṅ Ñi ma 'od zer, *Chos 'byuṅ Me tog sñiṅ po*, ff. 425'b, 430a–b and 435b. Cf. below, pp. 84, 93, 98, 117, 141–2.

information on the lineages and teachings of the Ho-shangs, including Mahā yan who is counted as the seventh master in line from Bo de dar mo tā ra (*sic*) in a succession beginning with Kāśyapa ('od sruṅs, f. 8a, 12a, 29a). In this text Kamalasila and the Hva śaṅ Mahā yan have been mentioned side by side (f. 8a, 17a); but it is noteworthy that no mention has been made of the Great Debate in which they are said by the other sources under consideration here to have been involved. Material very similar to that of the *bSam gtan mig sgron* is moreover contained in the *gter ma* text known as the *bKa' thaṅ sde lṅa*, in the chapter entitled *Blon po bka'i thaṅ yig.*[131] These texts clearly testify to the links between the Dhyāna traditions of the Ho-shangs and the rDzogs chen pas/rÑiṅ ma pas. But it is at the same time notable that the *bSam gtan mig sgron* has explicitly distinguished between the sTon mun or Cig car bas and both the rNal 'byor chen po (Mahāyoga) and the rDzogs chen and Atiyoga, placing the sTon mun or *cig car gyis 'jug pa* as a second stage between the first stage consisting of the Tsen men or *rim gyis 'jug pa* and the third and fourth stages of Mahāyoga and the rDzogs chen.

In the wake of the current interest in the history and teachings of the various forms of Ch'an under the T'ang, what may be called the Tibetan and Tibetological dimension of the Great Debate and its background in the Dhyāna traditions of India and Central Asia have since Tucci's masterly discussion of 1958 sometimes been relegated to the background.

Moreover, Y. Imaeda has gone so far as to express doubt as to whether an actual confrontation and debate ever really took place between Mo-ho-yen and Kamalaśīla;[132] and the same scholar has described what is probably in its core our earliest Tibetan historical record on the subject, the *sBa bžed*, as a relatively late work dating from the early fourteenth century.[133] These ques-

[131] The *Lo paṇ bka'i thaṅ yig* is cited as a source concerning the Hva śaṅ Mahāyāna and the Great Debate by Tshe dbaṅ nor bu (1698/9–1755) in his *rGya nag hva śaṅ gi byuṅ tshul grub mtha'i phyogs sṅa bcas sa bon tsam smos pa yid kyi dri ma dag byed dge ba'i chu rgyun* (reprinted in Vol. v of his works, Dalhousie, 1977), f. 7b4. But the text quoted actually corresponds to that of the *Blon po bka'i thaṅ yig*, f. 19a (ed. Tucci, *Minor Buddhist texts*, II, p. 68).

[132] See Y. Imaeda, *Journal asiatique* 1975, p. 140.

[133] Cf. Imaeda, *loc. cit.*, p. 126. For a recently published account of the Great Debate according to the *sBa bžed*, see F. Faber, *Acta Orientalia* 47 (1986), pp. 33–61.

tions will therefore be investigated in the following on the basis of some of the older Tibetan sources.

That a true debate took place towards the end of the eighth century at the Byaṅ chub gliṅ of bSam yas between Kamalaśīla and the Tibetan Gradualists on the one side and the Hva šaṅ Mahāyāna, i.e. Mo-ho-yen, supported by his Tibetan 'Simultaneist' followers on the other under the aegis of the Tibetan ruler Khri Sroṅ lde btsan is stated in both available texts of the *sBa bžed* (G, pp. 67–75 and S, pp. 57–62). This chronicle connected with the first Tibetan monastic centre of bSam yas (see G, p. 82.11) contains records of the sBa family, members of which are reputed to have participated in the Great Debate.[134] And the sBa records may well be our oldest *chos 'byuṅ* source on the subject; at all events the *sBa bžed* has been described as the 'matrix' (*phyi mo*) – i.e. the textual source – of all Tibetan chronicles (*rgyal rabs*) and religious histories (*chos 'byuṅ*) as well as the record (*bka' gtsigs*, etc.) of bSam yas.[135]

The Supplemented Version (*Žabs btags ma*) of the *sBa bžed* became widely available to modern scholarship only in 1961, when R. A. Stein published a facsimile edition of it. And another, unsupplemented version of the *sBa bžed* was published as recently as 1980 in Beijing by mGon po rgyal mtshan. The title *sBa bžed* appears in Tibetan sources also in the forms *rBa bžed, dBa' bžed, dPa' bžed* and *sPa bžed*.[136] The reference in each case appears to be

[134] The colophon of the *sBa bžed* G p. 82 mentions the view that, in the title *sBa bžed*, sBa refers to sBa gSal snaṅ, as well as to another view that this *rus*-name refers to sBa Saṅ ši. This colophon then adds that the *sBa bžed* is in fact widely regarded as the record of bSam yas (*bsam yas bka' thams* [= *thaṅ*?]). A version known as the *Mi sPa bžed* (*sic*) is connected with gSal snaṅ and Saṅ ši in Sum pa mkhan po Ye šes dpal 'byor's *dPag bsam ljon bzaṅ*, f. 101a5 (p. 155).

[135] See the title-page of the 1978 Dharamsala edition of the *Žabs btags ma* version.

[136] The form *dPa' bžed* is found in Sa skya Paṇḍi ta Kun dga' rgyal mtshan, *sKyes bu dam pa rnams la spriṅ ba'i yi ge* (sDe dge ed.), f. 72b4, while the *Thub pa'i dgoṅs pa rab tu gsal ba*, f. 50b2, has both *dBa' bžed* (but *dPa' bžed* in the N-GMPP Ms from Nepal, f. 72a5) and *'Ba' bžed*; and the same text mentions in addition a *rGyal bžed* (cf. above, n. 134). 'Gos gŽon nu dpal's *Deb ther sṅon po*, ka, f. 20a4, and Sum pa mkhan po's *dPag bsam ljon bzaṅ*, f. 101a5 (p. 155), have *sPa bžed (gtsaṅ ma)*. The spelling *rBa bžed* is found in Bu ston's *Chos 'byuṅ* (f. 93b2), and in dPa' bo gTsug lag phreṅ ba's *mKhas pa'i dga' ston*, ja, f. 120a5.

As for the family name, the forms sBa, rBa, dBa', dBa's 'Ba' and Bha are all found (as

to the sBa family – seemingly known earlier as dBa'(s) and also as 'Ba' – which played so prominent a part in the development of the bSam yas monastic centre, and indeed in the whole history of Tibet in the second half of the eight century, starting apparently at the end of the reign of Mes Ag tshom(s) and continuing throughout the reign of Khri Sroṅ lde btsan. The *sBa bžed* is in fact considered the work of a member of this family, sBa gSal snaṅ.[137] This man, who had once been governor of Maṅ yul province in southern Tibet and was in contact with a certain Ho-shang (Me mgo/'go), became closely associated with Śāntarakṣita by whom he is said to have been ordained under the name of Ye šes dbaṅ po.[138] Another name closely associated with Śāntara-

well even as dPa' and sPa).

Three versions of the *btsan po mṅa bdag gi bka' gtsigs* are mentioned in the sources. One is said to have been deposited in the Tibetan King's own hand (*rje'i phyag* [*sbal*]); another is said to have been in lHa sa; and the third is said to have been taken to Khams (see *sBa bžed*, G, p. 82 ~ S, p. 65). Several sources furthermore mention the *sBa bžed* properly speaking, presumably the one deposited according to some authorities with the ministers and officials; the *rGyal bžed*, presumably the one deposited with the King; and the *Bla bžed*, in other words the version deposited with the Tibetan clergy. See Sa skya Paṇḍi ta, *Thub pa'i dgoṅs pa rab tu gsal ba* (sDe dge ed.), f. 50b; Sog bzlog pa Blo gros ryal mtshan, *gSaṅ sṅags sṅa 'gyur la bod du rtsod pa sṅa phyir byuṅ ba rnams kyi lan du brjod pa, ṅes don 'brug sgra* (in *Collected works of Sog-bzlog-pa*, ed. Sanje Dorje, Vol. i, New Delhi, 1975), f. 6a, f.; Sum pa mkhan po Ye šes dpal 'byor, *dPag bsam ljon bzaṅ*, f. 101 (= p. 155); Brag dgon žabs druṅ dKon mchog bstan pa rab rgyas, *Deb ther rgya mtsho*, I, f. 4a; A khu Šes rab rgya mtsho, *dPe rgyun dkon po 'ga' žig gi tho yig*, ed. Lokesh Chandra, *Materials for a history of Tibetan literature*, Part iii (New Delhi, 1963), nos. 11015–17. See also A. Vostrikov, *Tibetan historical literature* (Calcutta, 1970), pp. 24–26. According to Sog bzlog pa, *op. cit.*, f. 6a4, the *Bla bžed* was composed, following the *sBa bžed*, by Bla chen po (dGoṅs pa rab gsal, or Ye šes 'od ?). The identity of the *Mi sPa bžed* mentioned by Sum pa mkhan po, *op. cit.*, f. 101a5 (p. 155) is not certain.

In connexion with the record of three versions of the King's commands, of which one was apparently the *sBa bžed*, compare the report that the King's decision after the Great Debate was preserved in three versions, one of which was deposited in the King's hand or archive (*phyag dbal/sbal*) and another of which was distributed among the ministers (*žaṅ blon*) (*sBa bžed*, G, p. 76; S, p. 62).

[137] This attribution cannot of course hold for the entire Supplemented Version – the *Žabs btags ma* – which recounts events from the time of the accession of Khri Sroṅ lde btsan's successor Mu ne btsan po down to the time of Atiša in the middle of the eleventh century. Even the unsupplemented version recounts the death of sBa Ye šes dbaṅ po (G, p. 78 ff., identified with sBa gSal snaṅ in a note on p. 76) and sBa Saṅ ši (identified with dPal dbyaṅs, G. pp. 76, 78).

[138] See Bu ston, *Chos 'byuṅ*, f. 125b7. (But compare f. 127a3 of the same work which connects this name with another monk.) See also *sBa bžed*, S, p. 51; Bu ston, *Chos 'byuṅ*, f. 127a5; dPa' bo gTsug lag phreṅ ba, *mKhas pa'i dga' ston*, ja, f. 103b–104a. Cf. Tucci, *Minor Buddhist texts*, II, pp. 17–18.

kṣita is that of sBa Ratna, who is also stated to have become a monk under the name of Ye šes dbaṅ po (*sBa bžed*, G, p. 64 note) and who is mentioned as an associate of Kamalaśīla during the Great Debate.[139] According to an alternative view mentioned in the colophon of the *sBa bžed*, the name sBa refers to the records of ('Ba') Saṅ ši (ta). The name Saṅ ši alternates in some places with the name ('Ba'/sBa) dPal dbyaṅs, and the two seem in fact to refer to one and the same person. dPal dbyaṅs – the successor of Ye šes dbaṅ po as chief monk (*riṅ lugs*) – is well known as another of the Hva šaṅ Mahāyāna's main opponents and interlocutors in the Great Debate.

Now it is true that Imaeda, followed tentatively by Demiéville, has dated the *sBa bžed* to the early fourteenth century.[140] This dating would seem at first sight to find support in the fact that the Supplemented Version of the *sBa bžed* (S, p. 54.11) refers to the *gSuṅ rab rin po che'i mdzod*, i.e. to Bu ston's *Chos 'byuṅ* completed *c.* 1323. But this reference is missing in the other version (G, p. 64); and Bu ston has himself referred to a *rBa bžed* in his own *Chos 'byuṅ* in another context (f. 93b2). Moreover, Bu ston's source for the section in his *Chos 'byuṅ* on the Great Debate may well have been a *sBa bžed*; at any rate, the accounts of it we find in both texts are clearly closely related. And the later accounts in many Chos 'byuṅ texts rely on either Bu ston or the *sBa bžed*, or on both. In his *mKhas pa'i dga' ston* completed in 1564, dPa' bo gTsug lag phreṅ ba (1504–1566) has quoted an 'Alternative Tradition' in a form that is practically identical with the one found in the unsupplemented version of the *sBa bžed* (G, pp. 72–73). Most important in this context, however, is the fact that Sa skya Paṇḍi ta Kun dga' rgyal mtshan (1182–1251) much earlier referred to a *dPa' bžed* (or *dBa' bžed*) in his discussions of the Hva šaṅ Mahāyāna's teachings.

[139] In the *sBa bžed*, S, p. 50, sBa Ratna is mentioned as the first Tibetan monk; but compare Bu ston, *Chos 'byuṅ*, f. 127a, and Tucci, *Minor Buddhist texts*, II, p. 19. Z. Yamaguchi (*Hirakawa felicitation volume*, Tōkyō, 1975, p. 641 ff.) has identified dPal dbyaṅs = sBa Saṅ ši with sBa Ratna. Bu ston, *Chos 'byuṅ*, f. 128a, distinguishes between dPal dbyaṅs and Bha (*sic*) Ratna. The *sBa bžed* (S, p. 50) may identify 'Ba' Khri gzigs with sBa Ratna, and (S, p. 51) 'Ba' Khri (b)žer (Saṅ ši ta) with dPal dbyaṅs (?). Compare *sBa bžed*, G, pp. 58–59, 76, where the equivalences sBa Khri gzigs = sBa dPal dbyaṅs = sBa Saṅ ši (ta) have been indicated in small type; cf. p. 64.

[140] Imaeda, *Journal asiatique*, p. 126; Demiéville in M. Soymié (ed.), *Contributions aux études sur Touen-houang*, p. 4.

In sum, despite the fact that the Supplemented Version of the *sBa bžed* published by Stein must for the reasons mentioned above be considered as a whole to be much later than the eighth century, and although the recensions of the *sBa bžed* now available to us differ in wording and in many details, there would nevertheless seem to exist no compelling reason to reject as completely spurious and unreliable the matter on which the recensions agree in substance. And there is reason to think that both these recensions contain ancient records or traditions (*bžed lugs*) that could go back to members of the sBa family which played so important a rôle at the time of the foundation of bSam yas and the controversy between the 'Gradualists' and 'Simultaneists' in late eighth-century Tibet, and that we thus have reflected (however indirectly) in our texts of the *sBa bžed* the views of major participants in these events.

Among other important earlier Tibetan historical sources, the *Bod kyi rgyal rabs*, an old chronicle in some three folios only by the Sa skya hierarch Grags pa rgyal mtshan (1147–1216), has not entered into doctrinal matters, and this very short work contains no reference to the Hva šaṅ and the controversy between Gradualists and Simultaneists. And in the *Chos la 'jug pa'i sgo* by the Sa skya hierarch bSod nams rtse mo (1142–1182), a work that does include briefly at the end some Chos 'byuṅ type material relating to Tibet, we also find no mention of these matters. It seems, then, that in the Sa skya historical tradition Sa skya Paṇḍi ta (1182–1251) was the first of the great hierarchs to direct his attention to the controversy between Śāntarakṣita's and Kamalaśīla's school and the Ho-shangs, which he has done in several of his writings.

In the history by Ne'u/Nel pa Paṇḍi ta Grags pa smon lam blo gros, the *sÑon gyi gtam Me tog phreṅ ba* (dated to 1283 or 1343) which on many points follows traditions different from those found in the *Chos 'byuṅ* of the author's contemporary Bu ston,[141]

[141] Cf. G. Roerich, *The Blue annals* (Calcutta, 1949); p. viii; H. Uebach, in M. Brauen and P. Kvaerne (eds.), *Tibetan studies* (Zürich, 1978), pp. 219–230; and in B. Aziz and M. Kapstein (eds.), *Soundings in Tibetan civilization* (New Delhi, 1985), p. 147 f.

we find an allusion to the debate (*rtsod pa*) between the sTon min and the rTse min (f. 22a1), the Tibetan transcriptions of the Chinese names of the two opposed tendencies of 'Simultaneism' and 'Gradualism'. Ne'u Paṇḍi ta has however provided no details about the doctrinal points at issue except to say, very interestingly, that the Hva šaṅ Mahāyāna taught a doctrine that was in agreement with the Mahāmudrā (*phyag rgya chen po 'thun pa'i grub mtha' bzuṅ*, f. 21b5). This point had already been made earlier by Sa skya Paṇḍi ta.[142] Ne'u Paṇḍi ta concludes his account of the matter by stating (f. 22a1) that the monk Mahāyāna was defeated and reporting that it was thereupon decreed that only Dharma (*chos 'ba' žig*) – that is, evidently, the Dharma taught by Śāntarakṣita and Kamalaśīla following Nāgārjuna – should hencetorth be practised in Tibet, and that non-Dharma (*chos ma yin pa*) should not be practised (f. 22a2).

The account of the controversy and ensuing debate between the 'Gradualists' and 'Simultaneists' provided by Bu ston Rin chen grub (1290–1364) in his *gSuṅ rab rin po che'i mdzod* (ff. 127a–129b) has hitherto been no doubt the best known one since it has been drawn upon by a number of later Tibetan historians. Bu ston recounts how, in view of disagreements between Śāntarakṣita's followers such as Ye šes dbaṅ po and the Hva šaṅ Mahāyāna, Kamalaśīla was invited to Tibet to replace his master Śāntarakṣita, who had recently died as the result of an accident. A debate was then organized with the King sitting in the centre as witness and arbiter, and with the Hva šaṅ placed to his right and Kamalaśīla accompanied by the Tsen min to his left. Bu ston explains that the Chinese term *tsen min (pa)* corresponds to *rim gyis pa* 'Gradualist', and that the Chinese term *ton mun (pa)* corresponds to *gcig car ba* 'Simultaneist'. According to Bu ston's account, the points at issue were the Hva šaṅ's teaching of the need for simultaneous engagement (*gcig car [du] 'jug pa*) while giving up all activity and thinking and the teaching of Kamalaśīla's school concerning the need for gradual engagement (*rim gyis*

[142] See below, p. 101ff. 'Brug pa Kun legs has also spoken of a *phyag rgya hva šaṅ gi lta ba* in his gSuṅ 'bum, kha, f. 14a (quoted by R. A. Stein, *Revue de l'histoire des religions* 179 [1971], p. 10 note). Compare also the colophon of the *bSam gtan mig sgron* ascribed to gNubs Saṅs rgyas ye šes (Leh, 1974), f. 254a, for references to the relation between the *(da lta'i) phyag chen* and the teaching of the Hva šaṅ Mahāyāna.

'jug pa) which is compared with the step-by-step ascent of a mountain. As part of the 'Simultaneist' teaching, mention is made of primal buddhahood (*dan po nas sans rgyas*, f. 129a–b).[143] As opponents of the Hva šan's Simultaneist teaching Bu ston mentions dPal dbyans and Ye šes dban po beside Kamalaśīla. And Co rMa rma is mentioned as an associate of the Hva šan. Already at the beginning of the debate the King is stated by Bu ston to have ordered that the loser should not remain. And after he had conceded defeat the Hva šan is accordingly said to have been sent home (*rgya'i yul du brdzans*), at which point he concealed books of his as 'treasures' (*gter du sbas so*). The King decreed that henceforth the system (*lugs*) of Nāgārjuna should be observed in the domain of theory, that in the domain of praxis the ten Dharma-practices (*chos spyod*) should be followed, and that the Ton mun system was not to be permitted. Finally, according to Bu ston, four Chinese executioners of the Hva šan (*hva šan gi rgya'i bšan pa mi bži*) killed Kamalaśīla by squeezing his kidneys; and Ye šes dban po then died after having given up food. As already noted, Bu ston's account is quite closely related to the version we find in the *sBa bžed*, and it is probably based on it.

Another Tibetan history, the *Deb ther dmar po* (*Hu lan deb ther*) composed in 1346 by Tshal pa Kun dga' rdo rje (dGe ba'i blo gros), merely mentions Kamalaśīla and the Hva šan Mahāyāna (f. 17b1 = p. 37) without, however, saying anything about a controversy or debate between 'Gradualists' and 'Simultaneists'.

The story of the Hva šan, Kamalaśīla and the Great Debate was thereafter taken up by other historians of the bKa' brgyud pa school. It is true that in his *Deb ther snon po* completed in 1478 the Karma pa historian 'Gos gŽon nu dpal (1393–1481) does not mention the Great Debate; nor does he refer to Kamalaśīla in connexion with events at that time although he speaks of Śāntarakṣita. But he alludes to Hva šans and to the story that one of them left behind in Tibet one of his boots as a presage of the spread of the Teaching in Tibet (ka, f. 21a); and he specifies that a Hva šan prophesied that the conversion of Tibet was to be the special responsibility (*'dul skal*) of Śāntarakṣita, and that nobody

[143] On this point see below, note 164.

else would be of help in this task (f. 21a5). Another historian from the Karma pa school, dPa' bo gTsug lag phreṅ ba (1504–66), has on the contrary dealt in detail with the Great Debate and with the rôle of Kamalaśīla in his *mKhas pa'i dga' ston* (ja, ff. 114a–122b). The treatment of the Great Debate and of Kamalaśīla's rôle in the *Chos 'byuṅ bstan pa'i padma rgyas pa'i ñin byed* by the 'Brug pa bKa' brgyud pa Padma dkar po (1527–1592) is very closely related to Bu ston's account and thus to that of the *sBa bžed*.[144]

Thus, in the earlier Tibetan historical literature up to the middle of the fourteenth century as available to us until recently, apart from the *sBa bžed* the exact school-links of which are not altogether clear, the encounter and controversy in Tibet between the 'Gradualists' and 'Simultaneists' and the Great Debate are found mentioned above all in sources connected with the Sa skya pa and, probably, the bKa' gdams pa schools. Later the subject was treated by bKa' brgyud pa authors too such as dPa' bo gTsug lag phreṅ ba, who has based his account on the *sBa bžed* (including the 'Alternative Tradition' reproduced in the unsupplemented recension of the *sBa bžed*) and has also quoted (f. 119b) Bu ston's *Chos 'byuṅ*.

II. The *Chos 'byuṅ Me tog sñiṅ po* of Ñaṅ Ñi ma 'od zer

The relative paucity and possible onesidedness of these older Tibetan historical materials have now been compensated in a most valuable and important way by the recent publication of the *Chos 'byuṅ Me tog sñiṅ po sBraṅ rtsi'i bcud*, a history of Buddhism ascribed to the twelfth-century rÑiṅ ma author Ñaṅ Ñi ma 'od zer.[145] For the most part, this work corroborates and supplements the accounts of the encounter between 'Gradualists' and 'Simultaneists' and of the Great Debate available from the sources mentioned above. But in certain respects it gives us a different view of some important details.

[144] Ed. Lokesh Chandra (New Delhi, 1968), f. 164b ff. For other later Tibetan sources on the Great Debate, see G. W. Houston, *Sources for a history of the bSam yas debate*.

[145] See: *Chos 'byuṅ Me tog sñiṅ po sBraṅ rtsi'i bcud*, MS A and B, in *Riṅ chen gter mdzod chen po'i rgyab chos*, Volumes 5 and 6 (Paro, 1979); and R. O. Meisezahl, *Die grosse Geschichte des tibetischen Buddhismus nach alter Tradition*, Monumenta tibetica historica 1/3 (St. Augustin, 1985).

The date of birth of Ñaṅ ral has been variously given as 1124 and 1136, and his death has been placed in either 1192 or 1204. He is renowned as a master of the rDzogs chen, and as a Discoverer (*gter ston*) of both rÑiṅ ma and Bon po texts (*gter ma*).[146] He thus belongs to a tradition quite different from the author(s) of the *sBa bžed*, from Bu ston and the other gSar ma pa authors of later Chos 'byuṅs who follow the *sBa bžed* and/or Bu ston in their accounts of the Great Debate, and from Sa skya Paṇḍi ta.

Ñi ma 'od zer's family name Ñaṅ/Myaṅ (both spellings have the same pronunciation) might possibly suggest a link, however distant, with the tradition of Myaṅ/Ñaṅ Tiṅ ṅe 'dzin (bzaṅ po),[147] the preceptor of the young Khri lDe sroṅ btsan (Sad na legs, reigned *c.* 800–815?), a disciple of Vimalamitra from whom he received the sÑiṅ thig teaching, and hence a very important early teacher of the rDzogs chen. As already noted above, Myaṅ Tiṅ ṅe 'dzin bzaṅ po figures as an opponent of sBa Ye šes dbaṅ po. Another master evidently connected with the Myaṅ/Ñaṅ tradition, Myaṅ/Ñaṅ Ša mi, is also known as the associate of a Hva šaṅ sometimes known as Me 'go/mgo and of sÑa Bye ma (*sBa bžed*, G, p. 67–68, and S, p. 57).

The *Chos 'byuṅ Me tog sñiṅ po* accordingly is one of our earliest datable Tibetan sources concerning the encounter between 'Gradualists' and 'Simultaneists' and the Great Debate. Its author is senior by at least half a century to Sa skya Paṇḍi ta, who has hitherto been our oldest securely datable authority on the subject. The *Chos 'byuṅ Me tog sñiṅ po* may then be surpassed in antiquity only by sBa records incorporated in the *sBa bžed*, and perhaps by

[146] On Ñaṅ ral and the question of 'ambivalent' – i.e. Buddhist (rDzogs chen) and Bon po -- *gter stons*, see A. M. Blondeau in L. Ligeti (ed.), *Tibetan and Buddhist studies commemorating the 200th anniversary of the birth of Alexander Csoma de Kőrös* (Budapest, 1984), p. 77 ff., and Meisezahl's introduction to his facsimile edition of the *Chos 'byuṅ*.

[147] Richardson, *A corpus of early Tibetan inscriptions*, p. 44, regards such a connexion as perhaps speculative. The *Myaṅ ban* Tiṅ ṅe 'dzin (bzaṅ po) founded the dBu ru Žva'i lha khaṅ 50 miles north-east of lHa sa on the Maṅ ra chu. As for the *Ñaṅ bdag* and *Ñaṅ ral* Ñi ma 'od zer, though born in lHo brag, his *gdan sa* is to be found in Myaṅ stod according to the *'Dzam gliṅ rgyas bšad* (f. 65a; Wylie, p. 71). And the Myaṅ clan to which Tiṅ ṅe 'dzin belonged may have originated in the upper valley of the Myaṅ chu around rGya mda' according to Richardson (*Corpus*, p. 44; see also *Bulletin of Tibetology* 4 (1967), p. 19 n. 10 on the location of Myaṅ). Eva Dargyay has listed Myaṅ Tiṅ ṅe 'dzin as an ancestor of Ñaṅ ral Ñi ma 'od zer in her *Rise of esoteric Buddhism in Tibet* (Delhi, 1977), p. 57, but without clearly giving her source.

another source stemming from the same school as Naṅ ral, the *bSam gtan mig sgron* ascribed to gNubs Saṅs rgyas ye šes the date of which is, however, not established with certainty and which does not in any case explicitly mention the Great Debate even though it has much to say on the two schools of thought that then confronted each other.

It is at all events very important for the question of the reliability of the Tibetan accounts of the Great Debate that the version given in the *Chos 'byuṅ Me tog sñiṅ po* is in many parts close to, and sometimes indeed practically identical in wording with, the *sBa bžed*. In particular, this text relates the defeat of the Hva šaṅ Mahāyāna by the 'Gradualists' headed by Kamalaśīla and his subsequent departure from Tibet. The only possible conclusion seems then to be that if Ñaṅ ral did not actually follow the *sBa bžed* in one of its recensions, he was making use of either a source of the extant recensions of the *sBa bžed* or of some other text closely related to it.

The *Chos 'byuṅ Me tog sñiṅ po* thus seems effectively to dispose of the suspicion that the account of the Great Debate and of the Hva šaṅ's defeat by Kamalaśīla's school to be found in the *sBa bžed*, in Bu ston's *Chos 'byuṅ* and in the many later sources that give this version of events was nothing but a tendentious sectarian fabrication of Atiša's bKa' gdams pas, and of other gSar ma pas such as the Sa skya pas and dGe lugs pas, which was concocted in order to discredit the traditions including the Dhyāna ones associated with the rÑiṅ ma pas/rDzogs chen pas.[148] It has to be recalled also that in his *Deb ther dmar po*, composed in 1346 after the Chos 'byuṅs of both Ne'u Paṇḍi ta and Bu ston, Kun dga' rdo rje has made no point of mentioning the Great Debate or the Hva šaṅ's defeat, something he might be expected to have done had this version of events been a fabrication of the gSar mas pas. It is equally noteworthy that whereas Sa skya Paṇḍi ta attached importance to criticizing the Hva šaṅ's teachings, the Great Debate and the Hva šaṅ's defeat have been mentioned by neither of his two great predecessors as hierarchs of Sa skya – Grags pa

[148] On the relationship between the *sBa bzed* and the rÑiṅ ma tradition, see also Sog bzlog pa, *Ñes don 'brug sgra*, f. 6a f.

rgyal mtshan in his *Bod kyi rgyal rabs* and bSod nams rtse mo in his *Chos la 'jug pa'i sgo* – although these two authors were contemporaries of the rÑiṅ ma pa Ñaṅ ral who has recounted these things.

The account given by the rDzogs chen pa Ñaṅ ral of the Great Debate and especially of the Hva šaṅ's defeat is all the more significant for the evaluation of the authenticity and reliability of the sources containing them because at least as early as the time of Kloṅ chen rab 'byams pa (1308–1363) rDzogs chen pa authorities have inclined to look on the Ḥva šaṅ Mahāyāna's teachings with favour (see below, p. 102).

On the following points the account found in the *Chos 'byuṅ Me tog sñiṅ po* concerning the Hva šaṅ Mahāyāna and the Great Debate deserves special mention. Some of them are quite close to what has been recorded in the *sBa bžed* and in the later Tibetan historical sources, but a few reflect noteworthy divergences from the hitherto available accounts.

(1) The discussions between the 'Gradualists' and 'Simultaneists' in Tibet at the end of the eighth century are presented as taking the form of a formal debate (*rtsod pa*) between two tendencies, each engaged in trying to reach a decisive conclusion in investigative argument (*gšags*), with the Tibetan ruler himself acting as the witness-arbiter (*dpaṅ po = sākṣin*) between Kamalaśīla and his Tibetan followers on the one side and the Hva šaṅ Mahāyāna and his supporters on the other.[149]

That this kind of discussion taking the form of a regular debate, familiar as it is to us from treatises on the Indian *vāda-*

[149] For the rôle of the *sākṣin* in a debate, see for example Dharmakīrti, *Vādanyāya* with Śāntarakṣita's comment (ed. Dwarikadas Shastri, Varanasi, 1972), pp. 69, 107. A king's court is recognized as a *vādādhikaraṇa* or suitable place for debate by Asaṅga, *Abhidharmasamuccaya*, p. 104. The arbiter-witness is also known as *sabhāpati* (e.g. in Vācaspatimiśra's *Nyāyavārttikatātparyaṭīkā* V. ii. 21). For later debates between Buddhists and Taoists under the Yüan, including one in which the young 'Phags pa took part in 1258 and which was presided over as crown prince by the future emperor Qubilai, see T. Thiel, *Monumenta Serica* 20 (1961), pp. 39–46.

That such a debate should have been organized and presided over (at least occasionally) by a king or prince is accordingly in no way unusual and *need* not be considered as later legend, or 'invention of tradition', by the Tibetan writers.

tradition, could have been already known in Tibet at the end of the eighth century is in accord with the likelihood that a high degree of scholastic knowledge and skill had been introduced in Tibet at that time by Śāntarakṣita (who indeed commented on Dharmakīrti's *Vādanyāya*) and Kamalaśīla, and with the fact that extensive scholastic knowledge is demonstrated a little later by such an early Tibetan scholar as sNa nam Ye šes sde.[150]

That just this scenario of a formal debate between Kamalaśīla and the Hva šaṅ Mahāyāna should have been accepted for the controversy between the 'Gradualists' and 'Simultaneists' by the author of the *Chos 'byuṅ Me tog sñiṅ po*, who belonged to a school for which the use of philosophical debate was however anything but characteristic, is of considerable significance for assessing the Tibetan account of these events. This fact could be explained in various ways. The author may simply have been relying on the *sBa bžed*, or on some closely related source belonging to a tradition that did make extensive use of debate in its philosophical exercises. Or these traditions may have been current in at least a section of the rÑiṅ ma school too. Or, again, it may be that events actually took the form described in the above-mentioned Tibetan sources. All that can be said at present is that this account of the controversy may reflect one of the earliest Tibetan views of these events handed down by the sBa family and accepted also by the author of the *Chos 'byuṅ Me tog sñiṅ po*, even though this precise scenario is not known to us from the Dunhuang documents; or, on the contrary, it may be a more or less dramatized reconstruction by Tibetan writers of a slightly later period (possibly at the start of the *phyi dar* or Second Propagation of Buddhism in Tibet) in accordance with a standard schema of Indo-Tibetan philosophical and religious discussion.

[150] Cf. for example D. Seyfort Ruegg, *Journal asiatique* 1979, p. 207 ff., on sNa nam Ye šes sde. And for a discussion of other scholastic treatises ascribed to early Tibetan authors, see Tucci, *Minor Tibetan texts*, II, p. 122 ff.

Subsequently, philosophical discussion in the form of debate appears to have been cultivated at the very latest by the time of Phya pa Chos kyi seṅ ge (1109–1169) at gSaṅ phu Ne'u thog. This seminary was founded in 1073 by rŇog Legs pa'i šes rab, the uncle of rŇog Blo ldan šes rab whose writings also attest a high degree of scholastic knowledge and who acted as abbot of this seminary. The forms of religio-philosophical discussion and debate have been set out in some detail by Sa skya Paṇḍi ta in his *mKhas 'jug* (Ch. iii), the oldest Tibetan text on the subject that appears to be available at present. Cf. now D. Jackson, *The Entrance Gate for the Wise (Section III)* (Vienna, 1987).

At all events, the fact that the *Chos 'byuṅ Me tog sñiṅ po* does mention a formal debate in which Kamalaśīla and his followers prevailed over the Hva šaṅ Mahāyāna lends no support to the opinion that the account found in the *sBa bžed* and in Bu ston's *Chos 'byuṅ* represents nothing but a deliberate and tendentious distortion of events by opponents of the 'Simultaneists' and of the rÑiṅ ma/rDzogs chen traditions motivated by sectarian bias. An argument *ex silentio* based on the absence of an explicit reference in the Chinese documents to a formal debate between the Ho-shang and Kamalaśīla or his Tibetan followers cannot be regarded as conclusive, especially in view of the clearly polemical character of Wang Hsi's *Cheng-li chüeh* studied by Demiéville.

(2) In agreement with other sources, the *Chos 'byuṅ Me tog sñiṅ po* (f. 433a–b) has placed the master dPal dbyaṅs among the opponents of the Hva šaṅ and the *cig char 'jug pa* or 'Chinese theory' (*rgya'i lta ba*) of the sTon min pas. This connexion is in accord with the attachment of dPal dbyaṅs to the 'Ba'/sBa family (for example in the *sBa bžed*). Tucci[151] has entertained the hypothesis that since a (certain) dPal dbyaṅs is stated to have belonged to the gÑan family, and indeed to have been a disciple of Vimalamitra and gÑags Jñānakumāra,[152] the attachment of the participant in the debate named dPal dbyaṅs to the party of Kamalaśīla and sBa Ye šes dbaṅ po may simply reflect a desire on the part of the author(s) of the *sBa bžed* to glorify their own family. But the fact that the *Chos 'byuṅ Me tog sñiṅ po* also regards this dPal dbyaṅs as an associate of Kamalaśīla and Ye šes dbaṅ po goes against this hypothesis; and the alternative view considered by Tucci, namely that we have here two different masters having the same name, is the likely one. It should be noted, moreover, that the words ascribed to dPal dbyaṅs in this *Chos 'byuṅ*, in one version of the *sBa bžed* (G, p. 70) and in the *mKhas pa'i dga' ston* (ja, f. 117b) are ascribed in the *Žabs btags ma* version of the *sBa bžed* (S, p. 59) to a certain Saṅ ši, a name (or title) borne by another member of the 'Ba' family (S, p. 17.15). (Strangely, the

151 G. Tucci, *Minor Buddhist texts*, ii, pp. 20–21, 150. Cf. Demiéville, in: M. Soymié (ed.), *Contributions aux études sur Touen-houang*, p. 11 (referring to Z. Yamaguchi).

152 See *mKhas pa'i dga' ston*, tha, f. 25a (p. 215.7); *Deb ther sṅon po*, ga, f. 2a (p. 104). On gÑan dPal dbyaṅs see R. Kimura, *Journal asiatique*, 1981, pp. 191–2.

Supplemented Version of the *sBa bžed* then (S, p. 60) ascribes to dPal dbyaṅs the intervention in the Great Debate which the unsupplemented version (G, p. 70–71) attributes to Ye šes dbaṅ po.)

(3) In its account of the Great Debate the *Chos 'byuṅ Me tog sñiṅ po* (f. 433b2) mentions, in the intervention ascribed to the master dPal dbyaṅs, a trifurcation of the 'middle Nikāyas' (? *dbus sde rnam gsum*). What is meant by this enigmatic expression is unfortunately not clear.[152a]

However, in this connexion both recensions of the *sBa bžed* – G (p. 70.16) where dPal dbyaṅs is also mentioned as the speaker, and S (p. 60.5) where Saṅ ši is named as the speaker – as well as Bu ston's *Chos 'byuṅ* (f. 129a6) and the *mKhas pa'i dga' ston* (ja, f. 118a1) all read *dbu ma rnam gsum*. Now, if the reference were to the three well-known schools of the Madhyamaka (*dbu ma*) recognized by the later Tibetan doxographers, this passage could hardly be dated before the eleventh or twelfth century when, as a consequence of the activity of Pa tshab Ñi ma grags (said to have been born in 1055) and his associates, the *Prāsaṅgika (Thal 'gyur ba) branch of the Madhyamaka first became established in Tibet in addition to the (Sautrāntika-)Svātantrika and the (Svātantrika-) Yogācāra-Madhyamaka branches already recognized by the ninth century. At all events, it seems highly unlikely that dPal dbyaṅs (or Saṅ ši) should have spoken of three branches of the Madhyamaka in Tibet at the end of the eighth century, when none of the known sources of that period seems ever to mention this third branch.

The reading *dbus sde* in the *Chos 'byun Me tog sñiṅ po* seems to place the problem in a different light, and it might even be supposed to reflect an earlier version of the passage in question (although it is not clear to what the expression *dbus sde* might refer). On the other hand, the reading *dbus sde* might represent a

[152a] The problem is compounded by the fact that in another historical work giving an account of the Great Debate and also ascribed to Ñaṅ ral – the Mi rje lhas mdzad *Byaṅ chub sems dpa' sems dpa' chen po chos rgyal mes dbon rnam gsum gyi rnam par thar pa, Rin po che'i phreṅ ba* published in 1980 at Paro – we read *dbu ma rnam pa lṅa ma mthun te ston min 1 char du 'jug mchis te* (f. 125b4–5). (The authorship of this work is not clear, and one folio is missing just before the last page of the reprint.)

correction, by Ñaṅ ral or by a source or a redactor of his, of the reading *dbu ma rnam gsum*. For the earlier rÑiṅ ma/rDzogs chen authors did not ordinarily recognize three branches of the Madhyamaka;[153] in addition, the author (or a redactor) of the *Chos 'byuṅ Me tog sñiṅ po* could well have been aware of the fact that this triple division of the Madhyamaka was not recognized in Tibet at the time of the Great Debate. Nevertheless, it must be noted that our *Chos 'byuṅ* itself explicitly mentions (f. 512a) both Candrakīrti – the main source of the *Prāsaṅgika branch of the Madhyamaka – and Pa tshab Ñi ma grags – reputedly its first major Tibetan proponent; but it has done so without mentioning the Thal 'gyur ba (*Prāsaṅgika) as a distinct, third branch of the Madhyamaka.

(4) Concerning the circumstances of Kamalaśīla's death after the Great Debate, the author of the *Chos 'byuṅ Me tog sñiṅ po* differs from the account we find in the *sBa bžed*, and he diverges completely from the version found in Bu ston's *Chos 'byuṅ* and the related sources.

According to the *sBa bžed* (G, p. 77–78; S, p. 64) and the *mKhas pa'i dga' ston* (ja, f. 122b6), Kamalaśīla was murdered by executioners (*gšed ma*) despatched by the *mu stegs pa*. This name, corresponding to Skt. *tīrthika/tīrthakāra*, designates a non-Buddhist, and in particular a Hindu sectarian. What *mu stegs pa* was intended to denote in this context is, however, uncertain.[154] And the difficulty is compounded from the point of view of the Tibetan tradition by the fact that, in the prophetic testament he is supposed to have given Khri Sroṅ lde btsan, Śāntarakṣita is recorded to have foretold that after his death there would no

[153] The *Prāsaṅgika school of Madhyamaka is not known to the *bSam gtan mig sgron*. Roṅ zom Chos kyi bzaṅ po (eleventh century) mentions only the mDo sde dbu ma and the rNal 'byor spyod pa'i dbu ma in his *Man ṅag lta phreṅ 'grel pa* (f. 28b), *lTa ba'i brjed byaṅ* (f. 11b–12a) and *Grub mtha' brjed byaṅ* (f. 5a–6a). However, Kloṅ chen rab 'byams pa (1308–1363) has recognized the *Prāsangika branch, for example in the *Grub mtha' mdzod* (f. 54b f. ~ 40a f.).

[154] Tucci has supposed that Kamalaśīla may have been killed by Bon pos (*Minor Buddhist texts*, II, p. 45). But since the reference is to executioners from China, could the *mu stegs pa* in this case have been Taoists (or even Buddho-Taoists)? On Taoism in Tibet at this time, see Demiéville in M. Soymié (ed.), *Contributions aux études sur Touen-houang*, p. 6. Compare for example the *Li'i yul luṅ bstan pa*, translated by F. W. Thomas, *Tibetan literary texts and documents concerning Chinese Turkestan*, I (London, 1935), p. 84.

longer be any *mu stegs pa*s in Tibet, but that instead a split would develop in the Buddhist Dharma itself.[155] Bu ston (or possibly a source of his) may have noticed this discrepancy between the account that Kamalaśīla was murdered by an agent of the *mu stegs pa* and what Śāntarakṣita had foretold in his testament, which he has recorded in his *Chos 'byuṅ*.[156] For according to Bu ston Kamalaśīla was murdered by four executioners from China belonging to the Hva šaṅ (*hva šaṅ gi rgya'i bšan pa mi bži*, f. 129b6), a version of events that was later followed by Padma dkar po (*Chos 'byuṅ*, f. 165a6) among others. In other words, Bu ston (or a source) may have engaged in a kind of rational reconstruction of events and concluded – given what Śāntarakṣita was held to have foretold – that it must have been the Ho-shang's party that was responsible for Kamalaśīla's alleged murder. In these circumstances, fully satisfactory grounds hardly exist for explaining Bu ston's version (along with that of Padma dkar po and others) by simply ascribing to him a desire to denigrate the Ho-shang.

It is of special interest to observe in this connexion that the *Chos 'byuṅ Me tog sñiṅ po* (f. 138a) not only knows nothing of Bu ston's version mentioning executioners sent by the Hva šaṅ as Kamalaśīla's murderers but distances itself from the *sBa bžed*'s account of a murder by agents of the *mu stegs pa* by qualifying it as a report by means of the verb *zer ba* 'it is said'. And it states instead that Kamalaśīla was killed by an Indian servant Dhanaśrī who was looking for gold.

(5) In the *Chos 'byuṅ Me tog sñiṅ po* (f. 429b–430a) it is related that at the start of the Great Debate at the Byaṅ chub gliṅ of bSam yas the King decreed that the loser should, as the price of defeat, receive a punishment (*chad pa gcod do*), which is however not specified. But no mention is made in this text of the banishment from Tibet by royal command of the Hva šaṅ Mahāyāna after he lost the debate. According to this account the

[155] *sBa bžed*, G, pp. 66, 72; and S, p. 56; Bu ston, *Chos 'byuṅ*, f. 127b; dPa' bo gTsug lag phreṅ ba, *mKhas pa'i dga' ston*, ja, f. 115b. Cf. *Chos 'byuṅ Me tog sñiṅ po*, f. 427b–428a.

[156] Bu ston, *Chos 'byuṅ*, f. 127b. It should however be noted that the teaching of non-activity which was Mo-ho-yen's, and to which Kamalaśīla refers in his *Bhāvanākrama* (iii, p. 20), has been connected by Kamalaśīla with teachings of the *mu stegs can* (*tīrthikas*) called *kun tu tshol ba*, evidently the Ājīvikas. See below, p. 142.

Hva šaṅ left, apparently voluntarily, not for China but for Bodh Gayā (rDo rje gdan) in India (f. 436a–b).

In the *sBa bžed* (G, p. 75 and S, p. 62) it is related that the Hva šaṅ returned to China (*slar rgya nag tu gšegs*) (cf. *mKhas pa'i dga' ston*, ja, f. 119a). The *rGyal rabs gsal ba'i me loṅ* (p. 182) too states that he departed (*bžud pa*) for China. For their part, Bu ston (*Chos 'byuṅ*, f. 128b2) and Padma dkar po (*Chos 'byuṅ*, f. 165a3–4) report that already at the very start of the Great Debate the Tibetan monarch decreed that the loser was not to remain in his realm; and these two sources relate that after losing the debate the Hva šaṅ was sent off (*rdzoṅ ba*) – i.e. probably, was banished – to China (Bu ston, f. 129b6; Padma dkar po, f. 165a5). Wang Hsi's *Cheng-li chüeh* on the other hand refers neither to a defeat nor to the banishment of Mo-ho-yen; and it mentions (f. 129a) an official edict authorizing the practice of his Dhyāna teaching. The Chinese material indicates furthermore that Mo-ho-yen returned to Dunhuang.[157]

The discrepancies in the accounts of the fate of Ho-shang Mo-ho-yen after the Great Debate have given rise to the hypothesis that he was involved in more than one debate, and that whereas he won the earlier debate he was finally defeated in a later one.[158] This is of course not impossible, but it would be as difficult to prove as it would be to disprove on the basis of the available evidence; it is at least equally possible that the divergence between the accounts reflects not the different outcome of two or more debates, but differing views of a single set of events.

(6) Of special interest is the account given in the *Chos 'byuṅ Me tog sñiṅ po* of the fate of the Hva šaṅ Mahāyāna's teaching in Tibet.

Both recensions of the *sBa bžed* (G, p. 75; 2, p. 62) and the *mKhas pa'i dga' ston* (ja, f. 119a) relate that the Tibetan ruler condemned the practice of the Hva šaṅ's Dharma (known as the

[157] See Demiéville, *Concile*, pp. 253 and 278, who has identified Mo-ho-yen with a Chinese Bhadanta living at Dunhuang after the time of the Great Debate and occupying a high post in the local administration there. Cf. Imaeda, *Journal asiatique*, 1975, p. 140–1.

[158] Demiéville distinguished at least three distinct sessions; see *T'oung Pao* 56 (1970), pp. 40–42. See also D. Ueyama, *Tōhō gakuhō* 35 (1964), pp. 141–214, with Demiéville's summary in *T'oung Pao* 56, pp. 29–43 (and pp. 43–44 on Z. Yamaguchi's critique of Ueyama); Imaeda, *Journal asiatique* 1975, pp. 126, 129, 140.

ston min pa cig char 'jug). And the *Žabs btags ma* version (S, p. 62), followed by the *mKhas pa'i dga' ston* (f. 119a), further specifies that the King decreed that henceforth the theory of Nāgārjuna should be accepted and that in the sphere of practice the Six Perfections should be adhered to. This version is followed in substance by Bu ston (*Chos 'byuṅ*, f. 129b) and Padma dkar po (*Chos 'byuṅ*, f. 165a). In the words of Ne'u Paṇḍi ta's *Chos 'byuṅ* (f. 22a), after the defeat of the Hva šaṅ, non-Dharma (*chos ma yin pa*) was not to be practised, and Dharma alone (*chos 'ba' žig*) – that is, evidently, the Dharma taught by Kamalaśīla following Śāntarakṣita and, ultimately, Nāgārjuna – was to be practised. Interestingly, the *Blon po bka'i thaṅ yig* (f. 28a), a section of the *bKa' thaṅ sde lṅa* which reproduces rDzogs chen traditions (cf. *Pelliot tibétain 116*), specifies that it was the Yoga-Madhyamaka (*rnal 'byor dbu ma'i gžuṅ*) that was to be followed, but without mentioning Kamalaśīla in this connexion; this source in fact states that the *ston mun cig car 'jug pa* is the Madhyamaka.

Now the *Chos 'byuṅ Me tog sñiṅ po* (f. 435b) relates that, after the Hva šaṅ Mahāyāna had conceded defeat in the Great Debate, the debate was reconciled on the side of Dharma (*rtsod pa chos phyogs su 'dum par byas so*). And the King declared that in substance there was no disagreement (*don la mi mthun pa tsam mi 'dug ste*) between the two parties to the debate, and that with respect to the method of practising the Path the Hva šaṅ's Dharma, known as the *cig char du 'jug*, is a teaching concerning persons whose faculties are highly developed (*dbaṅ po yaṅ rab sbyaṅs pa can gyis chos* [variant from Ms B: *lam*] *yin la*).[159] But, the King added, the ten Dharma-practices had been condemned [by the Hva šaṅ] starting with the case of those whose faculties are middling (*dbaṅ po 'briṅ man chad chos spyod bcu la skyon bskal*): Mind thus becomes drowsy (*sems ni byiṅ*), good equipment (*tshogs* = *sambhāra*) is not accumulated, and because others' mental training is interrupted the Dharma also declines and is interrupted. And, the King concludes, you [i.e. the Hva šaṅ] must practise meditative realisation (*bsgoms šig*). Henceforth, in the sphere of theory (*lta ba*), the theory of Nāgārjuna should be

[159] On the highly developed faculties (*dbaṅ po rnon po* = *tīkṣṇendriya*) required to penetrate the Hva šaṅ's teaching, see also above p. 66.

accepted, and in the sphere of praxis (*spyod pa*) the Six Perfections should be practised; the ten Dharma-practices (*chos spyod bcu*) should be exercised; in the sphere of meditative realization (*bsgom pa*) mental training is through the three kinds of discriminative understanding (*šes rab*=*prajñā*); Means (*thabs*=*upāya*) and Prajñā should be yoked together (*zuṅ du 'brel bar gyis*), and one should engage thus in meditative realization.

This version of the King's decree does not, it is true, actually disagree with the words found in the *sBa bžed*, most of which it contains while omitting only a few. But by including several additional phrases the *Chos 'byuṅ Me tog sñiṅ po* has nevertheless put another complexion on the Great Debate and the King's decree following it. Thus, the King's remark that the Hva šaṅ Mahāyāna's teaching does not disagree *in substance* with that of Kamalaśīla's school and that it is the teaching (*chos*) – or, according to a variant reading, the Path (*lam*) – followed by advanced disciples effaces the radical opposition between the 'Gradualist' and the 'Simultaneist'.[160]

Nevertheless, in the *Chos 'byuṅ Me tog sñiṅ po* there is recorded the King's decree to the effect that Nāgārjuna's theory was thenceforth to be accepted, and that the practice of the Pāramitās and the yoking together in *yuganaddha* of Upāya and Prajñā should be observed.

Interestingly, the *bSam gtan mig sgron* has quoted (f. 23b–24a) a verse from the *rTen 'brel sñiṅ po*, stating that it provides the source for the meditative realization of the sTon mun, in other words of the Hva šaṅ Mahāyāna's school. Now this *rTen 'brel sñiṅ po* must be the *Pratītyasamutpādakārikās* ascribed to Nāgārjuna; for the verse quoted corresponds to verse 7 of this text (which is paralleled by *Ratnagotravibhāga* i. 154 and *Abhisamayālaṃkāra* v. 21, and partially by Aśvaghoṣa's *Saundaranandakāvya* xiii. 44).[161] It thus appears that an important rDzogs chen text that

[160] This view of the matter is similar to the one attested in the *bSam gtan mig sgron*. And it is even attested in an intervention in the Great Debate ascribed either to sBa dPal dbyaṅs or Saṅ ši (see below, p. 86).

[161] This verse is quoted also in the *dMyigs su med pa tshul gcig pa'i gžuṅ* (*Pelliot tib. 116*), f. 164 (cf. F. Faber, *Acta Orientalia* 46 [1985], pp. 71–72), and in Vimalamitra's *Cig car 'jug pa rnam par mi rtog pa'i bsgom don* (D, f. 10b). For a recent discussion of the *Pratītyasamutpādahṛdayakārikās*, see C. Dragonetti, *WZKS* 30 (1986), pp. 109–22 (where

treats the 'Simultaneist' doctrine favourably has gone so far as to cite a text elsewhere usually ascribed to Nāgārjuna as a major source for the Hva šaṅ's school.[162] This significant linkage is not weakened, from the point of view of the Tibetan tradition, by the fact that the results of modern scholarship make it unlikely that Nāgārjuna was actually the author of this verse, which fits rather into a distinct doctrinal complex (with which the Hymnic Corpus ascribed to Nāgārjuna may, however, be connected).

Finally, the relationship between twenty-one Indian Ācāryas and five (Chinese) Hva šaṅs has been described in the *Chos 'byuṅ Me tog sñiṅ po* (f. 437b) as a peaceful one at the Byams pa gliṅ, after the defeat of the Hva šaṅ Mahāyāna in the Great Debate at the Byaṅ chub gliṅ of bSam yas and his departure for Bodh Gayā in India.

Even according to the sBa traditions, a leading member of this family – dPal dbyaṅs or Saṅ ši – remarked during the course of the Great Debate that although there indeed existed a difference as to 'means of access' (*'jug sgo*) between the 'Simultaneists' and 'Gradualists' the two were nonetheless broadly in agreement as to their doctrines concerning the attainment of buddhahood. In other words, their doctrines of the Fruit (*'bras bu*) were generally in harmony; and the disagreement between the two parties in the Great Debate concerned their respective theories of practice of the Path.[163] Kamalaśīla's followers also rejected the idea of original Awakening (*daṅ po nas saṅs rgyas*).[164]

(7) The *Chos 'byuṅ Me tog sñiṅ po* (f. 436b) rejects as false

they are tentatively ascribed to a certain Śuddhamati, a Mādhyamika author of perhaps before the sixth century).

162 Nāgārjuna is quoted elsewhere in texts belonging to the Dhyāna-tradition, for example in *Pelliot tibétain 116* (f. 164), where he is placed before a seven-membered line (*bdun rgyud*) beginning with Bo de dar ma ta la, and culminating in Ma ha yan.

Compare also Thu'u bkvan Blo bzaṅ Chos kyi ñi ma, *Grub mtha' šel gyi me loṅ*, rGya nag Chapter, f. 11b–13b, on the *sñiṅ po don gyi brgyud pa* and the *tsuṅ men (pa)*, a line that includes the Hva šaṅ Mahāyāna at its end, and Nāgārjuna, Āryadeva and Rāhula towards its beginning. See below, p. 117f.

163 See *sBa bžed*, G, p. 70.18–19, *mKhas pa'i dga' ston*, f. 118a2, and *Chos 'byuṅ Me tog sñiṅ po*, f. 433b3–4 (quoting dPal dbyaṅs); *sBa bžed*, S, p. 60.6–7 (quoting Saṅ ši): *'jug sgo tha dad kyaṅ saṅs rgyas (thob par 'dod par) (g)cig (žes) 'bras bu ('dod pa) (cig la) (doṅ gyi) (spyi) mthun pa* ... (The reading of the *Chos 'byuṅ Me tog sñiṅ po* is problematical here.)

164 See *sBa bžed*, S, p. 60.10 (quoting dPal dbyaṅs); G, p. 70.23; *mKhas pa'i dga' ston*, f. 118a3; *Chos 'byuṅ Me tog sñiṅ po*, f. 433b6 (quoting Ye šes dbaṅ po): *cig char (du) 'jug na (khyed) da duṅ (ruṅ) ci byed daṅ po nas saṅs rgyas na ci ñes*...

rumour the reports that the Hva šaṅ Mahāyāna immolated himself in fire after his defeat in debate or, alternatively, that in despair (*yid mug pa*) he left for home after leaving behind one of his boots as a token of the future spread of his teaching in Tibet.

Such a case of self-immolation, followed by death facing in the direction of the Sukhāvatī-heaven, of a Chinese master (*rgya nag mkhan po*) – according to the context apparently the Hva šaṅ Mahāyāna himself – is in fact reported in part of the 'Alternative Tradition' of the *sBa bžed* (G, p. 75; but not reproduced in dPa' bo gTsug lag phreṅ ba's *mKhas pa'i dga' ston*, f. 120). Both recensions of the *sBa bžed* have nevertheless elsewhere recounted that the Hva šaṅ left for China after having first constructed a temple in Tibet (G, p. 76; S, p. 62–63). The false rumour to which the *Chos 'byuṅ Me tog sñiṅ po* refers is then perhaps the account found in the 'Alternative Tradition' of the *sBa bžed*.

Such an auto-da-fé by setting fire to the head carried out by *a* Hva šaṅ after having lost an argument is however reported in both recensions of the *sBa bžed* (G, p. 68.1; S, p. 57.12), but only one version specifies that he thereupon died (G, p. 68.1; cf. also *mKhas pa'i dga' ston*, ja, f. 115a5 and 116b4). The Hva šaṅ who thus immolated himself is, however, given the suggestive name, or probably rather epithet, of Me mgo/Me 'go, literally 'Fire-head' (see also *sBa bžed*, S, p. 10.1 and p. 52). This appellation could well be based on the Chinese practice of lighting a lamp on the top of a monk's head at the time of ordination,[165] and it may then have been reinterpreted as signifying that the Ho-shang immolated himself.[166] The reports of this Hva šaṅ's auto-da-fé are doubtless influenced in addition by the practice of ritual self-cremation occasionally adopted by monks in East (and South East) Asia.[167]

It is interesting to observe that in this context the *Chos 'byuṅ*

165 Cf. J. J. M. de Groot, *Le code du Mahâyâna en Chine* (Amsterdam, 1893), pp. 218–220; cf. pp. 50–51, 220 ff.

166 For such suicides by Tibetans (!) in the *Cheng-li chüeh*, see Demiéville, *Concile*, pp. 41–42.

167 For a bibliography of this practice, see Tucci, *Minor Buddhist texts*, II, pp. 10, 284; E. Lamotte, *Traité de la Grande Vertu de Sagesse* (Louvain, 1949), p. 740 n. 1; J. Filliozat, *Journal asiatique*, 1963, pp. 21–51, and *Arts asiatiques* 15 (1967), pp. 65–88; P. Demiéville, *Choix d'études bouddhiques* (Leiden, 1973), pp. xxxviii–xxxix, 264–5. See below, pp. 149–50.

Me tog sñiṅ po (f. 429b4) relates that the Hva šaṅ Mi/Me go died (? *bro dor*),[168] while his associates – Ñaṅ Ša mi, rṄog and sÑa[169] – 'contracted illness' (*na tsha skyed*). The *Žabs btags ma* version of the *sBa bžed* (S, p. 57) also states that the three 'contracted illness'. Another version of the *sBa bžed* however specifies that they died as the result of self-mutilation (G, p. 67–68; cf. *mKhas pa'i dga' ston*, ja, f. 116b).

As for the report that the Hva šaṅ Mahāyāna departed for China after leaving his boot behind in Tibet, it is found also in the 'Alternative Tradition' of the *sBa bžed* (G, p. 75.8, not reproduced in the *mKhas pa'i dga' ston*, f. 120). The motif of the boot left behind is known also in connexion with another Hva šaṅ (perhaps one connected with sBa gSal snaṅ in the *sBa bžed*, G, p. 9 ~ S, p. 8).[170] The association of this motif with Bodhidharma is of course known from the Chinese Ch'an tradition; and in Tibetan sources it is found in connexion with the Dhyāna-master Bodhi-Dharmottāra in the *bSam gtan mig sgron* (f. 12b).[171]

(8) It is significant that in the *Chos 'byuṅ Me tog sñiṅ po* (f. 425'a6) the expression *dkar po chig thub* – a term presumably borrowed from the vocabulary of Tibetan pharmacology and denoting in the present context a spiritual sovereign remedy – is recorded as a description, based on a medical metaphor, of the Hva šaṅ Mahāyāna's 'spontaneist' and cognitively nativist teaching of face-to-face intuitive confrontation with and comprehension of Mind (*sems ṅo 'phrod pa*, etc.).

The same expression is found in addition in the 'Alternative

[168] See *Chos 'byuṅ Me tog sñiṅ po*, f. 426b4, where the expression *bro bor* is found. In standard classical Tibetan, *bro bor ba* and *bro dor ba* mean 'to swear an oath' (*mna' bskyal ba/skyel ba*). In the present context, however, not only does this meaning not fit well but the corresponding passages in the parallel sources indicate that the appropriate meaning is 'to die' (*ši* in *sBa bžed*, G, p. 68.1, and in dPa' bo gTsug lag phreṅ ba's *mKhas pa'i dga' ston*, ja, f. 116b4; *'das* in *mKhas pa'i dga' ston*, ja, f. 115a5).

[169] See above, p. 61.

[170] See also 'Gos gŽon nu dpal, *Deb ther sṅon po*, ka, f. 21a3 (Roerich, p. 41); bSod nams rgyal mtshan, *rGyal rabs gsal ba'i me loṅ* (ed. Kuznetsov), p. 182. Cf. *bSam gtan mig sgron*, f. 12 (in connexion with 'Bodhidharmottāra'); mGon po skyabs, *rGya nag chos 'byuṅ* (Sichuan ed., 1983), p. 122. See also G. Tucci, *Tibetan painted scrolls* (Rome, 1949), p. 615 n. 252, and *Minor Buddhist texts*, II (Rome, 1958), p. 44.

[171] Compare Thu'u bkvan Blo bzaṅ Chos kyi ñi ma, *Grub mtha' šel gyi me loṅ*, rGya nag Chap., f. 13a.

Tradition' of the *sBa bžed* (G, pp. 72–75), from where dPa' bo gTsug lag phreṅ ba has taken it (*mKhas pa'i dga' ston*, ja, f. 120a6–7). And it is known too from Sa skya Paṇḍi ta's treatment of the Hva šaṅ's teaching in connexion with his criticism of the Neo-Mahāmudrā (*da lta'i phyag rgya chen po*) and Chinese-style rDzogs chen (*rgya nag lugs kyi rdzogs chen*).[172] A corresponding medical concept is, moreover, found in Wang Hsi's *Cheng-li chüeh* (f. 146b); there, in the context of Mo-ho-yen's own presentation of his teaching on non-reflection and non-examination, the *Mahāparinirvāṇasūtra* is quoted on the subject of the medicine called *agada*, which is said to heal all illnesses.[173]

This attestation in the *Chos 'byuṅ Me tog sñiṅ po* – which as seen above is not unfavourable to the Hva šaṅ Mahāyāna – of the expression *dkar po chig thub* as a description of the 'Simultaneist' teaching, supported as it is by the presence of a parallel medical description ascribed to Mo-ho-yen himself in the *Cheng-li chüeh*, disposes of the suspicion that the comparison with the Hva šaṅ's teaching of certain other doctrines current in Tibet that also made use of the image of the *dkar po chig thub* as a spiritual panacea was arbitrary and nothing but a transparent polemical device used by Tibetan opponents of these later teachings such as Sa skya Paṇḍi ta (see below, Chap. iii).

In sum, largely concordant accounts of the Great Debate between the 'Gradualists' headed by Kamalaśīla and represented in addition by Ye šes dbaṅ po and dPal dbyaṅs – both members of the sBa family – on the one side and the Ho-shang Mo-ho-yen associated with Myaṅ/Ñaṅ Ša mi and other Tibetan followers on the other side have been handed down in the traditions of the sBa family (*sBa bžed*) followed by Sa skya Paṇḍi ta and Bu ston, and perhaps also by Ne'u Paṇḍi ta, and in the *Chos 'byuṅ Me tog sñiṅ*

[172] See Sa skya Paṇḍi ta, *sDom gsum rab dbye*, f. 25b–26b. Cf. *Thub pa'i dgoṅs pa rab tu gsal ba*, f. 48b–50b, 59b; and *sKyes bu dam pa rnams la spriṅ ba'i yi ge* f. 3a ff.

[173] See Fa-hsien's Chinese translation of the *Mahāparinirvāṇasūtra* (T 376, p. 893b), a passage that is however not found in the other Chinese translations according to Demiéville, *Concile*, p. 122 n. 7. In the *Mahāparinirvāṇsūtra* it is, moreover, the Sūtra itself that is compared with the *agada*. Cf. *Hōbōgirin*, p. 180, s.v. *Akada*.

po by the rDzogs chen master of the Ñaṅ family, Ñi ma 'od zer. Assuming that the ascriptions of these texts are not wholly without foundation – and no reason to think otherwise has so far emerged – the account of the Great Debate and the issues addressed in it can be securely traced back at least as far as the early thirteenth century, in other words to no less than a century before Bu ston and to a time just before Sa skya Paṇḍi ta. No cogent reason has appeared either for supposing that sBa traditions, at least in their core, are not even older. Indeed – except of course for the supplemented version of the *sBa bžed*, which continues down to the time of Atiša, and the very end of the unsupplemented version, which records events after the death of Ye šes dbaṅ po – the sBa traditions may go back essentially to the time of sBa gSal snaṅ (identified with Ye šes dbaṅ po) and dPal dbyaṅs, two of Mo-ho-yen's main opponents in the Great Debate.

As for the *Chos 'byuṅ Me tog sñiṅ po*, the question arises as to whether its author, *Ñaṅ ral* Ñi ma 'od zer, could have made use of records going back as far as Ñaṅ/Myaṅ Ša mi – an early advocate of 'Simultaneist' teachings and apparently an associate of the Hva šaṅ known as Me mgo/Me 'go, of sÑa Bye ma la/mÑa' Bi ma,[174] and perhaps of Mo-ho-yen himself[175] – and *Myaṅ ban* Tiṅ ṅe 'dzin bzaṅ po – a supporter of the Ho-shangs and an opponent of Ye šes dbaṅ po.

Now, if the *sBa bžed* and sources such as the writings of Sa skya Paṇḍi ta, Bu ston's *Chos 'byuṅ* and the *mKhas pa'i dga' ston* which agree with it have transmitted records of the sBa family going back to the time of the Great Debate whilst the *Chos 'byuṅ Me tog sñiṅ po* might perhaps be conjectured to reflect, at least to some degree, ancient traditions of the Myaṅ/Ñaṅ family, it will be all the more significant that the account of the events surrounding the Great Debate found in the latter *Chos 'byuṅ* agrees fairly closely with the account in the sBa traditions. At all events, on several points of importance in the present context, the *Chos 'byuṅ Me tog sñiṅ po* hardly differs more from one or the other of the *sBa bžed* versions than these differ from each other. Hence, if Ñaṅ ral was not actually following a version of the sBa records, it

[174] See above, pp. 61, 88. [175] See *sBa bžed*, G, pp. 65–68, and S, pp. 55–57.

must be concluded that he was drawing either on a closely related text or on some older common source.[176]

Therefore, and despite some important differences such as the ones noted above, the very considerable degree of agreement between the sBa records and the *Chos 'byuṅ Me tog sñiṅ po* lends support if not to the assumption that the controversy and debate between Kamalaśīla's school and the Hva šaṅ(s) actually took place in *exactly* the way related in these sources, then at least to the likelihood that these accounts are not mere fabrications by post-twelfth-century gSar ma pa writers motivated by hostility to the teachings of the eighth-century 'Simultaneists' and the rDzogs chen pas.

It has to be borne in mind too that if Kamalaśīla and the Hva šaṅ Mahāyāna figure in a kind of complementary theoretical opposition to each other, Śāntarakṣita and Padmasambhava – a major source of the rÑiṅ ma tradition – stood in a relation of complementary suppletion according to the sources. Thus, in our sources there can be no question of an undifferentiated blanket rejection of all that is rÑiṅ ma or rDzogs chen; and it will not be possible either to hold that the rejection of the Hva šaṅ and his teachings was simply inspired by hostility to rDzogs chen with which his teachings bear a certain typological affinity that did not go unrecognized by rÑiṅ ma pa authorities (see below, p. 102).

In the historiography of Tibetan religion and philosophy matters are seldom so simple as to be explainable merely by a conspiracy theory. If alterations and distortions of historical events have actually taken place, then both the causes and the

[176] In his *rGya nag hva šaṅ gi byuṅ tshul grub mtha'i phyogs sña bcas sa bon tsam smos pa*, f. 14a, Tshe dbaṅ nor bu has referred also to the *sBa bžed* in connexion with the differences between the Chinese Ho-shangs and the Indian Siddhāntas, as well as to the *bSam gtan mig gi 'grel pa* (i.e. the *bSam gtan mig sgron*) of gNubs Rin po che.

Furthermore, as already noted, monks of the dBa'/sBa and Myaṅ families were already linked as disciples of Śāntarakṣita according to the Turkestan (Ša cu) document published by F. W. Thomas (see above, n. 107 and n. 110). Later, a certain sBa sgom was the disciple of Myaṅ Šes rab 'byuṅ gnas of the dBu ru Žva'i lha khaṅ founded by Myaṅ Tiṅ ṅe 'dzin, and a contemporary of Myaṅ Byaṅ chub grags (Myaṅ Ša ba can); see gŽon nu dpal, *Deb ther sṅon po*, ga, f. 33b (= p. 173–4).

For a later rÑiṅ ma view of the Great Debate as reported in the *sBa bžed* and as discussed by Sa skya Paṇḍi ta, in addition to Tshe dbaṅ nor bu's work already cited above see Sog bzlog pa Blo gros rgyal mtshan, *gSaṅ sṅags sṅa 'gyur la bod du rtsod pa sṅa phyir byuṅ ba rnams kyi lan du brjod pa, ṅes don 'brug sgra*, ff. 6a ff. and 117a–120b.

processes of these changes are probably fairly complex. Much historical, religious and philosophical analysis remains to be done on the eighth-century encounter in Tibet between 'Gradualism' and 'Simultaneism' for which the documentation is multifarious and sometimes opaque. An attempt in this direction will be made in the two following essays.

III

Models of Buddhism in Contact and Opposition in Tibet: Religious and Philosophical Issues in the Great Debate of bSam yas

WHAT then were the fundamental questions at issue in the encounter between Śāntarakṣita's and Kamalaśīla's Yogācāra-Madhyamaka school on the one side and on the other the doctrines of the Ho-shangs teaching in Tibet and the Dunhuang area with Mo-ho-yen (Mahāyāna/Mahā yan) amongst the best known of them?

In his *Bhāvanākrama* (III, ed. Tucci, pp. 13–14) Kamalaśīla has given the following summary of some teachings that represent the views of an unnamed opponent:

> A certain [teacher] has the following opinion: 'It is because of the force of good and bad deeds (*śubhāśubhakarman*), produced through mental construction (*cittavikalpa*), that sentient beings (*sattva*) revolve in the round of existences (*saṃsāra*), experiencing the fruits of deeds (*karmaphala*) such as heaven (*svargādi*).[177] Those who on the contrary neither think on anything (*na kiṃcic cintayanti*) nor perform any deed whatever are completely freed (*parimuc-*) from the round of existences. Therefore nothing is to be thought on (*na kiṃcic cintayitavyam*), nor is salutary conduct (*kuśalacaryā*) consisting in generosity and the like (*dānādi*) to be practised. It is only in respect to foolish people (*mūrkhajana*) that salutary conduct consisting in generosity and the like has been indicated (*nirdiṣṭā*).'

[177] Cf. Wang Hsi's *Cheng-li chüeh*, f. 134a ff. (translated by Demiéville, *Concile*, pp. 75 ff.); *Stein 468* (cf. L. Gómez, in R. Gimello and P. Gregory [eds.], *Studies in Ch'an and Hua-yen* [Honolulu, 1983], p. 107); *Pelliot tibétain 21* (cf. L. Gómez, *Studies*, p. 124).

Several lines further on in the same text Kamalaśīla again cites (p. 14) the assertion that the practice of generosity and the other virtues is not to be carried out, and he later quotes the thesis (p. 20): 'No deed whatever, salutary or otherwise, is to be performed'.

Kamalaśīla also cites (p. 15) the teaching according to which one 'enters' all factors through non-mind and non-mentation (*sarvadharmeṣv asmṛtyamanasikāreṇa praviśati*).[178] And in another *Bhāvanākrama* (I, ed. Tucci, p. 212) Kamalaśīla quotes the *Avikalpapraveśadhāraṇī*'s observation that 'by non-mentation one sets aside the phenomenal marks of visible matter and so forth' (*amanasikārato rūpādinimittaṃ varjayati*). According to Kamalaśīla's explanation, what is here intended by the term *amanasikāra* is not simple absence of mentation (*manasikārābhāvamātra*) but, rather, that non-objectifying or non-apprehension which belongs to him who analyses through discriminative knowledge (*prajñayā nirūpayato yo 'nupalambhaḥ* = *śes rab kyis brtags na mi dmigs pa gaṅ yin pa*).[179]

[178] Cf. *Cheng-li chüeh* f. 135a f. (Demiéville, p. 76 f.); *Stein 468* (Gómez, p. 108) and *709* (Gómez, p. 114); *Pelliot tibétain 823* (Goméz, p. 126). Cf. *bSam gtan mig sgron*, f. 73a f.

[179] Kamalaśīla has taken up this point in his *Avikalpapraveśadhāraṇī-Ṭīkā* (P, f. 156b–157b). There he observes first that when something is perceived by being presented in cognition (*snaṅ bar 'gyur bas mṅon du 'gyur pa*), it is something that may then be removed through non-mentation (*amanasikāra*). Next he argues that such *amanasikāra* is not mere absence of mentation [in the sense of absolute, non-presuppositional and non-implicative, negation, or *prasajyapratiṣedha*]. For, non-existence being no thing (*dṅos po med pa*), it cannot serve as the cause for anything at all; and without correct analytical examination (*bhūtapratyavekṣā*) it is impossible not to attend (*manas-kṛ-*) to the phenomenal signs (*nimitta*) of matter (*rūpa*) and the other [*skandhas*] presented in cognition. Nor, however, does something other than this mentation constitute *amanasikāra* [in the sense of relative, presuppositional and implicative negation, or *paryudāsa*]; for it would then follow that some other thing such as *rūpa* and the other [*skandhas*] too could be *amanasikāra*, [*amanasikāra*] being then not the counter-agent (*pratipakṣa*) against them [as is required by the theory]. Accordingly, what was intended [when *amanasikāra* was spoken of in the *Avikalpapraveśadhāraṇī*] is that an *amanasikāra* that is the characteristic (*lakṣaṇa*) of *bhūtapratyavekṣā* – the contrary of that *manasikāra* [which is to be counteracted] – constitutes *amanasikāra*.

Alternatively, because *amanasikāra* is a product (*phala*) [of analytical examination], it has been stated that *bhūtapratyavekṣā* is to be designated metonymically by the term '*amanasikāra*'. That is, by merely indicating its product, it becomes evident by implication (*arthasāmarthya*) that [analytical examination as the cause of *amanasikāra*] is to be effected. So it is possible fully to remove the phenomenal signs (*nimitta*). For, granted that the Yogin thus analytically examines phenomenal signs such as *rūpa* presented in his cognition [even though] in a form that is erroneous (*viparyasta*) owing to the force of misknowledge

In his *Bhāvanākrama* (III, p. 25–26) Kamalaśīla also cites the thesis that the Six Perfections (*pāramitā*) are contained in Dhyāna, so that through the cultivation (*sevanā* = *bsten pa*) of the latter all the Perfections are cultivated, whereas generosity (*dāna*) and the others should not be cultivated separately.[180] This thesis contrasts with the view (based on the Prajñāpāramitā-Sūtras) according to which, in order to be true Perfections, the other *pāramitās* must be under the direction of the Perfection of discriminative understanding (*prajñāpāramitā*).

Now, he who suitably joins together *dhyāna* and *prajñā* is called *prajñottaradhyāyin* (*śes rab mchog gi bsam gtan pa*), i.e. a meditator for whom discriminative understanding is paramount.[181] At this high stage of attainment, mind (*manas*) – or *manasikāra* according to *Bhāvanākrama* II (ed. Goshima, p. 47) – characterized as it henceforth is by the cessation of analytical reflection (*uparatavicāra*) is wholly without linguistic conceptual construction (*nirjalpaikarasa* = *brjod pa med pa ṅaṅ gcig tu gyur pa*);[182] and it operates of itself (*svarasavāhin* = *raṅ gi ṅaṅ gis 'jug pa*), so that the Yogin will then abide in determining reality without conceptual effort (*anabhisaṃskāratas*).[183] When Mind (*citta*) is thus *svarasavāhin* and proceeds in balance (*samapravṛtta* = *mñam par 'jug pa*) there will be equanimity because of the relaxation of mental inflexion (*ābhogaśithilīkaraṇād upekṣaṇīyam*).[184] This is what is known as the Path

(*avidyā*), once they are not cognitively objectified (*ālamb-*) [any longer], conceptual attraction (*abhiniveśa*) [to them] is removed. When they have been removed, absence of phenomenal sign (*animitta*) is comprehended ... [157b5]. In this way, the characteristic of *bhūtapratyavekṣā* is considered in this connexion to be *amanasikāra*. Although it is [indeed] of the nature of dichotomizing construction (*vikalpa*), it will [nevertheless] be consumed by the fire of correct Gnosis (*yaṅ dag pa'i ye śes* = *samyagjñāna*) produced by it, just as e.g. two fire-sticks are consumed by the fire produced by rubbing them together. Thus, he who wishes to produce Gnosis free from *vikalpa* must first cultivate Insight (*vipaśyanā*), the characteristic of *bhūtapratyavekṣā*. Thereby phenomenal signs will be fully removed.

This image of the fire-sticks burnt up by the fire that issues from them is taken from the *Kāśyapaparivarta* § 69; see *Bhāvanakrama* III, p. 20, and below, pp. 114, 206. And on the *nirvikalpa/avikalpa(praveśadhāraṇī)*, in addition to Kamalaśīla's *Bhāvanākramas* (I, p. 212 and III, p. 11), compare Sthiramati's *Triṃśikābhāṣya* 22d, 28–30. See also K. Matsuda, *Bukkyō seminā* 34 (1981), pp. 40–49.

[180] Cf. *Pelliot tibétain 116* (171 f.) and *117*; *Stein 709* (Gómez, pp. 80, 87).

[181] *Bhāvanākrama* III (ed. Tucci), p. 8; II (ed. Goshima), p. 47. (This concept has to be distinguished from *dṛṣṭyuttaradhyāyitā* in Asaṅga's *Abhidharmasamuccaya*, p. 68, which constitutes a ground for Affects [*saṃkleśa*].)

[182] *Bhāvanākrama* III, p. 5.6–7. [183] *Bhāvanākrama* III, p. 8.

[184] Cf. *Bhāvanākrama* I (ed. Tucci), pp. 266–7; II, pp. 49–53.

where Quieting and Insight operate in conjunction (*śamathavipaśyanāyuganaddhavāhī mārgo niṣpannaḥ* = *ži gnas daṅ lhag mthoṅ zuṅ du 'brel ba'i lam grub pa*).[185]

The concept of the balanced process of Mind in *śamatha* and *vipaśyanā*, as a consequence of which there is neither drowsiness (*laya* = *byiṅ ba*) nor excitation (*auddhatya* = *rgod pa*) of Mind, is further illustrated by the image of a pair of oxen going along yoked together (*yuganaddhavāhibalivardadvaya* = *glaṅ gñis zuṅ du 'brel ba*).[186] Crucial in this context is exact analysis (*bhūtapratyavekṣā* = *yaṅ dag par so sor rtog pa*) leading to analysis of the factors of existence (*dharmapravicaya* = *chos šin tu rnam par 'byed pa*) and discriminative understanding (*prajñā* = *šes rab*), and to Insight (*vipaśyanā* = *lhag mthoṅ*).

According to Kamalaśīla, then, there should indeed be a simultaneous operation (*cig car 'jug pa*) of Means (*thabs* = *upāya*) consisting in generosity, etc., and of Prajñā, this being the Path of their joint processing (*yuganaddhavāhī mārgaḥ*).[187]

Such practice leads to the Bodhisattva's achievement of objectifying the entirety of things (*vastuparyantatālambana* = *dṅos po'i mtha' la dmigs pa*),[188] to his birth in the Tathāgata-Family (*tathāgatakula*), to his entry into faultless determination (*skyon med pa* = *niyāma*),[189] and thus ultimately to buddahood.

The opposed doctrines, which are found most clearly reported in the third *Bhāvanākrama* and which Kamalaśīla has rebutted in detail by means of a very extensive array of quotations from the Sūtras and some Śāstras, are not, as already mentioned, explicitly ascribed by him to the Ho-shang Mo-ho-yen or to any other contemporary. Indeed, as is frequently the case in Indian philosophical treatises, no explicit information is provided as to whether they were the actual views held by some particular contemporary of the author. The fact that they are envisaged in the Mahāyānist canonical texts cited by Kamalaśīla leads one to suppose that they are quite old opinions. However, there are

[185] *Bhāvanākrama* III, p. 9. [186] *Bhāvanākrama* III, p. 10; cf. I, p. 207, and II, p. 35.
[187] *Bhāvanākrama* II, p. 71. [188] Cf. *Bhāvanākrama* III, p. 30.6.
[189] *Bhāvanākrama* II, p. 77, quoting the *Daśabhūmikasūtra* i, p. 12.

clear links between Kamalaśīla's *Bhāvanākramas* and *Avikapla-praveśadhāraṇī-Ṭīkā* and Mo-ho-yen's views as found in the Tibetan fragments from Dunhuang and in Wang Hsi's *Cheng-li chüeh*.

The two tendencies confronting each other have regularly been described, and clearly contrasted, in the older Tibetan historical texts by means of the designations *rim gyis pa* or *rim gyis 'jug pa* for Kamalaśīla's school and *(g)cig c(h)ar ba* or *cig c(h)ar* [*du*] *'jug pa* for Mo-ho-yen's school. The term *rim gyis pa*, a noun derived from the locution *rim gyis* 'gradually', corresponding to Skt. *krameṇa*, may accordingly be rendered by 'gradualist', the emphasis in this tendency being on the step-by-step serial cultivation (*bhāvanā*) through reinforcement (*abhyāsa*) of the Path of Awakening with its successive gradations (*rim pa* = *krama*). And *rim gyis 'jug pa* can be rendered as 'gradual engagement' or 'gradual process' (*'jug pa* = *pravṛt-*). To render accurately the second term *(g)cig c(h)ar ba* is somewhat more difficult. Since in this tendency emphasis is put on the immediate, instantaneous, simultaneous and holistic – i.e. the single-moment – nature of Awakening, and because the term employed is derived from the expression *cig c(h)ar du* 'in one instant, simultaneously' which is used to render the Sanskrit words *yugapat* and *sakṛt* and which may be glossed by *dus gcig tu* 'at one time, at once' (Skt. *ekavāram*), the term can be rendered either as 'instantaneous/instantaneist' or as 'simultaneous/simultaneist'. The frequently employed renderings 'sudden' for *cig c(h)ar* and 'Subitist' for *cig c(h)ar ba* are of course appropriate also to the extent that these words – together with Skt. *sakṛt* and *ekavāram* – are additionally associated with the idea of suddenness; but only occasionally (see below) is the word *cig c(h)ar* actually used to describe actions that are sudden and abrupt (*glo bur*) as distinct from those that are either simultaneous with each other or instantaneous.

In our Tibetan sources 'Gradualism' is in addition often referred to by the expression *(br)tse(n) min/mun*, and the 'Gradualist' by the word *(br)tse(n) min/mun pa*. And 'Simultaneism' is known as the *(s)ton min/mun*, and the 'Simultaneist' as a *(s)ton min/mun pa*. These words, which are clearly not Tibetan in origin, correspond respectively to the Chinese expressions *chien men (p'ai)* '(school of) gradual entrance' and *tun men (p'ai)* '(school of) immediate entrance'.[190] Another contrasting pair of expressions in Chinese are *chien wu* 'gradual Awakening' and *tun wu* 'sudden Awakening'. It is however not certain that simultaneity and suddenness are in fact totally identical notions in the history of the Dhyāna schools; but the clarification of this point is crucial for the history of Ch'an rather than for that of the Tibetan doctrines being considered here.[191]

The 'Gradualist' procedure is compared in Tibetan sources with a progressive, step-by-step ascent toward a mountain peak, or with a monkey's gradual climbing to the top of a tree from below (*mas 'dzeg*). On the contrary, the 'Simultaneist' procedure is compared with an eagle's sudden or abrupt (*glo bur*) descent on to the top of a tree from above (*yas babs, yas 'bab*).[192] This pair of metaphorical descriptions is thus intended graphically to illustrate a distinguishing feature of two contrasting procedures.

The Hva šaṅ Mahāyāna is stated to have said that not thinking on anything whatever, not conceptualizing anything whatever and not practising anything whatever constitute an objectifying that involves simultaneous engagement (*dmigs pa gcig char 'jug pa*), so that this is as (one) on the tenth Bodhisattva-stage (*sa* = *bhūmi*).[193] He is also shown as sometimes asserting that his method is taught for persons whose faculties are superior (*dbaṅ po rnon po* = *tīkṣṇendriya*), whereas the Dharma-practice based on generosity and so forth (*dānādi*) has been taught rather for those whose faculties are blunt.[194]

[190] Cf. n. 120.

[191] On this terminology cf. Demiéville, *Concile*, pp. 10, 14–15, 18–19, 35; n. 50–51, 74–75, 184, and 279; R. A. Stein, *Revue de l'histoire des religions* 179 (1971), pp. 3–30. (See now also P. Gregory [ed.], *Sudden and Gradual* [Honolulu, 1987].)

[192] This comparison is placed in the mouth of the Hva šaṅ in the 'Alternative Tradition' of the *sBa bžed* (G, p. 74), and in Ñaṅ Ñi ma 'od zer, *Chos 'byuṅ Me tog sñiṅ po* (ed. R. O. Meisezahl) f. 430b. See however the critique of these examples, as well as of the corresponding meanings, in the 'Alternative Tradition' of the *sBa bžed* (G, p. 74); in dPa' bo gTsug lag phreṅ ba, *mKhas pa'i dga' ston*, ja, f. 120b2–3 and f. 122a–b (which refers to the 'Alternative Tradition'); and in the *Chos 'byuṅ Me tog sñiṅ po*, f. 432a. These examples are also mentioned by Sa skya Paṇḍi ta in his *sDom gsum rab dbye*, f. 25b, and (together with Kamalaśīla's critique) in his *Thub pa'i dgoṅs pa rab tu gsal ba*, f. 49b.

[193] *sBa bžed*, G, p. 68.20; S, p. 58.7; *Chos 'byuṅ Me tog sñiṅ po*, f. 430b5.

[194] Cf. *sBa bžed*, G, p. 68.17; S, p. 58.5; *Chos 'byuṅ Me tog sñiṅ po*, f. 425'b5, 430b3, and 435b3. See pp. 66, 84, 93, 117, 141–2.

A feature characteristic of the teachings ascribed in our Tibetan sources to the Hva šaṅ Mahāyāna is the eradication of all discursive thinking in any and every form and an emphasis on non-mentation (*yid la mi byed pa* = *amanas(i)kāra*) and non-minding (*dran pa med pa* = *asmṛti*) as the necessary – and indeed sufficient – condition for achieving the meditator's goal of understanding (*rtogs pa*) or face-to-face recognition (*ṅo 'phrod/sprod pa*) of Mind (*sems*).

This denial of the fitness of mental activity and analysis for the understanding of reality is the more remarkable as the Buddha himself is regularly presented as having enjoined his disciples to attend (Pali: *sunotha*) and apply their minds (Pali: *manasi karotha*) to his teaching; indeed, thorough application of mind (*yoniso manasikāro*) has been one of the salient and most highly prized features in Buddhism. In the Abhidharma *manaskāra* has been defined as inflexion of thinking (*cetasa ābhogaḥ*), and it is listed among the *cittamahābhūmika-dharmas* alongside *mati* (defined as *prajñā dharmapravicayaḥ*, 'discriminative understanding and analysis of the *dharmas*'), *smṛti* (defined as *ālambanāsampramoṣa*, 'non-forgetting of the object of thought'), and *samādhi* (defined as *cittasyâikāgratā*, 'one-pointedness of mind').[195] A negative valuation of *manas(i)kāra* was, however, a characteristic of the Siddha movement, especially for example with Maitrīpāda (*c.* 1000 CE), as well as of Dhyāna/Ch'an. It can be accounted for by its association with discursive thinking and mental construction (*vikalpa*), which have to be brought to a stop before direct and immediate understanding of reality can be achieved, and perhaps also by the fact that mentation is absent in certain superior forms of Samāpatti and Vimokṣa meditation. Clearly, what the Hva šaṅ was seeking was a 'return' to inborn and spontaneous Mind, in the form of its immediate face-to-face recognition, rather than an application of mind to what is communicated from outside, even if this communication be from the Buddha himself; for such mediated, 'other-conditioned' (*parapratyaya*) verbal-conceptual communication is inextricably tied up with mental construction

[195] Vasubandhu, *Abhidharmakośabhāṣya* ii. 24. Compare Asaṅga, *Abhidharmasamuccaya* (ed. Pradhan), p. 6.

(*rtog pa* = *kalpanā*) and binary conceptualization (*rnam par rtog pa* = *vikalpa*).

A noteworthy metaphorical description of the Ho-shang Mo-ho-yen's teaching was, as already mentioned above, by means of the expression *dkar po chig thub* found in both the 'Alternative Tradition' of the *sBa bžed* and Ñaṅ ral's *Chos 'byuṅ Me tog sñiṅ po*, as well as in later Tibetan sources. In the vocabulary of Tibetan pharmocology, this term evidently designates a certain substance (either mineral or vegetable) considered as a sovereign remedy, or at least as a pre-eminent antidote effective all by itself.[196] Just so, according to the 'Alternative Tradition' of the *sBa bžed*, understanding of Mind in face-to-face recognition was regarded by the Hva šaṅ as a spiritual *dkar po chig thub* that acts alone, like a panacea (*sems rtogs na dkar po chig thub yin pas des chog zer nas*, G, p. 72). In dPa' bo gtsug lag phreṅ ba's *mKhas pa'i dga' ston* it is further specified that the doctrine of pure understanding of Mind (*sems rtogs pa*) known as *dkar po chig thub*, which suffices for the achievement of Awakening, involves the denial (*skur pa 'debs pa* = *apavāda*) of both salvific means (*thabs* = *upāya*) and discriminative knowledge (*šes rab* = *prajñā*; ja, f. 120a7); and it is added that the teaching according to which Awakening results from 'recognition in confrontation' of Mind is stated to have been described as this same *dkar po chig thub* (*deṅ saṅ chos rnal ma rnams bor nas sems ṅo 'phrod pas 'tshaṅ rgya bar 'dod pa dkar po chig thub tu 'gro ba'i rgyu mtshan de yin gsuṅ*, ja, f. 120b6).[197] This description is confirmed by Ñaṅ ral's *Chos 'byuṅ Me tog sñiṅ po*, which cites the teaching that when there is understanding issuing from face-to-face recognition there is Awakening, and that it is therefore necessary to recognize Mind face-to-face, this mode of knowing being the *dkar po chig thub* (*raṅ ṅo šes nas rtogs na saṅs rgya/ de'i phyir sems ṅo 'phrod dgos/ de šes na dkar po chig thub yin*, f. 425'a5–6). As already noted above, Wang Hsi's *Cheng-li chüeh* (f. 146b) includes a passage where Mo-ho-yen compares his

[196] Cf. L. van der Kuijp, *Journal of the International Association of Buddhist Studies* 9 (1986), p. 149.

[197] Elsewhere in the *mKhas pa'i dga' ston*, the expression *sems ṅo rtogs pa* has been used. The Tibetan expressions *sems rtogs pa*, etc. – as well as *sems la blta ba*, etc., in the Dunhuang documents – correspond to Chinese *k'an hsin*, on which see Demiéville, *Concile*, pp. 43 n. 1, 51–52, 78, 125–6, 158. Cf. below, n. 461.

teaching of non-reflection and non-examination with the *agada*-medicine mentioned in the *Mahāparinirvāṇasūtra*, which describes itself as this antidote that heals all illness.

The idea of the understanding and face-to-face recognition of Mind being a sort of spiritual medicine that is self-potentiating and effective entirely by itself – the *dkar po chig thub* – has been discussed and severely criticized by Sa skya Paṇḍi ta Kun dga' rgyal mtshan (1182–1251) in his *Thub pa'i dgoṅs pa rab tu gsal ba* (ff. 48b, 50a, 56b)[198] and *sDom gsum rab dbye* (ff. 25b–26a), as well as in his *Phyogs bcu'i saṅs rgyas daṅ byaṅ chub sems dpa' rnams la žu ba'i 'phrin yig* (f. 6b), *sKyes bu dam pa rnams la spriṅ ba'i yi ge* (ff. 3a–4a) and Epistle to Glo bo Lo tsā ba Šes rab rin chen (f. 28a–b). With the exception of Ñaṅ Ñi ma 'od zer's *Chos 'byuṅ Me tog sñiṅ po* (and *Byaṅ chub sems dpa' sems dpa' chen po chos rgyal mes dbon rnam gsum gyi rnam par thar pa rin po che'i phreṅ ba*?), these works of Sa skya Paṇḍi ta appear to be the oldest securely datable Tibetan sources discussing the Hva šaṅ Mahāyāna's teachings now available.

In the account of the Hva šaṅ's teachings in the *sDom gsum rab dbye* (ff. 25b–26a), this unique 'medicine' is even mentioned in the prophetic testament that Śāntarakṣita is deemed to have delivered to Khri Sroṅ lde btsan and in which he recommended that after his death his disciple Kamalaśīla should be called to Tibet when a split would occur in the Dharma, so that he might then combat the teaching of the Hva šaṅ described as the *dkar po chig thub*. For his version Sa skya Paṇḍi ta seems to have relied on the 'Alternative Tradition' of the *sBa bžed*, where Śāntarakṣita's prophecy is quoted by Ye šes dbaṅ po and in which the *dkar po chig thub* is also expressly named (G, p. 73.3).[199]

In his account of what he termed the method (*gžuṅ lugs*) of the Chinese Bhikṣu and Master (*mkhan po*), Sa skya Paṇḍi ta has

[198] Cf. R. Jackson, *Journal of the International Association of Buddhist Studies* 5 (1982), pp. 91–93.

[199] The expression *dkar po chig thub* does not, however, appear in the version of Śāntarakṣita's testament given in Bu ston's *Chos 'byuṅ* (f. 127b), in dPa' bo gTsug lag phreṅ ba's *mKhas pa'i dga' ston* (ja, f. 115b), and in Padma dkar po's *Chos 'byuṅ* (ed. Lokesh Chandra, f. 164b). (See however *mKhas pa'i dga' ston*, ja, f. 120a).

joined what he called 'today's Mahāmudrā' (*da lta'i phyag rgya chen po*) – described as almost (*phal cher*) a Chinese Dharma system (*rgya nag chos lugs*) – and the Chinese-style rDzogs chen (*rgya nag lugs kyi rdzogs chen*).[200] And using the metaphor of (the eagle's sudden) descent from above (*yas 'bab*) along with the designation *cig char ba*, he has pointed out defects in all three doctrines together.[201]

Exactly what Sa skya Paṇḍi ta had in mind when speaking of a 'Neo-Mahāmudrā' is perhaps not altogether clear from this passage of the *sDom gsum rab dbye*. His purpose was evidently to contrast it with an older Mahāmudrā teaching, that is, probably, with the classical one he accepted (ff. 26a–b); and his criticism does not therefore appear to be indiscriminately directed against all forms of Mahāmudrā. Indeed, in this connexion, he has explicitly recognized the version connected with Nāgārjuna; and he has also separately mentioned both Nāropa's and Maitrīpāda's Mahāmudrā teachings (f. 26a5).

Now we know that sGam po pa bSod nams rin chen (1079–1153) – an early Tibetan master who combined the bKa' brgyud pa traditions, one of whose fundamental teachings is

[200] It is to be noted that the rDzogs chen master Śrī Siṃha is sometimes described as *rgya nag po'i slob dpon* 'the master of/from China'.

[201] A connexion between the Hva šaṅ Mahāyāna's teaching and the *phyag chen* (*mahāmudrā*) has been mentioned in Ne'u Paṇḍi ta's *Chos 'byuṅ* (f. 21b: *hva šaṅ ma hā ya na byon pas/ phyag rgya chen po 'thun pa'i grub mtha' bzuṅ*). 'Brug pa Kun legs (1455–1529) has also spoken of a *phyag rgya ha šaṅ gi lta ba* in his gSuṅ 'bum (kha, f. 14a), quoted by Stein, *Revue de l'histoire des religions* 179 (1971), p. 10. (And a connexion with the [*da lta'i*] *phyag chen* is at least suggested in the colophon of the *bSam gtan mig sgron* [f. 254a].)

On the rDzogs chen side, Kloṅ chen rab 'byams pa (1308–1363) has mentioned the closeness of the Hva šaṅ's teachings to aspects of *rdzogs chen* (see the *gNas lugs mdzod 'grel*, f. 33b ~ 23b). See also the *Blon po'i bka'i thaṅ yig* of the *bKa' thaṅ sde lṅa*. And Tshe dbaṅ nor bu (1698/9–1755), *rGya nag ha šaṅ gi byuṅ tshul grub mtha'i phyogs sṅa bcas sa bon tsam smos pa* (Volume V of his collected writings, Dalhousie, 1977), ff. 8b, 10b and 12b, has distinguished in the Hva šaṅs teachings between what is correct and what is not. In particular, Tshe dbaṅ nor bu alludes to a *partial* similarity (*cha 'dra ba*, f. 8b4–5), as does the *bSam gtan mig sgron* (f. 93b3). According to an opinion rejected by Sog bzlog pa (b. 1552/3), gNubs Saṅs rgyas ye šes conflated (*sres pa*) the doctrine of the Hva šaṅ with that of the *Man ṅag lta ba'i phreṅ ba* ascribed to Padmasambhava (see the *gSaṅ sṅags sṅa 'gyur la bod du rtsod pa'i sṅa phyir byuṅ ba rnams kyi lan du brjod pa, Ṅes don 'brug sgra* [New Delhi, 1975], f. 9a–10a). Further, A ro Ye šes 'byuṅ gnas held both the seven-fold lineage-tradition of India and the seven-fold lineage-tradition of the Chinese Hva šaṅ(s), which he taught to two disciples who then passed them on to Roṅ zom Chos kyi bzaṅ po (eleventh century) (see 'Gos gŽon nu dpal, *Deb ther sṅon po*, ga, f. 30b).

precisely the Mahāmudrā, with the tradition of Atiśa – in fact made use of the expression *dkar po chig thub* for his teaching. Thus, in his *Dus gsum mkhyen pa'i žus lan*, *dkar po chig thub* is a name for a form of spiritual realization (*ñams*) that is undetermined as to the length of its preparation and cognitive origin, and which remains constant and is linked with the yogic signs of hyperthermia.[202] And in his *Phag mo gru pa'i žus lan* sGam po pa has referred to the *dkar po chig thub* as that by the knowledge of which alone total freedom ensues (*gcig šes kun grol*); through it the fetters of grasping at the cycle of existences (*'khor bar 'dzin pa'i sgrog*) burst of themselves, and the level of Great Bliss in Own-Mind is attained (*raṅ sems bde ba chen po'i sa non bya ba yin*).[203] This passage on the *dkar po chig thub* follows one in which the 'Gradualist' (*rim gyis pa*) and the 'Simultaneist' (*cig car ba*) are distinguished as to the degree of their spiritual practice, the *cig car ba* being described as more advanced on a continuous scale of development than the *rim gyis pa*. Here the concept of the *dkar po chig thub* does not appear linked specifically and exclusively with the Mantra domain of Tibetan Buddhist thought.

Žaṅ Tshal pa brTson 'grus grags pa (1123–1193) was another early bKa' brgyud pa master who made use of the expression *dkar po chig thub* in his teachings.[204] He is in fact considered as the main propagator of the *dkar po chig thub* in the bKa' brgyud pa

[202] *Collected works (gSuṅ 'bum)*, Delhi, 1975, tha, f. 187b f.; *rTsibs ri'i spar ma* (La dvags khrid dpon 'Khrul žig Padma chos rgyal, *dKar rñiṅ gi skyes chen du ma'i phyogs rdzogs kyi gdams ṅag gnad bsdus ñer mkho rin po che'i gter mdzod*), ca/3, f. 1b–2b.

[203] *Collected works*, da, f. 236b; *rTsibs ri'i spar ma*, ca/2, f. 4b.

For Phag mo gru pa in this connexion, see also Sog bzlog pa, *Ṅes don 'brug sgra*, f. 118a; D. Seyfort Ruegg, 'A Karma bKa' brgyud work on the lineages and traditions of the Indo-Tibetan dBu ma (Madhyamaka)', in *Orientalia Iosephi Tucci memoriae dicata*, III (Rome, 1988), p. 1259.

[204] See the *Phyag rgya chen po lam zab mthar thug* (in the *rTsibs ri'i spar ma*, ṅa/2), f. 26b1 = *Phyag rgya chen po'i lam mchog mthar thug* (in Koṅ sprul's *gDams ṅag mdzod*, ña/21), f. 13b7. This text deals also with the bKa' brgyud pa theory of the three kinds of person (*gaṅ zag*), the *rim gyis pa*, the *thod rgal ba* and the *gcig char ba*. Cf. Padma dkar po (1527–1592), *Phyag rgya gan mdzod*.

On Žaṅ Tshal pa/'Tshal pa/mTshal pa brTson 'grus grags pa (Žaṅ rin po che), see Tshal pa Kun dga' rdo rje, *Deb ther dmar po*, p. 126 f.; 'Gos gŽon nu dpal, *Deb that sṅon po*, ña, f. 136 f.; Thu'u bkvan Blo bzaṅ Chos kyi ñi ma, *Grub mtha' šel gyi me loṅ*, bKa' brgyud chapter, f. 19b and f. 25b. Cf. Stein, *Revue de l'histoire des religions* 179 (1971), p. 10 n. and M. Broido, *Journal of the International Association of Buddhist Studies* 8 (1985), p. 49 n. 3. For his works, see *Writings (bKa' thor bu) of Žaṅ gYu brag pa brTson 'grus grags pa* (Palampur, 1972) (e.g. p. 712 for the *dkar po chig thub*).

school.[205] 'Gos gŽon nu dpal mentions in particular his teacher sGom pa's instruction on setting aside all conceptual and analytical investigation when engaging in true meditative realization (*brtag dpyad ma byed par bsgoms šig*).[206]

Now Sa skya Paṇḍi ta has expressed the view that the Mahāmudrā is to be realized only on the basis of Mantra sources (*sDom gsum rab dbye*, f. 25b5), and he thus appears to exclude the validity of anything like a Sūtra-based version of Mahāmudrā. When speaking of a Neo-Mahāmudrā, then, Sa skya Paṇḍi ta may have been adverting to sGam po pa's Sūtra-based form of the Mahāmudrā.[207] And if it was indeed to these teachings of the bKa' brgyud pa tradition of sGam po pa that he was referring under the name of *da lta'i phyag rgya chen po*, Sa skya Paṇḍi ta was then presumably not directly criticizing the highly problematic would-be Mahāmudrā that was propagated in the Kingdom of Western Tibet in particular in the tenth and eleventh centuries, and which Atiša was invited there to help combat. According to the **Bodhipathadīpa-Pañjikā* ascribed (perhaps incorrectly) to Atiša himself, this deviant and pernicious doctrine, which was sometimes known under the name of Mahāmudrā, would seem to have had a strong – and in this case totally unauthentic – 'spontaneist' and 'innatist' tendency. (Nevertheless, Sa skya Paṇḍi ta might be expected to have wished in particular to attack this infamous doctrine – one with which sGam po pa's Sūtra-based form of Mahāmudrā could have had nothing in common, especially in view of the fact that sGam po pa belonged also to Atiša's bKa' gdams pa lineage. See below, p. 121.)

In his extensive commentary on the *sDom gsum rab dbye* – the *sDom pa gsum gyi rab tu dbye ba'i rnam bšad* (f. 104a ff.) – Go rams pa bSod nams seṅ ge (1429–1489) has contrasted the authentic Buddhist Mahāmudrā and the Neo-Mahāmudrā criticized by Sa skya Paṇḍi ta, describing the first – his school's own (*raṅ lugs*) – as

[205] See for example lCaṅ skya Rol pa'i rdo rje, *Grub pa'i mtha'i rnam par bžag pa gsal bar bšad pa thub bstan lhun po'i mdzes rgyan*, kha, f. 21a (=p. 300).

[206] *Deb ther sṅon po*, ña, f. 137b (G. N. Roerich's translation, *Blue annals*, p. 714, is misleading here). This sGom pa Tshul khrims sñiṅ po (1116–1169) was the nephew and disciple of sGam po pa (ña, f. 27a–b).

[207] Cf. D. Seyfort Ruegg, 'A Karma bKa' brgyud work on the lineages and traditions of the Indo-Tibetan dBu ma (Madhyamaka)', in: *Orientalia I. Tucci memoriae dicata*, III, pp. 1256, 1258–62.

an Indian system (*rgya gar gyi lugs*) and the second – a doctrine held by others (*gžan lugs*) – as a Chinese system (*rgya nag lugs*). The last doctrine he has in fact defined as a specious Insight (*lhag mthoṅ ltar snaṅ*) because it is a view that posits the Empty alone (*stoṅ rkyaṅ du lta ba*). This consists in the suppresssion of thought-construction in a sort of cataleptic fixation on the Empty (*stoṅ pa had de 'jog pa'i rtog pa kha tshom pa ñid*) (ff. 104b1). In this context Go rams pa, quoting the *sBa bžed* (f. 106a1), devotes a long discussion to the teachings of the Hva šaṅs and the Great Debate of bSam yas between Kamalaśīla and Mahāyāna (ff. 105b–110a). His evaluation of the Hva šaṅ's doctrine is basically in agreement with that of the *sBa bžed* (G, p. 73), which alludes in this connexion to the impurity of view (*lta ba'i sñigs ma* = *dṛṣṭikaṣāya*) consisting in taking pleasure in Emptiness.[207a] Go rams pa however goes further, connecting (f. 110a) the doctrine of the Hva šaṅ criticized by Sa skya Paṇḍi ta with the deviant doctrines, also known under the name of Mahāmudrā, which spread at the time of Kings Yum brtan and 'od sruṅs after the breakdown of the old Tibetan kingdom consequent on the death of Glaṅ da ma. In view of this connexion it may then be that Go rams pa even linked in his mind the debased pseudo-Mahāmudrā combatted in Western Tibet by Atiśa and Rin chen bzaṅ po with the Hva šaṅ's teachings which, he says, were recovered at that time from their places of concealment (*gter sa*), although he has not explicitly made this connexion in his comment.

Šākya mchog ldan (1428–1507), another master of the Sa skya pa school, has proceeded in a more complex (and also somewhat more conciliatory) fashion when discussing the Hva šaṅ's teaching and the Neo-Mahāmudrā. This creative and rather innovative thinker was also an advocate of the theory of the Emptiness of the heterogeneous (*gžan stoṅ*), which he describes as being in harmony with the Mahāmudrā in contradistinction to the doctrine of the Emptiness of own-nature (*raṅ stoṅ*).[207b] He was thus linked

[207a] Sa skya Paṇḍi ta, *Thub pa'i dgoṅs gsal*, following the *sBa bžed*, mentions both the *dṛṣṭikaṣāya* of taking pleasure in Emptiness (f. 49a3) and the rejection of all activity (*bya byed*) on the path to Awakening (f. 49b2). Bu ston's reference to the Hva šaṅ's nihilism (*chad lta*) in his *Chos 'byuṅ* (f. 128a1) relates rather to quietism and ataraxia.

[207b] Šākya mchog ldan, *Luṅ rigs gñis kyi phyag rgya chen po bžed tshul la 'khrul pa sel ba'i bstan bcos, zuṅ 'jug gi gru chen* (gSuṅ 'bum, vol. tsa/14), f. 14b2–3.

with the Tibetan tradition of *tathāgatagarbha*-exegesis that interpreted the Buddha-nature in a 'spontaneist' and 'innatist' fashion.

Now, in several works Šākya mchog ldan distinguishes between Fixation-Bhāvanā (*'jog sgom*) and Inspection-Bhāvanā (*dpyad sgom*), pointing out that it is necessary to determine whether Fixation is to be preceded by Inspection or not.[207c] The *dpyad sgom* used in dispelling imputation (*sgro 'dogs = samāropa*) is connected roughly with Prajñāpāramitā-philosophy and the Madhyamaka, the bKa' gdams pa Po to ba being cited as a master of this method (tsa/14, f. 24b). As for *'jog sgom*, it would correspond mainly to intuitive awareness (*ñams myoṅ*), the coincidence of Bliss and the Empty (*bde stoṅ*) in Mantrayāna and the Mahāmudrā. And while noting that still other systems of meditation have been developed based on traditions that are neither Mahāmudrā nor Madhyamaka, Šākya mchog ldan points to the fact that they have been rejected by Sa skya Paṇḍi ta in his *Thub pa'i dgoṅs gsal* (tsa/18, f. 4a). Šākya mchog ldan furthermore connects analytic Inspection (*dpyad pa*) with the scholar-paṇḍit, i.e. the specialist in scholastic philosophy (*mtshan ñid pa*) who engages in *pratyavekṣā*; Fixation-Bhāvanā is on the contrary linked by him with that kind of Yogin who takes everything just as it is, without engaging in mental construction and analysis, i.e. with the type of practiser known as the *ku sā li pa* (tsa/18, f. 4b; tsa/14, ff. 15b–16a; tsa/21, f. 7a–b).

With regard to the problem of the kinds of Mahāmudrā, Šākya mchog ldan concludes that the theory of the non-duality of *saṃsāra* and *nirvāṇa* as explicated by Sa skya Paṇḍi ta and the Mahāmudrā-teaching of 'Candraprabhā-Kumāra' (i.e. sGam po pa) are, notwithstanding the difference in their names, one in sense and import (*don gcig*). This is so in spite of the fact that the former doctrine as described by Šākya mchog ldan is concerned with the eradication and stoppage of imputation (*samāropa: sgro*

[207c] Šākya mchog ldan, *Phyag rgya chen po'i šan 'byed ces bya ba'i bstan bcos* (*Phyag rgya chen po gsal bar byed pa'i bstan bcos, Tshaṅs pa'i 'khor lo*), gSuṅ 'bum, vol. tsa/14), ff. 8b–13a (addressed to a certain Sa skyoṅ mchog, i.e. the Rin spuṅs pa ruler); *Luṅ rigs gñis kyi phyag rgya chen po bžed tshul la 'khrul pa sel ba'i bstan bcos, zuṅ 'jug gi gru chen*, gSuṅ 'bum, vol. tsa/14), ff. 13a–25a (addressed to Karma dBaṅ phyug dpal); and *mKha' spyod dbaṅ po'i spyan druṅ du 'bul ba'i mol mchid*, gSuṅ 'bum, vol. tsa/18, ff. 1b–5a (addressed to Žva dmar IV, Chos grags ye šes, 1453–1524?); and Replies to the Rin spuṅs sde pa Šākya rgyal mtshan and sDe pa gar pa, gSuṅ 'bum, tsa/21, f. 5b ff.

'dogs chad pa, 'gog pa) by means of analytic inspection and reasoning (*rigs pa*) based on learning and reflection, and that it follows in particular the second of the Buddha's three turnings of the Wheel of Dharma (i.e. the Prajñāpāramitā) and its teaching of the Emptiness of own-nature (*raṅ stoṅ*) as explicated by Candrakīrti; whereas sGam po pa's Mahāmudrā is concerned rather with intuitive awareness in Gnosis (*ye šes kyis ñams su myoṅ ba*) born of the Consecrations and is in accord with the last of the Buddha's three turnings of the Dharma-Wheel which is of definitive sense (*ṅes don*) and where Emptiness of the heterogeneous (*gžan stoṅ*) has been taught (tsa/18, f. 2b). Indeed, Candrakīrti is considered the author not only of the analytical-philosophical *Madhyamakāvatāra* but also of the mystical-philosophical *Pradīpoddyotana* (tsa/18, f. 4a2).

It thus appears that Šākya mchog ldan sought to harmonize the whole of the authentic Mahāmudrā with the doctrinal position adopted by Sa skya Paṇḍi ta in his *Thub pa'i dgoṅs gsal* and *sDom gsum rab dbye*, and also to re-establish the *gžan stoṅ* tradition known from the hermeneutics of the *tathāgatagarbha*-doctrine and the Kālacakra beside the *raṅ stoṅ* of the main line of the Madhyamaka school (after an early version of the *gžan stoṅ*, anterior to that taught by the Jo naṅ pa Dol bu pa [1292–1361], had been rejected by Sa skya Paṇḍi ta).

It has at the same time to be borne in mind that the Neo-Mahāmudrā has been criticized by Sa skya Paṇḍi ta and his followers in the main line of the Sa skya school on the ground that it was based in large part on the non-Tantric Prajñāpāramitā tradition rather than on the authentic pure Tantric tradition of the 'standard' Mahāmudrā. Now, given that Šākya mchog ldan fully accepted sGam po pa's Mahāmudrā, it is perhaps not clear how, as a follower of Sa skya Paṇḍi ta, he considered that the two prongs of the latter's criticism of the Neo-Mahāmudrā – *viz.* as not based on the authentic pure Tantric tradition and as close to the Hva šaṅ's teaching – combine to constitute a compelling refutation of this Neo-Mahāmudrā. Šākya mchog ldan's reorganization of the doctrinal categories and his shifting of the hermeneutical frame accepted by Sa skya Paṇḍi ta and the main line of the Sa skya school indeed makes it difficult fully to reconcile the views of this fifteenth-century Sa skya pa with the position of the thirteenth-century Sa skya hierarch on the Neo-Mahāmudrā and its connexions with the Hva šaṅ's teachings. Go rams pa's critique of the Hva šaṅ's teaching together with the Neo-Mahāmudrā may accordingly be considered typical of the main-line Sa skya school.

Šākya mchog ldan's above-mentioned attempt to harmonize Sa skya Paṇḍi ta's teaching with that of sGam po pa in the matter of the Mahāmudrā would seem to suggest at all events that he considered that it was indeed the latter's Mahāmudrā doctrine that was the object of the Sa skya hierarch's criticism.

As for the Hva šaṅ, according to Šākya mchog ldan his mistake lay in having failed duly to differentiate between surface-level *saṃvṛti* and ultimate *paramārtha*, theory and practice, *jñāna* and *vijñāna*, the level of learning and reflection (*thos bsam*) and that of meditative realization (*bsgom pa*), and the indirect provisional *neyārtha* and the definitive *nītārtha*, as a consequence of which he came to believe that mere non-mention (*ci yaṅ yid la mi byed pa tsam: amanasikāra-mātra*) constitutes the essential (tsa/14, f. 10b5–6; tsa/21, f. 5b). Šākya mchog ldan concludes that in the true Mahāmudrā freedom from conceptual construction and non-mentation are altogether unlike the Hva šaṅ's meditation (tsa/14, f. 11a1–2) and are not dull quietude (*lteṅs po'i gži gnas*, tsa/18, f. 3b; tsa/21, ff. 5b, 6b).

Mi bskyod rdo rje (1507–1554) – the eighth hierarch of the Karma branch of sGam po pa's bKa' brgyud pa school – however evidently understood Sa skya Paṇḍi ta's ctiticism of Neo-Mahāmudrā as being directed against the non-mentation (*yid la mi byed pa*) teaching of Maitrīpāda and also Saraha, sGam po pa's great predecessors in this Indo-Tibetan lineage. Like sGam po pa's, their teachings were considered to be linked also with the Sūtra and not solely with the Mantra department of Indo-Tibetan thought.[208] Nevertheless, as already noted above, it would seem that Sa skya Paṇḍi ta wished rather to distinguish the Neo-Mahāmudrā he was criticizing from Nāgārjuna's and evidently also from Nāropa's and Maitrīpāda's (*sDom gsum rab dbye*, f. 26a).

With regard to Žaṅ tshal pa as the propagator of the *dkar po*

[208] See D. Seyfort Ruegg, 'A Karma bKa' brgyud work ...' (n. 203), pp. 1258–62.

chig thub in the bKa' brgyud pa school,[209] Thu'u bkvan Blo bzaṅ Chos kyi ñi ma writes in his *Grub mtha' šel gyi me loṅ* that up to the time of Žaṅ Rin po che *dkar po chig thub* had not been well known as a term (*tha sñad*) in that school, but that from his time onwards it became very well known (bKa' brgyud pa chapter, f. 19b). And he adds (f. 25b) that of the many refutations found in Sa skya Paṇḍi ta's *sDoṅ gsum rab dbye* the chief ones turn out to be directed against the *dkar po chig thub* teaching of Žaṅ Tshal pa and the *dgoṅs gcig* teaching of 'Bri guṅ pa; indeed, he notes, many writers have emulated Sa skya Paṇḍi ta and concluded that this teaching of Žaṅ Tshal pa had the meaning of non-mentation (*yid la mi byed pa*). Very interestingly, however, Blo bzaṅ Chos kyi ñi ma then observes that if an impartial person considers the sayings of Žaṅ Tshal pa, it becomes apparent to him that they do not in fact belong to the position (*phyogs*) of non-mentation; hence the refutation in the *sDom gsum rab dbye* was clearly an over-hasty statement (*thub chod kyi gsuṅ*). As for the fundamental view of Mar pa, the source of the Dvags po bKa' brgyud, Blo bzaṅ Chos kyi ñi ma describes it as Prāsaṅgika-Madhyamaka (f. 17b4).

The fact that the Hva šaṅ Mahāyāna is represented as having upheld at the Great Debate the principles of non-mentation and of not thinking on anything (*ci yaṅ mi sems pa*) probably accounts for Sa skya Paṇḍi ta's association of him with what he terms the 'almost' Chinese Dharma-system of Neo-Mahāmudrā, and also with Chinese-style rDzogs chen.[210] As he has written in his *sDom gsum rab dbye*, despite the fact that the Neo-Mahāmudrā and the Chinese-style rDzogs chen have different names they are in substance without difference with respect to their simultaneism (*cig char ba*) and subitistic procedure (*yas 'bab*) (f. 25b); and the Neo-Mahāmudrā based on the literal wording of the tradition of the Chinese Master (*rgya nag mkhan po'i gžuṅ lugs kyi yi ge tsam*) was for the most part (*phal cher*) a Chinese Dharma-system (f. 26a). It is not impossible that in his account Sa skya Paṇḍi ta was thinking as much in terms of typological strands and family resemblances between teachings as in terms of direct and immediate historical influences. That he may not have meant to reject *all*

[209] See above, pp. 103–04.

[210] See also the discussion of Sa skya Paṇḍi ta's view in Sog bzlog pa, *Nes don 'brug sgra*, ff. 117a–120b.

the teachings of Chinese Buddhism is perhaps suggested by the fact that with respect to the rejection of the Hva šaṅ Mahāyāna's teachings in Tibet he has written '*that* Chinese system' (*rgya nag lugs de*, f. 26a3).

As for the doctrine of the Hva šaṅ Mahāyāna as criticized and rejected by the main line of the Sa skya pa school, what was at issue was clearly not only quietism in the sense of the abandonment of praxis and the first four perfections (*pāramitā*) – though it was this too – but also a faulty form of *vipaśyanā* consisting in the *dṛṣṭikaṣāya* of taking pleasure in Emptiness – that is, in a frozen and more or less unconscious or cataleptic fixation in the Empty.

The current of thought in Tibet, and earlier in India, that thus emphasized, to the practical exclusion of all other exercises, the cultivation of non-construction (*akalpa*[*nā*], *avikalpa*, etc.) and the spontaneous and gnoseologically innate recognition of Mind together with its Quieting (*śamatha*) was opposed by a school of thought that laid much stress on correct analysis (*bhūtapratyavekṣā* = *yaṅ dag par so sor rtog pa*) leading to the full development of the investigation of the factors of existence (*dharmapravicaya* = *chos rnams šin tu rnam par 'byed pa*) and of discriminative knowledge born from meditative realization (*bhāvanāmayī prajñā*) together with Insight (*vipaśyanā* = *lhag mthoṅ*).

Among the early bKa' gdams pa masters, Atiša's disciple Po to ba Rin chen gsal (1031?–1105) has stated in his *Be'u bum* that if, after having determined non-substantiality (*bdag med* = *nairātmya*) by reasoning on the stages of learning and reflection (*thos bsam* = *śruta* and *cintā*), one then simply realizes non-construction (*mi rtog*) on the stage of meditative realization (*sgom pa* = *bhāvanā*), this would represent a faulty realization of Emptiness which is irrelevant (*'brel med* = *asambaddha*) and cannot function as the true counteragent (*gñen po* = *pratipakṣa*) against the positing of a hypostatized entity like a personal self (*gaṅ zag* = *pudgala*).[211] Another early bKa' gdams pa who considered that the extreme form of the non-mentation doctrine was incompatible with the Madhyamaka is Gro luṅ pa, the disciple of rṄog Blo ldan šes rab

[211] This passage is quoted from Tsoṅ kha pa, *Lam rim chen mo* (lHa sa ed.), f. 510b.

(1059–1109).[212] It should nevertheless be noted that Dīpaṃkaraśrījñāna's *Ekasmṛtyupadeśa* (*Dran pa gcig pa'i man ṅag*) is described as an instruction on simultaneous engagement (*cig car 'jug pa* = *yugapadvṛtti*); both discriminative understanding and means are involved in this instruction, as is the sequence (*krama*) of objectification followed by non-objectification (*dmigs pa med pa*) described as effortless and spontaneous (*anābhoga*).

In his classical treatise on the Path of Awakening, Tsoṅ kha pa has devoted much discussion to the relationship in meditative realization (*sgom pa* = *bhāvanā*) between the settling function of Fixation-Bhāvanā (*'jog sgom*) and the analytical function of Inspection-Bhāvanā (*dpyad sgom*) derived from analysis (*dpyod pa* = *vicāra*).[213] Typologically speaking, it is no doubt true that non-mentation and non-analysis as advocated (according to Tibetan accounts) by 'Simultaneists' such as the Hva šaṅ Mahāyāna bear a resemblance to Fixation-Bhāvanā and to Quieting (*ži gnas* = *śamatha*). The distinction lies in the fact that alongside Fixation-*Bhāvanā* and Quieting the procedure for philosophical thought and meditation adopted by Kamalaśīla and his Tibetan followers requires in addition the application of the discriminative understanding of investigative analysis (*so sor rtog pa'i šes rab* = *pratyavekṣā-prajñā*) and Insight (*lhag mthoṅ* = *vipaśyanā*).

For Tsoṅ kha pa the essential point is then that these two forms of *bhāvanā* should be treated as complementary. For otherwise there might be simple acquaintance (*go ba tsam*), but there could be no full realization of the theory (*lta ba*) of non-substantiality and Emptiness, i.e. the 'analytically inspected sense' (*dpyad pa'i don*) (*Lam rim chen mo*, f. 501b2). Neither acquaintance (*go ba*) not followed by analytical inspection nor the mere assertion (*dam bca' ba tsam*) of impermanence and the like can be effective alone;[214]

[212] For Gro luṅ pa's understanding of non-mentation (*yid la mi byed pa*), see his *bDe bar gšegs pa'i bstan pa rin po che la 'jug pa'i lam gyi rim pa rnam par bšad pa* (*bsTan rim*), f. 377a–b etc. Cf. D. Seyfort Ruegg, in: *Orientalia I. Tucci memoriae dicata*, iii, p. 1257, for Karma Mi bskyod rdo rje's view of the matter.

[213] Tsoṅ kha pa, *Lam rim chen mo*, ff. 495a6–516a2. (Cf. A. Wayman, *Central Asiatic Journal* 21 [1977], pp. 139–44 [and *Journal of the American Oriental Society* 78 (1958), pp. 214–16].)

[214] On the problem of the thesis (*dam bca'* = *pratijñā*) in the Madhyamaka and Mahāyana, see D. Seyfort Ruegg, 'On the thesis and assertion in the Madhyamaka/dBu ma', in: E. Steinkellner and H. Tauscher (ed.), *Contributions on Tibetan and Buddhist religion and philosophy* (Vienna, 1983), pp. 205–41, especially pp. 223–4 with reference to the Hva šaṅ.

and ascertainment (*ṅes pa*) of non-substantiality must therefore be firmly and repeatedly established by means of both fixation and inspection in co-ordination (f. 502b–503a). Only from effecting the serial alternation (*re mos su byed pa*) of fixation and inspection can there arise the Gnosis that is free from conceptual construction (*mi rtog pa'i ye śes = nirvikalpaka-jñāna*) (f. 504b5).

Tsoṅ kha pa's gnoseological model for understanding reality is derived from his interpretation of a distinction made many centuries earlier by Dharmakīrti[215] between a cancelling or sublating counteragent (*bādhaka*) whose function is ascertainment (*niścaya*) and a mental construction to be cancelled (*bādhya*, as being mere imputation, *samāropa*), and from Dharmakīrti's further distinction between negative determination (*vyavaccheda = rnam par gcod pa* 'exclusion') and positive determination (*pariccheda = yoṅs su gcod pa* 'delimitation').[216] Now, in Tsoṅ kha pa's model, the settling Fixation-*Bhāvanā* corresponds to the phase of cancellation (*gnod byed = bādhaka : vyavaccheda*) whilst the analytical Inspection-Bhāvanā corresponds to the phase of positive determination (*sgrub byed = sādhana : pariccheda*). The first, representing as it does only the non-construction of a hypostatized entity (*bden par yod pa mi rtog pa*), cannot effect the ascertainment of non-substantiality (*nairātmya*); and in addition there is required, as the ascertaining counteragent against conceptual construction, the understanding (*rtogs pa : adhigama*) of non-hypostatization (*bden med*) and of the non-substantiality (*bdag med*) of both a personal self (i.e. *pudgalanairātmya*) and the factors of existence (i.e. *dharmanairātmya*) (f. 504b–505a).

In support of this type of philosophical and meditative realization in two co-ordinate phases, Tsoṅ kha pa has quoted many passages from Kamalaśīla's *Bhāvanākramas*. In addition, he has cited *Madhyamakahṛdayakārikā* iii. 21 where Bhāvaviveka has spoken of *prajñā* following on concentration of mind; *Madhyamakāvatārabhāṣya* vi. 120 where Candrakīrti has described how stoppage (*'gog pa : nirodha*) of hypostatization is followed by

[215] Dharmakīrti, *Pramāṇavārttika* i. 49ab.

[216] See Dharmakīrti's *Hetubindu* (ed. E. Steinkellner), p. 25* f. For a further application of this model by Tsoṅ kha pa to the case of understanding reality, see D. Seyfort Ruegg in E. Steinkellner and H. Tauscher (eds.), *Contributions on Tibetan and Buddhist religion and philosophy*, pp. 225–7.

analytical inspection (*rnam par dpyad pa* : *vicāra*); and *Bodhicaryāvatāra* viii. 4 where, following the Prajñāpāramitā-Sūtras, Śāntideva has treated successively the Perfections of Dhyāna and Prajñā (f. 503a–b).

Now, on the ground that by following the Hva šaṅ's instructions (as widely understood by the Tibetans) one would be trying to reach the signless (*mtshan med* : *ānimitta*) and non-construction (*mi rtog pa* : *akalpa*[*nā*]) merely by suppressing all mentation involved in the proliferating activity of mind (*sems 'phro ba* : *cittaṃ prasarati*) without ever engaging in deconstructive analysis (*rigs pa'i dpyod pa*), Tsoṅ kha pa has rejected the Hva šaṅ's view as being contrary to what has been recommended in the *Ratnameghasūtra*, as interpreted by Kamalaśīla in his *Bhāvanākrama* II (pp. 29 and 45–46) and III (pp. 3, 7, and 18) (f. 503b–504b).[217]

In sum, according to Tsoṅ kha pa, not only is there to be non-construction of any hypostatized entity and of substantiality in the form of a *pudgala* and *dharma*s, but there must be comprehension of non-hypostatization (*bden med*) and two-fold non-substantiality (*bdag med*). Accordingly, (negative) *absence* of construction of a hypostatized entity and twofold substantiality must be carefully distinguished from (positive) *understanding* of non-hypostatization and non-substantiality (f. 504b–505a).

Now, the *nirvikalpa-jñāna* of the Ārya is of course immediate understanding (*mṅon sum du rtogs pa*) of the sense of non-substantiality, empty of the cognitive object (*yul* = *viṣaya*) that is falsely hypostatized in the one or other form of substantiality, i.e. of *pudgala* or *dharmas*. Nevertheless, even though it is conceded that the required meditative realization by means of the post-analytical (*dpyad nas*) understanding that a hypostatically posited entity does not exist does in fact involve conceptual construction, the latter still proves to be an altogether homogeneous cause (*šin tu rjes su mthun pa'i rgyu*) for non-constructive Gnosis (*nirvikalpa-*

[217] Interestingly, however, the *bSam gtan mig sgron* ascribes to the Hva šaṅ Mahāyāna the teaching that one should *not* suppress notions (*'du šes dgag par yaṅ mi bya*, f. 83a4). This version of his teaching appears at first sight different from what is usually found in other sources, both Tibetan and Chinese. It may refer to his rejection of the Śrāvaka's mere suppression of notions (*saṃjñā*) and feeling (*vedita*). See *Pelliot tibétain 117* and *Stein 709* (cf. L. Gómez in R. Gimello and P. Gregory (eds.), *Studies in Ch'an and Hua-yen*, pp. 110–112); and Demiéville, *Concile*, pp. 63 n. 67, 71 (cf. pp. 75–76, 130, 140); below, p. 202 f.

jñāna) (f. 505b4–6). The procedure may therefore be illustrated by the idea suggested in the *Kāśyapaparivarta* (§ 69) that exact analysis (*bhūtapratyavekṣā*) gives birth to *prajñā* and is then consumed by this *prajñā*, just as fire created by attrition of two pieces of wood is as it were consumed in the blaze thus produced (f. 505a).[218]

If on the contrary, following the Hva šaṅ's instruction, one were to suppose that any and every conceptual construction (*rtog pa*) – inclusive, therefore, of *pratyavekṣā* (*so sor rtog pa*) – binds one to Saṃsāra, and then to request the Hva šaṅ's instruction (*gdams ṅag*) on non-conceptualization (*mi rtog pa*) with the sincere intention of realizing it meditatively, this procedure could, in terms of the Hva šaṅ's own assumption, only result in binding one to Saṃsāra (cf. *Bhāvanākrama* III, p. 15) (f. 506b). In other words, if taken seriously, the Hva šaṅ's method will be self-defeating.

Even if we hold mental cognition (*blo*) to be in error, the point is to discover how we are to know this unless and until we realize that the cognitive object perceived by it is not substantially real. This unreality of the cognitive object, grasped hypostatically, cannot be established by mere assertion (*dam bca' ba tsam*); and the realization of reality depends on bringing together unalloyed scriptural sources (*luṅ* = *āgama*) and arguments (*rigs pa* = *yukti*) establishing it. What is required, therefore, is non-construction preceded by already accomplished inspection through *prajñā* pertaining to *pratyavekṣā* (*so sor rtog pa'i šes rab kyi dpyad pa sṅon du soṅ ba'i mi rtog pa*), mere non-construction alone being quite inadequate for this (f. 507a).

Tsoṅ kha pa has referred as well to Sūtras such as the *Samādhirāja* and the *Saṃdhinirmocana* where the synergic co-ordination of Quieting (*śamatha*) and Insight (*vipaśyanā*) have been taught. Chapter viii in particular of the last Sūtra is regarded by the Yogācāra-Mādhyamika Kamalaśīla as a *locus classicus* on the subject of this co-ordination or syzygy. Tsoṅ kha pa has

218 This highly important theme, mentioned by Kamalaśīla (*Bhāvanākrama* III, p. 20), is discussed also in the *Madhyamakaratnapradīpa*, a work ascribed to Bhavya, in Chapter VII entitled *bhāvanākrama* (P, f. 352b), which also alludes to the question of non-mentation. See above, pp. 94–95 note; below, p. 206.

elsewhere referred to the account of the Great Debate[219] according to which this very Sūtra was contemptuously rejected by the Hva šaṅ (f. 306a).

It is therefore concluded by Tsoṅ kha pa that settling Fixation-Bhāvanā consisting in retention free from dispersal (*mi 'phro bar 'dzin pa'i 'jog sgom*) and Inspection by *prajñā* consisting in analysis (*so sor rtog pa'i šes rab kyis dpyod pa*) should first be made to alternate in meditative realization. In this way *śamatha* and *vipaśyanā* reach equilibrium (*cha mñam*), where there is an excess of neither the settling aspect (*gnas cha*: *sthiti*) nor of analytical investigation (f. 509b). Tsoṅ kha pa observes that *śamatha* and *vipaśyanā* are realized separately, and are made to alternate (*spel mar byed pa*) with each other, there being no rule at this stage that Inspection and Fixation should be realized [together] in a single mental continuum (*rgyun gcig*) (f. 510a5).

But in a later stage there follows the yoking together (*zuṅ du 'brel ba*: *yuganaddha*), or syzygy, of *śamatha* and *vipaśyanā*, when they merge and operate together (*samapravṛtta*: *mñam du 'jug pa*). The Path being then characterized by this yoked pair functions of itself (*raṅ gi ṅaṅ gis 'jug pa* = *svarasavāhin*), without effort (*mṅon par byed pa* = *abhisaṃskāra*) and mental inflection (*rtsol ba* = *ābhoga*) (f. 514a–b). Here the force of analytical Inspection-Bhāvanā (*dpyad sgom*) consisting in *pratyavekṣā* makes it possible to achieve Quieting (*śamatha*) (f. 514b6). And whilst inspection (*dpyod pa*) is *vipaśyanā*, this inspection once brought to perfect completion (*dpyad pa mthar thug pa*) is apprehension of Emptiness (*śūnyatā*) qualified by *śamatha* (f. 515a1).

This Fixation-Bhāvanā that initially alternates and then finally coincides with analytical Inspection, in the form first of a regular sequence and then of a syzygy of *śamatha* and *vipaśyanā*, is not, therefore, to be confused with 'Darkness-Bhāvanā' (*mun sgom*) and with non-construction known as *tsom 'jog gi mi rtog pa* (f. 496a6). These last two expressions are used to describe that one-sided form of totally non-analytical, and practically cataleptic, non-mentation and non-construction so often attributed in the Tibetan treatises to the Hva šaṅ, when *asmṛti* and *amanasikāra*

219 See *sBa bžed*, G, p. 66.16 ~ S, p. 56.8; dPa' bo gTsug lag phreṅ ba, *mKhas pa'i dga' ston*, ja, f. 116a2.

are advocated to the exclusion of exact analytical inspection (*bhūtapratyavekṣā*) and the resulting transcending discriminative understanding (*prajñā*).

In Tsoṅ kha pa's opinion, Nāgārjuna, Bhāvaviveka, Candrakīrti, Śāntideva, Kamalaśīla and Atiśa Dīpaṃkaraśrījñāna have all agreed on the matter of guidance in meditative realization (*'khrid tshul*) concerning the linkage that should obtain between Fixation-Bhāvanā and Inspection-Bhāvanā. And according to him the same fundamental method was, in addition, taught by Maitreya(nātha) and Asaṅga, and finally by Ratnākaraśānti (eleventh century) who faultlessly upheld their method in his *Prajñāpāramitopadeśa* (f. 511a).

The doxographer Blo bzaṅ Chos kyi ñi ma (1737–1802) has stated in his *Grub mtha' šel gyi me loṅ* that the Hva šaṅ Mahāyāna figures not as a sTon mun pa (as he does in the sources considered above) but as a special kind of Tsuṅ men pa. Yet Blo bzaṅ Chos kyi ñi ma observes straightaway that the Hva šaṅ Mahāyāna's doctrine does not prove to be identical with the general theory (*spyi'i lta ba*) of the Tsuṅ men pa.[220]

The same author then remarks that, according to the Tsuṅ men pa, the results of wholesome and unwholesome *karman* sustained by neither release (*ṅes 'byuṅ* = *niḥsaraṇa*) nor the *bodhicitta* can respectively engender bliss and pain, but that they nevertheless do not differ in so far as neither turns into the cause of Liberation and Omniscience. In the same way, black and white clouds are different in colour; but still they do not differ in their effect of obscuring the sky.[221] Not observing the appropriate distinction, however, the Hva šaṅ Mahāyāna has mistakenly asserted that good mental construction (*bzaṅ rtog*) and evil mental construction (*ṅan rtog*) are alike in being fetters. In the instruction on the meditative practice of real Tsuṅ men pa theory, there is mention

[220] Thu'u bkvan Blo bzaṅ Chos kyi ñi ma, *Grub mtha' šel gyi me loṅ*, rGya nag Chapter, ff. 11b–13b. I am indebted to Professor R. A. Stein for pointing out to me that Tib. *tsuṅ* corresponds here to Ch. *tsung* 'school', i.e. to the Ch'an as the school *par excellence*.

[221] Cf. *sBa bžed*, G, p. 68.18 and S, p. 58.5–6; *Stein 709*, f. 7a3 (cf. Gómez in *Studies in Ch'an and Hua-yen*, p. 114); *Chos 'byuṅ Me tog sñiṅ po*, f. 430b4; *Chos 'byuṅ mKhas-pa'i dga' ston*, ja, f. 117a2.

of inactivity (*ci yaṅ mi bya*) and non-mentation (*gaṅ yaṅ mi bsam*); but they concern the person who has attained direct understanding of reality (*gnas lugs mṅon du gyur pa'i gaṅ zag gi dbaṅ du byas pa yin pa*). However, the Hva šaṅ Mahāyāna has asserted that starting already with the level of the beginner (*las daṅ po pa* = *ādikarmika*), liberation results from total absence of thinking (*ci yaṅ yid la mi byed pa*).[222] The assertion made by this one Hva šaṅ is therefore wrong. But it is nevertheless impossible to hold that all theories of a Ho-shang (*hva šaṅ gi lta ba thams cad*) are consequently false.[223]

According to Blo bzaṅ Chos kyi ñi ma (f. 11b ff.), the *tsuṅ men* belongs to the tradition (*brgyud pa*) of the *sñiṅ po don*.[224] The term *tsuṅ men* is explained (f. 14a) as designating a tradition of realization in practice (*sgrub brgyud*), as distinct from a Vinaya one or an exegetical one (*bšad brgyud*).[225]

The *sgrub brgyud sñiṅ po don gyi brgyud pa* is said by Blo bzaṅ

222 See Demiéville, *Concile*, p. 77, and above, pp. 66, 84, 93, 98. But compare *Concile*, pp. 76, 86–88, 120–1, 157, 162, 164, as well as *Stein 709*, f. 40b.

223 *Grub mtha' šel gyi me loṅ*, rGya nag chapter, f. 13b. Blo bzaṅ Chos kyi ñi ma seems to have followed an account found in the *rGya nag chos 'byuṅ* of mGon po skyabs (eighteenth century), f. 72a ff. (of the sDe dge ed.; p. 118 ff. of the Sichuan People's Publishing House ed. of 1983).

224 While the expression *sñiṅ po don* or *sñiṅ po'i don* is often used in Tibet to refer to the *Dohā* traditions of the Siddhas and the bKa' brgyud, according to mGon po skyabs (p. 118) – who also mentions the Mahāmudrā (*phyag rgya chen po*) – the allusion is to a teaching given to Āryadeva by Nāgārjuna; see Tāranātha, *rGya gar chos 'byuṅ* (p. 67), who adds that the *sñiṅ po'i don* was passed on to Rāhulabhadra by Āryadeva (p. 68). Tshe dbaṅ nor bu (*rGya nag hva šaṅ gi byuṅ tshul*, f. 9a) relates the reference to the *ṅes don sñiṅ po'i mdo sde*, i.e. to the Sūtras of the Third Cycle teaching the *tathāgatagarbha*, such as the *Mahāparinirvāṇasūtra*, which deal with *don bsgom* (ff. 9a, 15a). This is also the *tsuṅ men* tradition going back, through the Hva šaṅ Mahāyāna, to Kāśyapa and Bodhidharma, even though it is sometimes referred to as the *tun min* (e.g. in the *bSam gtan mig sgron*, f. 8b). It resembles *in part* the rDzogs chen according to Tshe dbaṅ nor bu (f. 8b); however, it has to be distinguished from the latter in so far as it belongs to the *mdo lam* rather than the *sṅags lam* (f. 9b–10a). Tshe dbaṅ nor bu nevertheless concludes that the *don bsgom pa*, the *amanasi(kāra)* method of India and the two *bsam gtan gyi 'jug sgo* of the rGya nag mkhan po are virtually without difference (*phal cher mi mthun pa med do*, f. 12a).

225 It should be noted that mGon po skyabs differentiates between the *tsuṅ men* (pp. 118–123 of the Sichuan ed. of his *rGya nag chos 'byuṅ*) as a *bka' yi brgyud pa* comprising the twenty-eight Ch'an masters from Mahākāśyapa to Bodhidharmottara (see below) – and to which he has attached the *sñiṅ po don* also known as *rig stoṅ phyag rgya chen po* – and the *zab mo lta ba'i brgyud pa* in connexion with which he has discussed the *tun min* (= *gcig char 'jug pa'i sgo*) as opposed to the *tsi yan men* (= *rim gyis 'jug pa'i sgo*) (pp. 123–4). mGon po skyabs (p. 119) furthermore associates the *tsuṅ men* tradition with the *Ratnaguṇasaṃcayagāthās*, Kambala's *Ālokamālā*, and Dignāga's *Pramāṇasamuccaya*.

Chos kyi ñi ma (f. 12a) to descend through Bodhidharmottara (or Dharmo), the twenty-eighth in a line of spiritual transmission starting with Kāśyapa.[226] However, since in China Bodhidharmottara did not expound his doctrine literally (*sgra ji bžin pa*), but only by means of indirect allusion (*ldem dgoṅs kyi gsuṅ* : *saṃdhāvacana*) and symbols (*brda* : *saṃketa*), it is related that those who heard him did not have confidence (*mos pa*) and that they took him to be a teacher of nihilism (*chad lta mkhan*); and so he did not remain in China but went away to the North. The story of Bodhidharma's single shoe is also mentioned, as is the relevant iconography (f. 13a). And it is noted that by some he was identified with Pha dam pa rgya gar or Dam pa saṅs rgyas, an Indian master of the Ži byed doctrine who is reputed to have also gone to China. Our author nevertheless expresses uncertainty about the value of this identification because he knows of no reliable source for it (f. 13a).

In agreement with mGon po skyabs, Blo bzaṅ Chos kyi ñi ma then adds that the *sñiṅ po don* (or *tsuṅ men*) appears as a Tradition of Symbol-Mahāmudrā (*phyag rgya chen po brda'i brgyud pa*), one that is moreover in substantial agreement with the Tibetan bKa' brgyud pa (f. 13b). He thus approaches what Sa skya Paṇḍi ta has said in his critique of 'Chinese-style' rDzogs chen and Neo-Mahāmudrā, but apparently without a critical (or polemical) intent.

It is to be noted furthermore that, like mGon po skyabs, Blo bzaṅ Chos kyi ñi ma distinguishes this *sñiṅ po don* – and with it the *tsuṅ men* – from the *tun men/min* (*cig car 'jug pa'i sgo*) – the correlate of the *tsi'an men/tsi yan min*[227] (*rim gyis 'jug pa'i sgo*) – which he attaches to the distinct tradition of Profound Theory (*zab mo lta ba'i brgyud pa*) descending through Nāgārjuna and the

226 This information concerning the Hva šaṅ Mahāyāna's connexion with Bodhidharmottara's lineage and the *tsuṅ men* is found also in Tshe dbaṅ nor bu, *rGya nag hva šaṅ gi byuṅ tshul*, ff. 5b, 8a, 10b. On f. 9 Tshe dbaṅ nor bu describes 'Bodhidharmottara' as the source of the *tsuṅ men* (see also f. 10b2: *bsam gtan* [?] *mkhan hva šaṅ tsuṅ men rnams*). But, at the same time, Tshe dbaṅ nor bu maintains the connexion of Bodhidharma and his *brgyud 'dzin* Hva šaṅ Mahāyāna with the *cig char 'jug pa* following what he refers to as the *Lo paṇ bka' thaṅ* (in fact the *Blon po bka'i thaṅ yig*, f. 19a); see also f. 7b–8a. On the question of the line of twenty-eight Dhyāna masters, see further below, pp. 152–3.

227 The spellings *tse ya(n) men/man* are found in Tshe dbaṅ nor bu, *rGya nag hva šaṅ gi byuṅ tshul*, ff. 3b and 10b.

younger Bḥavya (f. 9b–11a).[228] It is in addition of great interest to see that this author considers (f. 11b) it incorrect to regard the latter two traditions as opposed doctrinal systems (*grub mtha'* = *siddhānta*); according to him, they are rather to be seen as methods of spiritual instruction (*'khrid tshul*) by which a disciple may be guided in accordance with his nature.[229] The same was in addition said by a great teacher cited by Blo bzaṅ Chos kyi ñi ma to apply to the distinction between *cig car ba* and *thod rgal*, which have been counted as two types in the practice of the Path (*lam gyi rim pa*) (f. 11b).

This linking of the Hva šaṅ Mahāyāna with a form of the *tsuṅ men* is clearly of considerable interest. Study of Mo-ho-yen's school-affiliations has suggested that, at least to begin with, he may have been a follower of the somewhat more gradualist Northern School of Ch'an linked with Shen-hsiu (seventh century), and that he only later moved closer to the Southern School represented by Shen-hui (670–762 or 684–758). However, the fact that he is sometimes listed as the seventh master in a line beginning with Dharmottāra/Bodhidharma can be interpreted as indicating rather that he in fact belonged strictly speaking neither to the Northern School, where it was P'u-chi (651–739) who was counted as the successor of the sixth Chinese Patriarch Shen-hsiu, nor to the Southern School, where Shen-hui is counted as the successor of the sixth Chinese Patriarch Hui-neng. Moreover, affinities between Mo-ho-yen and the Pao-t'ang School of Ch'an in Sichuan have also been noted by scholars. And it appears that his teaching was not wholly that of any of the well-known schools of Ch'an and that it was close to Ch'an movements in Sichuan and the Dunhuang area.[230]

In the records studied by Demiéville, furthermore, Mo-ho-yen is shown relativizing, and transcending, instantaneous (*tun*) and gradual (*chien*) tendencies within Ch'an.[231] Indeed, in a source

[228] See below, pp. 206–09.

[229] See also mGon po skyabs, *rGya nag chos byuṅ*, p. 173.

[230] Cf. S. Yanagida, in W. Lai and L. Lancaster (eds.), *Early Ch'an in China and Tibet*, pp. 20 ff., 36–37; D. Ueyama, *op. cit.*, pp. 327–49; J. Broughton in R. Gimello and P. Gregory (eds.), *Studies in Ch'an and Hua-yen*, pp. 1–68; G. Mala, 'Empreinte du Tch'an chez les mystiques tibétains' in *Le Tch'an (Zen)* (Hermès 4, Nouvelle Série, Paris, 1985), p. 387 ff.

[231] See Demiéville, *Concile*, p. 75; in *Essays in the history of Buddhism presented to Professor Z. Tsukamoto* (Kyōto, 1961), pp. 5, 26–27; *T'oung Pao* 56 (1970) pp. 83–86; and

often used by him, the *Laṅkāvatārasūtra*, we already find a relativization of the pair *yugapad* 'simultaneous' and *kramavṛtti* 'progressive engagement' (ii, pp. 55–56, 82 and 84). Vimalamitra is credited furthermore in the bsTan 'gyur with one treatise on the *cig car ba* doctrine and another on the *rim gyis pa* doctrine; and to the extent that these two works are attributable to a single author (whether he is named Vimalamitra or not), this too could attest an attempt at relativizing and reconciling the opposition between 'Simultaneism' and 'Gradualism' (or, eventually, at more or less inclusivistically integrating and 'recovering' the one in the other). At all events the *Cig car 'jug pa rnam par mi rtog pa'i bsgom don* ascribed to Vimalamitra contains materials corresponding to Kamalaśīla's *Bhāvanākramas*.[232]

In its furthest consequences the innatist and 'spontaneist' doctrine – especially if misunderstood – could, in certain circumstances, lead to ethical relativism or antinomianism.

It is interesting to observe that in connexion with the twin practices of ritualized sexual union and mactation (*sbyor sgrol*) – associated in the eleventh century in the Kingdom of Western Tibet with the so-called Ar tsho Ban de (or A ra mo Ban de) – antinomianism did in fact rage in tandem with immanentism

in: M. Soymié (ed.), *Contributions aux études sur Touen-houang*, pp. 1–7, 10–11; S. Yanagida, *loc. cit.*, p. 16; D. Ueyama, *loc. cit.*, p. 343; J. Broughton, *loc. cit.*, pp. 3, 8–10. Cf. J. McRae, *The Northern School and the formation of early Ch'an Buddhism* (Honolulu, 1986).

L. Gómez (in: R. Gimello and P. Gregory, *Studies in Ch'an and Hua-yen*, p. 95) has compared Mo-ho-yen's teachings with Tsung-mi's doctrine of sudden enlightenment followed by gradual cultivation. Tsung-mi belonged to the lineage of Shen-hui and hailed from Sichuan (cf. Yanagida, *loc. cit.*, p. 31). Wu-chu (Tib. Bu cu) of the Pao-t'ang Ch'an school of Sichuan inclined towards 'Subitism', whereas Master Kim (Chin Ho-shang, i.e. Wu-hsiang/Musang), the Korean master who taught in Sichuan, inclined towards 'Gradualism' (see Demiéville, in M. Soymié [ed.], *Contributions aux études sur Touen-houang*, pp. 3–7). On the 'sudden' tendency in the Northern School, in particular with Chih-ta who was a disciple of Shen-hsiu (rather than a later, and perhaps fictitious, master to be placed after Shen-hui), see B. Faure, *Cahiers d'Extrême-Asie* 2 (1986), pp. 123–132.

232 Tucci, *Minor Buddhist texts*, II, pp. 117, 120–1, speaks of interpolation. And Gómez in *Studies in Ch'an and Hua-yen*, p. 147 n. 8, regards 'all Bhāvanākrama passages in the Cig car ['*jug pa rnam par mi rtog pa'i bsgom don*] as interpolations, and not as instances of plagiarism or concessions to the gradualists'; see also Gómez, in *Early Ch'an in China and Tibet*, p. 397 and p. 430 n. 21. F. Faber has argued against attributing this treatise ascribed to Vimalamitra to (his) Vimalamitra (*Acta orientalia* 46 [1985], p. 49–50).

according to historical sources which tell us that Atiša was invited to Western Tibet in the middle of the eleventh century in order to combat this pseudo-Tantric doctrine in collaboration with Rin chen bzaṅ po. In this case the aberrations in theory and practice were apparently connected not with Chinese Ho-shangs but with a debased form of Mahāmudrā-teaching that was current in the border land with Kaśmīr, where a syncretism had evidently developed between Śivaism and Buddhism in which the doctrine and practice of both are said to have become perverted.[233]

Still, it is perhaps significant that the Supplemented Version of the *sBa bžed*, the *Žabs btags ma*, which has in its first part devoted so much space to the Great Debate and the circumstances surrounding it, deals at the end of its supplement (S, p. 90) with Atiša's confutation of those deviant Tantriks who – not having understood the intended purport (*dgoṅs pa* = *abhiprāya*) of texts the meaning of which requires to be elicited (*draṅ don* = *neyārtha*) but clinging rather to the bare words (*sgra* = *vyañjana*) – held that there was no need to have recourse to generosity (*sbyin pa* = *dāna*) and the other salvific means (*thabs* = *upāya*); for it is, they maintained, by Emptiness alone that one is Awakened. And in view of the resemblance between some of the problems at issue in the Great Debate and in the false doctrines propagated in Western Tibet by the Ar tsho Ban de which Atiša was called on to combat – and in particular the idea of dispensing with means as antidotes and the emphasis laid on the spontaneous innateness of buddhahood – it might even seem that the supplement to the *sBa bžed* was meant as it were to update this older text with a view to confronting a new, but in some respects comparable, situation.

[233] Cf. D. Seyfort Ruegg in: *Tantric and Taoist studies in honour of R. A. Stein* (*Mélanges chinois et bouddhiques* 20 [1981]), pp. 212–26; and *Acta indologica* 6 (1984), pp. 369–81.

Such antinomianism could, it is true, be derived from 'over-interpretation' of what has been said in even such classical texts of Buddhism as the *Kāśyapaparivarta* (§§ 48–49, on the wise and skilful Bodhisattva's being untouched by the pain of the passions) and Asaṅga's *Mahāyānasaṃgraha* (§ 10.28.11–12, on the theory of the destruction of the *kleśas* through the *kleśas* themselves), which have in fact been cited in just this connexion by the *bSam gtan mig sgron* (see below p. 122). See also *Mahāyānasūtrālaṃkāra* xiii. 11, and Sthiramati, *Madhyāntavibhāgaṭīkā* ii. 14 (p. 76) on *kleśa* as a factor of Awakening (*bodhyaṅga*). See in addition dPal brtsegs, *lTa ba'i rim pa* (cf. Tucci, *Minor Buddhist texts*, II, p. 139); and passages from Vimalamitra discussed by L. Gómez in W. Lai and L. Lancaster (eds.), *Early Ch'an in China and Tibet*, pp. 403–4.

However, it is important to note that no comparison has actually been drawn in the *Žabs btags ma* between the religious situation prevailing in Central and Eastern Tibet at the end of the eighth century, at the time of the Great Debate, and the dangerous debasement that menaced the Dharma in Western Tibet in the first part of the eleventh century. At most there may have been a kind of conflation of the problematics of each case.

It is nevertheless very curious to find cited in the *bSam gtan mig sgron* (f. 90a) a passage from a certain *rGya luṅ* ('Chinese Treatise') according to which even murder is a sin (*sdig pa*) only if the murderer conceives of the murdered person as a sentient being (*sems can*). On the contrary, if one does not do so – that is, in so far as one is able to recognize that all sentient beings are *māyā*-like and dream-like – there can, in the absence of any real sentient being, be no murder. This is compared with the case of killing in dream, where actually there is no killing at all of anybody; and dream and waking are then held to be alike in terms of the view in question. This doctrine seems, however, not to be often met with in our sources connected with the eighth-century Great Debate of bSam yas.[234]

In other words, despite a certain similarity in ideas, the actual practices and events in the two cases under consideration no doubt appeared altogether different to the authors of our sources. And they therefore did not equate the Hva šaṅ's rather etherealized spontaneous and innatist spiritualism and quietism – which dispensed with the difficult and prolonged 'allopathic' technique of the 'Gradualists' in favour of a spontaneous 'Nature-cure' of Mind[235] – with the deviant ideas and debased practices ascribed to the Ar tsho Ban de, who are reported to have engaged in ritual sexuality and mactation in the guise of a method that also repudiated the customary doctrines and praxis of 'Gradualist' Buddhism.

[234] Compare the citation from the *mkhan po* Phag do šan ši published by K. Okimoto, *Indogaku bukkyogaku kenkyū* 24/2 (1976), p. 994, who also has some information on a *rgya lun (chen po)* (pp. 993–2). In the *bSam gtan mig sgron*, f. 10a2, Dar mo ta ra is credited with a *rGya luṅ chen po*.

[235] Cf. the comparison of the rDzogs chen Man ṅag sde with moxabustion by Kloṅ chen rab 'byams pa, *Grub mtha' mdzod*, f. 126a5 (~p. 348.4–5): *yin sñam yid dpyod du ma lus par gnad thog tu phebs pas me btsa lta bu'o.*

In many Tibetan historical writings, and above all in philosophical and doxographical works, the expressions theory (*lta ba*) of the Hva šaṅ, Dharma-system (*chos lugs*) of the Hva šaṅ and tradition (*gžuṅ lugs*) of the Hva šaṅ have come to be used in a sense that is for all practical purposes dehistoricized and universalized. These expressions have thus come to be widely employed as generic designations for a *type* of theory or teaching that is characterized as quietist, spontaneist, innatist and simultaneist.[236]

Since disagreement may exist as to the extent to which Mo-ho-yen (and Ch'an) actually adhered exclusively, or mainly, to such views, this typological use of the expressions is perhaps not entirely justified historically. Yet it can be convincingly derived from the view, reliably ascribed to Mo-ho-yen, that all sentient beings are by their nature *buddhas* and that in coming to an awareness of their intrinsic and innate buddhahood – i.e. the Buddha-nature or *tathāgatagarbha* – any activity or 'reinforcement' of a religious and ethical as well as of an intellectual and discursively philosophical character is therefore altogether superfluous and irrelevant,[237] and may even be a hindrance on the level at least of the advanced practiser.[238] In this perspective, the Triple Vehicle (*triyāna*) is set aside in favour of the Unique Vehicle (*ekayāna*) – or even the Non-Vehicle (*ayāna*) – free from all verbalizations and conceptualization.[239] This interpretation of the Ho-shang's teaching is underpinned by his statements that liberation is achieved in immediate and face-to-face recognition of Mind free from all discursive and ratiocinative mentation, that is, in pure tranquillity unaccompanied by analysis and discriminative understanding.

Under this analysis, the Hva šaṅ's doctrine of the Buddha-nature and *tathāgatagarbha* would not issue in the eternalist view –

[236] L. Gómez in *Early Ch'an in China and Tibet*, p. 428 n. 14, describes the term quietism to refer to Ch'an as an unfortunate legacy of Demiéville's *Concile*. However, if not taken as referring specifically to seventeenth-century European thought, the word does not appear to be unsuitable. The hesychast too does not eschew all activity.

[237] See Demiéville, *Concile*, pp. 95, 107–08, 116–19, 151.

[238] See above, p. 117.

[239] See Demiéville, *op. cit.*, pp. 66, 119, 151.

with which these concepts have elsewhere been associated – and it could easily be (mis)understood as practically nihilistic. In Bu ston's *Chos 'byuṅ*, the Hva šaṅ's teaching is in fact assimilated to the nihilist view (*chad lta* = *ucchedadṛṣṭi*).[240]

In sum, virtually irrespective of its primary historical reference, the expression 'Hva šaṅ's theory' (or the like) has been used at least from the time of Sa skya Paṇḍi ta in the thirteenth century up to the present by Tibetan writers as a standard *topos*, and as a convenient *typological* designation for what a historian of religion and philosophy might call gnoseological nativism, soteriological spontaneousness, philosophical ataraxia (without of course presupposing any specific reference to Pyrrho or Stoical Pyrrhonism) and ethico-religious quietism (again without any specific reference to Molinos and Madame Guyon and to seventeenth-century European thought). In a large section of the Tibetan tradition it has in this way acquired currency as a term in the description of spiritual theory and practice.

Were it not for the fact that the historical existence of the Hoshang Mo-ho-yen is established by Chinese and Tibetan documents from Dunhuang and that Kamalaśīla and his teacher Śāntarakṣita are well-known figures in the history of Buddhism many of whose writings are extant in the original Sanskrit as well as in Tibetan translation, a historian might indeed have been excused for inferring from the available rather schematic accounts of the Great Debate, and from the almost paradigmatic rôles played in it by the Hva šaṅ Mahāyāna and Kamalaśīla, that this event and these names correspond not to historical facts and persons, but to emblematic figures embodying so to say a pair of contrasting religio-philosophical positions in typological and structural opposition. Certainly, in not a few Tibetan historical and doxographical traditions, the Ho-shang Mo-ho-yen has been partly dehistoricized and has developed into a practically emblematic figure occupying a paradigmatic, and structurally antithetical, position as the 'Simultaneist' *par excellence* in opposition to the

[240] See Bu ston, *Chos 'byuṅ*, f. 128a1; compare the 'Alternative Tradition' of the *sBa bžed* (G, p. 73) on *stoṅ pa ñid la dga' ba*. See however, *bSam gtan mig sgron*, f. 83a–b, on not falling into annihilation (*chad pa* = *uccheda*) and on *not* suppressing *saṃjñā* and *not* falling into absence of *saṃjñā*.

'Gradualist' Kamalaśīla. And even though the historical documentation available to us of course excludes such an inference, we still have to bear in mind that the figures in question have come to exemplify two important, and old, positions that have often been in tension, either virtual or actual, in the history of Buddhism. (Compare the cases of Musīla and Nārada, and of Mahākoṭṭhita/Mahākoṭṭhika and Sāriputta, in the old Buddhist canon mentioned below, Chap. iv)

The fact that, for the Tibetan historical and doxographical traditions, important facts concerning the Ho-shang Mo-ho-yen were uncertain and wrapped in the mists of time and legend must have greatly contributed to his becoming a somewhat shadowy and emblematic figure. For example, it was evidently not clear to the rÑiṅ ma master Tshe dbaṅ nor bu (1698/9–1755) whether he should be placed in the time of Khri Sroṅ lde btsan or earlier, at the end of the reign of this king's predecessor Mes Ag tshom(s) and whether it was he or a disciple of his who debated with Kamalaśīla.[241] Furthermore, as already noted, although the Hva šaṅ Mahāyāna is usually regarded by the Tibetan traditions as a 'Simultaneist', there seems to have been some uncertainty as to whether he should be identified as a *ston mun pa* or as a *tsuṅ men pa*.

Originally, and historically, 'Simultaneism' was possibly just as much complementary with as antithetical to 'Gradualism'. Ñaṅ ral's *Chos 'byuṅ Me tog sñiṅ po* has presented the teachings of the Hva šaṅ Mahāyāna and Kamalaśīla as being without difference in substance, notwithstanding the fact that they were pitched at different levels (f. 435b).[242] And in the *bSam gtan mig sgron* ascribed to gNubs Saṅs rgyas ye šes, simultaneous engagement (*cig car 'jug pa*) is a stage that follows on gradual engagement (*rim gyis 'jug pa*) and leads on first to Mahāyoga (*rnal 'byor chen po*) and

[241] See Tshe dbaṅ nor bu, *rGya nag hva šaṅ gi byuṅ tshul*, f. 8a–b, where Mahāyāna is placed in the latter part of the reign of Mes Ag tshom can (i.e. Khri lDe gtsug btsan, the father of Khri Sroṅ lde btsan) together with his disciples sBa gSal snaṅ (!) and Myaṅ Tiṅ ṅe 'dzin bzaṅ po and is therefore tentatively distinguished from the Hva šaṅ who debated with Kamalaśīla and who would then have been Mahāyāna's disciple. For an account of *ho-shangs* in Tibet at the time of Mes Ag tshoms, see for example the *sBa bžed*. And on the Hva šaṅ Me 'go/mgo at that time see Chap. ii above.

[242] See above, pp. 84–85. On the similar opinion of dPal dbyaṅs see above, p. 86.

then to Atiyoga and rDzogs chen; and although this work mentions the Hva šaṅ Mahā yan and Kamalaśīla in parallel, it does not refer to the Great Debate, nor does it present these two masters as opponents.[243] Kamalaśīla has, moreover, himself admitted the simultaneous operation (*cig car 'jug pa*) of *prajñā* and *upāya* in his *Bhāvanākrama* (II, p. 71).

Conclusion

The encounter in late eighth-century Tibet between two distinct, and contrasting, religio-philosophic currents has sometimes been presented in the Tibetan sources as well as by modern scholars as a confrontation between Indian and Chinese Buddhism. And by some modern scholars it has been described as a Sino-Indian or Indo-Chinese controversy, a conflict between Indian and Chinese culture, and sometimes even as a struggle at the Tibetan court between Indians and Chinese pursuing their respective political or religio-political interests.[244] The question arises as to whether such descriptions define the nature of the issues involved as precisely as is possible given the documentation available to us.

To take the last description first, although it is not impossible that political factors did play a part in these developments, it seems likely that the opposition between the two parties at the time of the Great Debate stemmed as much, if not more, from rivalries and conflicts between Tibetan magnates and their families (such as the sBa and Myaṅ, members of which had become Buddhist monks) as from national or ethnic rivalry between Indians and Chinese as such. The sBa family with which we have so often been concerned in the course of this discussion for example included some members – sBa gSal snaṅ and perhaps the enigmatic Saṅ ši (ta) – associated with Chinese and Korean Ho-

[243] In Don dam smra ba'i seṅ ge (15th–16th century ?), *bŠad mdzod yid bžin nor bu* (ed. Lokesh Chandra, New Delhi, 1969), f. 163a, there is a reference to Kamalaśīla and the Tsen min pa, as well as to the need to yoke together *śamatha* and *vipaśyanā* and to follow the theory of Nāgārjuna; but there is no mention of the Hva šaṅ Mahāyāna as Kamalaśīla's opponent. The *rdzogs chen* and *atiyoga* are, however, mentioned.

[244] Compare recently Demiéville in M. Soymié (ed.), *Contributions aux études sur Touen-houang*, p. 7, who refers back to his views expressed in his *Concile*.

shangs,[245] and other members – Ye šes dbaṅ po (who is, however, identified as gSal snaṅ once he had become a monk) and dPal dbyaṅs (who may or may not be identical with Saṅ śi) – who were closely linked with Kamalaśīla. As for Mo-ho-yen, two of his main supporters are reported to have been Khri Sroṅ lde btsan's 'Bro consort (the 'Bro bza' Jo mo Byaṅ chub rje) and his maternal aunt (*sru* Yaṅ dag), while other supporters of the Hva šaṅ were the chamberlain (*gzims mal pa*) Co rMa rma and a member of the rṄog family.[246] Myaṅ Tiṅ ṅe 'dzin bzaṅ po is also sometimes numbered as one of Ye šes dbaṅ po's chief opponents.

In the eighth century Tibet was in fact a major independent Central Asian power in its own right, especially after imperial power in China was shaken by the An Lu-shan rebellion. And there is no concrete evidence to show that the Tibetans, who figure so prominently in this encounter and the associated controversies, were pursuing anything but their own religious concerns, along perhaps with the political interests of their families and regions. At all events, and contrary to what has sometimes been suggested or implied, there is no reason to suppose that the Tibetans then represented nothing but the proverbial *tabula rasa* merely waiting to be converted or manipulated by Chinese or Indians. For their part, the Indians and Chinese in Tibet at the time would presumably have derived any political influence they may have possessed above all through the Tibetans with whom they were associated. And it is not evident that they would have been on their own in a position to further their national or ethnic interests in Tibet under the guise of a religio-philosophical controversy in which many of the points at issue had a long history in Buddhist thought. In sum, no conclusive evidence has been adduced to demonstrate that this controversy was essentially an eighth-century expression of Sino-Indian geo-political or politico-ideological rivalries and conflicts.

As to the view that the controversy was the consequence of cultural confrontation between Indian and Chinese Buddhism, and ultimately between Indian and Chinese civilization, it has to be borne in mind that there then existed no totally homogeneous

[245] See *sBa bžed* cited above, n. 100. [246] See above, p. 60 ff.

and monolithic Indian and Chinese Buddhism. On the one side the Chinese Ch'an traditions – which today are usually regarded as so typically Chinese – not only differed among themselves, but they had their origins, at least in part, in Dhyāna teachings from India and Central Asia and their counterparts in the teachings of certain Indian Siddhas and Yoga-masters. On the other side, the scholastic traditions of India had their Chinese extensions and equivalents, before and during the T'ang, in the San-lun (Madhyamaka) School, in Paramārtha's She-lun (*Mahāyānasaṃgraha*) School, in Paramārtha's and Hsüan-tsang's Chü-she (*Abhidharmakośa*) traditions, and in Hsüan-tsang's Fa-hsiang (*dharmalakṣaṇa*) School, as well as more generally in certain component strands of such major Chinese Buddhist schools as the T'ien-t'ai and Hua-yen. Furthermore, T'an-k'uang – an (elder?) contemporary of Mo-ho-yen at Dunhuang who evidently was in communication by correspondence with Khri Sroṅ lde btsan himself – was linked for example with the Abhidharma and Dharmalakṣaṇa (i.e. Vijñānavāda) traditions in China.[247]

What the student of comparative religion and intercultural transmission finds here is, then, neither a straightforward case of political conflict in Tibet between India and China, nor even a clear-cut case of cultural confrontation and hostility between homogeneous and monolithic national forms of Buddhism contending for the minds and hearts of Tibetans more or less passively waiting to be converted to the one or the other. Rather, we discover a complex of currents and trends – many of them old and respectable in the history of Buddhism – represented, in varying proportions, in the Buddhist traditions of India and China, and of course subsequently in Tibet itself.

Now, as already noted above, it is quite true that Tibetan sources have themselves underscored the fact that the two tendencies facing each other in Tibet arrived there in the main the one directly from India and the other through China, and that they were propagated respectively by Indian and Chinese masters. And the question of historically Chinese and Indian

[247] For the rôle of T'an-k'uang in the context of the Great Debate, see D. Ueyama in W. Lai and L. Lancaster (eds.), *Early Ch'an in China and Tibet*, p. 327; W. Pachow, *A study of the twenty-two dialogues on Mahāyāna Buddhism* (Taipei, 1979).

components in Tibetan Buddhism does unquestionably arise. Moreover, according to Tibetan sources, a certain *ho-shang* endowed with clairvoyance (*mṅon šes can*) foretold early in the reign of Khri Sroṅ lde btsan that Tibet was to be the special domain of teaching (*'dul skal*) of Śāntarakṣita (rather than of the *ho-shangs*).[248]

It would however appear that the Tibetan authors were thinking in terms neither of religio-political and politico-ideological interests and hegemony nor of national forms of Buddhism – a modern concept that would probably have been scarcely intelligible to these authors – but of lines of magisterial transmission and of doctrinal traditions differentiated according to their connexions with regions and lineages. Such classifications are of course well known within India and China; and in Tibet many schools (*chos lugs*) and teaching transmissions (*brgyud pa*) have been differentiated in just this way according to the names of places and regions (e.g. Sa skya pa, Jo naṅ pa, dGa' ldan pa, etc.). In other words, geographical regions and family lineages are very likely to have been involved to a degree now difficult precisely to determine in the encounter between currents and tendencies of thought with which we are here concerned. But to see this involvement as basically and essentially reducible to putative ethnic or national forms of Buddhism, or to great-power rivalry in Tibet, is to go beyond the evidence and to impose on it categories of thinking and analysis that are largely anachronistic. On the evidence available, such factors (to the extent that they existed) appear as incidental to the central issues at stake.

In the course of the later development of the Tibetan Buddhist traditions, nevertheless, the connexion of the Hva šaṅ Mahāyāna, and of the other *hva šaṅs*, with China may well have had an impact on the reception of their doctrines in Tibet. For the fact that the *ston mun pa* or 'Simultaneist' teachings are known to have been transmitted by Chinese and Korean Ho-shangs may have resulted in their being questioned or rejected by Tibetan writers on the ground of not being part of the main stock of Buddhism and its lines of transmission to Tibet. This would at the very

[248] See *sBa bžed*, G, pp. 7–8; S, pp. 6–7 (cf. G, pp. 11–12; S, p. 12.5); 'Gos gŽon nu dpal, *Deb ther sṅon po*, ka, f. 21a5.

least have made it easier for any Tibetan masters disposed to do so for reasons of theory or practice to take their distance from them.

Already at the end of the eighth and the beginning of the ninth centuries, the Tibetan rulers were evidently striving toward a normalization of the Buddhist teachings being propagated in their realm. This effort is reflected in the decrees attributed to them according to which the (Mūla)Sarvāstivāda should be the standard Nikāya-tradition in Tibet,[249] the philosophical theory of Nāgārjuna's Madhyamaka should be followed there,[250] and the dissemination of the Vajrayāna should be restricted.[251] These decisions – whether they were actually made by the monarch himself or by his advisers in the Dharma, or are part of some subsequent Tibetan 'invention of tradition' – do not, however, amount to the anathematization of all other Śrāvakayānist Nikāyas apart from the (Mūla)Sarvāstivādins, of all schools of philosophy other than Nāgārjuna's Madhyamaka, and of the Buddhist Tantras. And, similarly, the monarch's decree forbidding the dissemination of the Hva šan's teachings, assuming again that such a decree was actually issued by him, can perhaps be best understood as part of a further attempt at standardization rather than as an anathematization inspired by Kamalaśīla and his Tibetan followers. It has also to be recalled that at this time Tibetan civilization was in many of its aspects combining Chinese with Indian and Central Asian elements.[252] And in the ninth century translations of important Sūtras and major Śāstras (such

249 See Bu ston, *Chos 'byuṅ*, f. 130a–b (Obermiller, p. 197), referring to the time of Ral pa can. On the rôle of the Mūlasarvāstivāda Nikāya in Tibet, see D. Seyfort Ruegg, 'Über die Nikāyas der Śrāvakas und den Ursprung der philosophischen Schulen des Buddhism nach den tibetischen Quellen', in H. Bechert (ed.), *Zur Schulzugehörigkeit von Werken der Hīnayāna-Literatur*, Part I (Symposien zur Buddhismusforschung III, 1. Göttingen, 1985), pp. 121 f.

250 See above, pp. 62, 73, 84–86. Khri lDe sroṅ btsan's decree, reproduced in the *sGra sbyor bam gñis* (ed. N. Simonsson, *Indo-tibetische Studien*, i, Uppsala, 1957), p. 244 (compare Padma dkar po, *Chos 'byuṅ*, ed. Lokesh Chandra, f. 166b), names both Nāgārjuna and Vasubandhu as authorities.

251 See *sGra sbyor bam gñis*, p. 260 (compare Padma dkar po, *Chos 'byuṅ*, f. 168b), in the time of Khri lDe sroṅ btsan; Bu ston, *Chos 'byuṅ*, f. 130a–b, in the time of Ral pa can = Khri gTsug lde btsan (!).

252 See recently R. A. Stein, 'Tibetica antiqua' I–III, *Bulletin de l'Ecole française d'Extrême-Orient* 72 (1983), pp. 149–236, 73 (1984), pp. 257–72, and 74 (1985), pp. 83–133.

as the *Saṃdhinirmocanasūtra-Ṭīkā* by the Korean Wŏn ch'uk [613–696], P 5517 = D 4016) were being made from Chinese, notably by 'Go(s) Chos grub (Fa-cheng).[253] But the norm accepted for Tibetan Buddhism from the eighth century onwards has tended to be the twin criteria of the existence of an original Indian canonical source and of a valid Indo-Tibetan tradition of transmission.[254]

A further interesting point of difference between the Indian (and Indo-Tibetan) tradition and the Chinese tradition of Buddhism was that the former relied at least as much on Śāstra as on Sūtra sources whereas the latter was perhaps based more on Sūtras. It is no doubt to this tendency that Mo-ho-yen was referring when he contrasted his own Sūtra-based teachings and the predominantly Śāstraic content of the Buddhism being propagated by the 'Brahman monk' (*p'o-lo-men seng*).[255]

In sum, on the basis of the materials discussed above it appears appropriate to distinguish within Buddhism a 'Gradualist' current characteristic of the Sūtras and Śāstras that set out what might be termed the 'allopathic' use of counteragents (*gñen po* = *pratipakṣa* 'antidote') and salvific means (*thabs* = *upāya*) in a progressive course of gnoseological and soteriological reinforcement (*bhāvanā*, *sevanā* and *abhyāsa*); a gnoseologically 'innatist' and a soteriologically 'spontaneist' tendency characteristic in particular of the Siddhas and some Dhyāna-masters who followed above all certain Sūtras which dispense with 'allopathic' means and tend to have recourse mainly, or exclusively, so to say to a 'Nature-cure' based on the holistically immediate and face-to-face 'recognition' of Mind; and, finally, a current best known from the Vajrayāna (but not altogether absent from certain Sūtras and Śāstras) that makes use of what might be called 'homoeopathic' procedures by which obstacles such as the defilements/afflictions (*kleśa* = *ñon*

[253] Cf. S. Inaba in L. Kawamura and K. Scott (eds.), *Buddhist thought and Asian civilization* (Festschrift H. V. Guenther, Emeryville, 1977), pp. 105–13.

[254] For the use of this criterion in editing the canon, see D. Seyfort Ruegg, *The life of Bu ston Rin po che* (Rome, 1966), pp. 27–28.

[255] See Demiéville, *Concile*, p. 160 and pp. 25, 39–42.

moris) are overcome or cured through themselves.[256] And it is necessary to differentiate these currents – which have existed within Buddhism in a relationship of both suppletive and antithetical complementarity – from deviations and aberrations in theory and practice that arose from misunderstanding, debasement and misuse of either of the last two currents, and which are therefore distinct from them.

Although one or the other of these currents has no doubt predominated at a given place and time, it would be excessive to maintain that quintessentially and typically the first is Indian and the second is Chinese, and accordingly to represent the Great Debate and the encounter of theories and practices that accompanied it as a conflict between an Indian (or Indic) and a Chinese (or Sinitic) Buddhism. Similarly, however typical the 'Left-hand path' (*vāmācāra*) and the Cīnakrama may have been of certain Himalayan areas, it would not seem possible to consider the grave difficulties that arose in the Kingdom of Western Tibet in the eleventh century, and which led to Atiśa's being invited there to combat them, only as a clash between Indian and 'Himalayish' tendencies; for the problems involved extended far beyond these geographical and cultural areas.

In terms of any debate between 'nature' and 'nurture' – and in gnoseology and soteriology between nativism and reinforcement – the 'Simultaneist' with his principle of immediacy, spontaneousness and holism and his theory of the innateness of buddhahood would appear to stand on the side of 'nature' and gnoseological nativism, whereas the 'Gradualist' with his method of progressively eliminating all obscurations and defilements by means of counter-agents clearly emphasizes the need of 'nurture' and the reinforcement in meditative realization and cultivation of the factors conducive to buddhahood. These two approaches can also be applied to the understanding of the doctrine of the *tathāgatagarbha*, that is, the buddhomorphic nature of all sentient beings. For according to the 'Simultaneist' this teaching signifies

[256] Concerning the confluence of the last two currents in the teachings of Ta-mo-to-lo (*Dharmatrāta) according to Pao-t'ang Ch'an, see P. Demiéville, *Peintures monochromes de Dunhuang* (Paris, 1978), pp. 47–48.

For European thought, a connexion has been made between quietism and affectivity in A. Lalande, *Vocabulaire technique et critique de la philosophie*[9] (Paris, 1962), p. 874.

that all sentient beings are already *buddhas*; whilst according to the 'Gradualist' who insists on the need for methodical cultivation the same teaching signifies that on the 'causal' level (*gži*) beings are all potentially *buddhas*, that is, that their inborn capacity of achieving the 'fruit' (*'bras bu*) of buddhahood is proleptic and still unfulfilled. Nevertheless, as said in the *Mahāparinirvāṇasūtra* quoted by Kamalaśīla in his *Bhāvanākrama* (II, p. 19), the Matrix or Germ (*gotra*) of the *tathāgata* (*de bžin gšegs pa'i rigs*) is perceived only when Quieting (*śamatha*) and Insight (*vipaśyanā*) are in balance, as is the case with *tathāgatas* or *buddhas*. For when the mental tranquillity of concentration (*samādhi*) predominates and the discriminative function of *prajñā* is weak, as in the case of an Auditor (*śrāvaka*), one does not see the *tathāgatagotra* at all; conversely, if *prajñā* predominates and *samādhi* is weak, as is the case with Bodhisattvas still on the Path of Awakening, it is seen only indistinctly. That Kamalaśīla has thus called attention to the relevance of the *tathāgatagarbha* and *gotra* theories to his other concerns in his *Bhāvanākrama* is in keeping with the fact that in his *Madhyamakāloka* – which he is reputed to have composed in Tibet for the benefit of the monarch[257] – he introduced this theory into the main Madhyamaka tradition.

As regards the Vajrayāna, it appears to combine elements of the rapid way of 'nature' and nativism with a recognition that means, both ritual and cognitive, have to be brought into play gradually.

It is of special importance to note that both 'Gradualism' and 'Simultaneism' can find support in the Sūtra literature of Buddhism, and that in the Śāstras also many traces can be found of the idea of gnoseological nativism and soteriological spontaneousness as well as of holism and instantaneousness or 'Subitism'.

In Tibetan literature noteworthy indications are found concerning the manner in which the Tibetans have themselves regarded the interrelation and classification of the component elements of their religion and culture in terms of architectural organization in space.

[257] See *sBa bžed* G, p. 77 and S, p. 63; Ñi ma 'od zer, *Chos 'byuṅ Me tog sñiṅ po*, f. 437a6.

In the plan of the great temple complex of bSam yas – where at least part of the Great Debate took place in the Byaṅ chub gliṅ, which was constructed as a cosmogram on the model of the Indian temple of Otantapuri, and where for centuries members of the various Tibetan religious communities have found their monastic centre and have congregated[258] – the exposition of Dharma (*chos 'chad pa*) was kept up in the western temple (*gliṅ*) of Vairocana, the Dhyāna (*bsam gtan*) tradition of the 'Chinese Hva šaṅ' was cultivated in the western temple Mi g-yo bSam gtan gliṅ, Tantric rituals comprising Maṇḍalas and Abhiṣeka were performed in the southern temple of bDud 'dul sṅags pa gliṅ, Discipline (*khrims*) was placed in the eastern rNam dag khrims khaṅ temple, and the grammatical and literary arts were studied in the eastern Tshaṅs pa temple.[259] Here, then, we find a kind of diagram horizontally co-ordinating the various component traditions constituting Tibetan Buddhism.

In the vertical disposition of its successive storeys and their decoration, the central temple (dBu rtse) of bSam yas is said to have reflected a sort of symbiosis – or at all events a collocation – in ascending order of Tibetan, Chinese and Indian modes.[260] Thus, whilst the Tibetan style was represented on ground level in this sanctuary built in Tibet for the benefit of the Tibetan people, and whilst the Indian style characterized the pinnacle, the Chinese style is said to have been used in the middle storey. In this way, the component elements of Tibetan religious culture appear

[258] See G. Tucci, *To Lhasa and beyond* (Rome, 1956), p. 120.

[259] Bu ston, *Chos 'byuṅ*, f. 127b; cf. bSod nams rgyal mtshan, *rGyal rabs gsal ba'i me loṅ*, Chap. xviii, f. 83b–84a.

The classical Tibetan tradition has usually co-ordinated scholastic instruction (*bšad pa*) and spiritual realization (*sgrub pa*), meditation being associated with the former as well as with the latter. As for the grammatical and literary arts, they are regarded as general and 'exterior', i.e. as not specifically Buddhist, sciences (*vidyāsthāna*) and accomplishments of the Bodhisattva. Cf. *Bodhisattvabhūmi* i. 8 (p. 105) and i. 14 (p. 212).

[260] See *sBa bžed*, G, pp. 38–45, and S, pp. 31–36; Tshal pa Kun dga' rdo rje, *Deb ther dmar po (Hu lan deb ther)*, f. 17b (p. 37); *Padma bka'i thaṅ yig*, Ch. lxxxvi (transl. Toussaint, p. 342–3); *rGyal rabs gsal ba'i me loṅ*, Ch. xviii, f. 82b–83a. Cf. A. Ferrari et al., *mKhyen brtse's guide to the holy places of Central Tibet* (Rome, 1958), p. 113; Tucci, *To Lhasa and beyond*, p. 119 f.; R. A. Stein, *La civilisation tibétaine*[3] (Paris, 1987), p. 201. Reference can also be made to the remarks on the plan and models of the P'u-ning-ssu of Jehol (Chengde) in A. Chayet, *Les temples de Jehol et leurs modèles tibétains* (Paris, 1985), pp. 29, 67; and to P. Mortari Vergara Caffarelli, *Rivista degli studi orientali* 53 (1979), pp. 163–96 (with a bibliography of the question).

vertically ordered in a synthesis. However, no connexion appears to have been specified between the middle storey in Chinese style of the dBu rtse and the teachings of Dhyāna and the Hva šaṅ Mahāyāna.

The ground-plan of the bSam yas temple-complex thus suggests a horizontal co-ordination of philosophical exposition and Dhyāna, and even their structured complementarity and integration. And although the storey in Indian style was placed vertically above the one in Chinese style in the central temple, it is noteworthy that the elevation of this sanctuary has been interpreted by the sources cited as symbolizing neither a subordination nor an inclusivistic subjection of the Dhyāna propagated by Mo-ho-yen to the type of Buddhism taught by Śāntarakṣita and Kamalaśīla, or to that represented by Padmasambhava. It is to be recalled that, similarly, the teachings of Śāntarakṣita and Padmasambhava are traditionally regarded in Tibet as being in complementary harmony in the sense that their different methods serve the same end. And the close association of both Śāntarakṣita and Padmasambhava with Khri Sroṅ lde btsan has been symbolized for the Tibetan tradition by the *sdom brtson dam pa* device at least since the time of Sa skya Paṇḍi ta, who painted on a wall of bSam yas this emblem in which Śāntarakṣita is represented by a bird, Padmasambhava by a lotus and the Tibetan monarch by a flaming sword.

In summary, when we attempt to piece together from the Tibetan sources the circumstances in which the Great Debate of bSam yas took place, we find no clear and conclusive evidence to show that either Kamalaśīla or Mo-ho-yen was seeking a confrontation. Rather, having become aware of the presence in Tibet of tensions and polarized approaches within the Buddhist traditions connected on the one side with the teachings of certain Ho-shangs and on the other with the doctrines of Śāntarakṣita, the Tibetan monarch and his advisers are said to have taken the initiative in bringing representatives of the two currents together in a discussion because of their concern for the sound establishment and regularization in the kingdom of Buddhist theory and practice. And with this end in view Kamalaśīla was invited to

Tibet, supposedly in accordance with the advice that his master Śāntarakṣita had given just before his death.

It would moreover seem that, on the levels of both Ground (*gži*) and Fruit (*'bras bu*), there was little in Mo-ho-yen's teaching (to the extent to which it is available to us to judge) that could have been totally unfamiliar to Kamalaśīla from recognized Indian sources, despite the Chinese garb in which it was being presented by its propagators.[261] Equally, much of what Kamalaśīla's teaching stood for was well known to large sections of the Chinese Buddhist traditions, and thus it may not have been quite unfamiliar to Mo-ho-yen. It is however unlikely that Mo-ho-yen and Kamalaśīla could discuss or even converse directly with each other; and it is practically certain that interpreters, presumably Tibetans for the most part, would have had to act as translators in any meeting between them.

In this situation there lay the risk that what was a polarity – and a well-recognized and more or less creative tension – between two currents of thought and two approaches to the Buddhist Path could become magnified in a way not fully explained by any fundamental contradictions in either the commonly held canonical sources or in philosophical doctrine. And the ensuing rift would then have focused less on philosophy, or even on a theory of spiritual and philosophical praxis, than on methods and formulations bearing on the Path. In this way a polarity and tension present even in some of the oldest sources of Indian Buddhism could have assumed the proportions of the radical cleavage that we find in a large number of Tibetan accounts of the Great Debate starting with the *sBa bžed* and continuing in the discussions by Sa skya Paṇḍi ta and his successors.

It has at the same time to be borne in mind that part of the tradition of Tibetan Buddhism was markedly less critical of Mo-ho-yen's teachings. This attitude we find partially reflected in the *Chos 'byuṅ Me tog sñiṅ po* by the rDzogs chen master Ñaṅ ral Ñi ma 'od zer. And another rDzogs chen pa, Kloṅ chen rab 'byams pa, called attention to the similarity between certain of the

[261] See the remark on the basic agreement between the two parties in the Great Debate in regard to the Fruit (*'bras bu*) and the attainment of buddhahood, and on the difference between them as to the method of procedure (*'jug sgo*), in *sBa bžed*, G, p. 70.18–19 (attributed to dPal dbyaṅs) and S, p. 60.6–7 (attributed to Saṅ ši).

teachings of the Hva śaṅ Mahāyāna and the doctrine of *rdzogs chen*, as did in a slightly less pronounced way Tshe dbaṅ nor bu also. These masters have done so notwithstanding their recognition of the fact that whereas *rdzogs chen* is deeply Mantrayānist the teachings ascribed to the Hva śaṅ Mahāyāna are basically Sūtrayānist.[262]

In addition, a closeness in certain respects between some of the Hva śaṅ Mahāyāna's teachings and Mahāmudrā (*phyag rgya chen po*) was admitted by some bKa' brgyud pa masters, though certainly not by all. A link is indeed suggested by a convergent use of the metaphor of the Sovereign Remedy (*dkar po chig thub*) for the Hva śaṅ's teaching on non-mentational face-to-face recognition of Mind and the non-mentation (*yid la mi byed pa*) teaching of the bKa' brgyud pa, which with sGam po pa and some of his followers had a Sūtra branch in addition to the generally recognized Mantra branch.

It however remains true that neither all the rÑiṅ ma rDzogs chen pas nor gSar ma bKa' brgyud pas such as dPa' bo gTsug lag phreṅ ba and Padma dkar po have identified themselves with the Hva śaṅ's tradition. The closest approach to such an identification is perhaps to be found in the *bSam gtan mig sgron* ascribed to gNubs chen Saṅs rgyas ye śes and in the *Blon po bka'i thaṅ yig* of the *bKa' thaṅ sde lṅa*. That differences in fact existed between the Hva śaṅ Mahāyāna and the forms of Buddhism adopted in Tibet appears to be recognized by most of the Tibetan Buddhist tradition; nevertheless some representatives of this tradition have placed greater emphasis on the differences, taking them as the grounds for a radical cleavage, whereas other Tibetan masters have adopted a noticeably more conciliatory stance toward the teachings they connected with the Hva śaṅ.

262 Some 'Tantric' features however already appear in certain forms of Ch'an; cf. for example R. Kimura, *Journal asiatique* 1981, p. 192 (after gÑan dPal dbyaṅs); D. Ueyama, in W. Lai and L. Lancaster (eds.), *Early Ch'an in China and Tibet*, p. 349 n. 30; B. Faure, in P. Gregory (ed.), *Traditions of meditation in Chinese Buddhism* (Honolulu, 1986), pp. 115–16, 121. Moreover, the *tathāgatagarbha* theory, which is of such great importance in these traditions, is in some respects 'proto-Tantric', while some of its later developments are very clearly Vajrayānist.

IV

The Background to Some Issues in the Great Debate

KAMALAŚĪLA's treatment of the progressive Path of meditative realization (*bhāvanā*) and Awakening combining Quieting and Insight strongly suggests that he considered what might be described as the problem of innateness, immediacy, holism and spontaneity in relation to his theory of gradual development and reinforcement – in a sense of 'nature' in relation to 'nurture' – to be both an old and a recurring one in Buddhist thought.

Concepts such as manifestation or revelation (*abhivyakti*, etc.) in contrast to production or creation (*ārambha*, *utpatti*, etc.), the pre-existence of an effect in its cause (*satkāryavāda*) as opposed to production for the first time of a not previously existing effect (*asatkāryavāda*, *ārambhavāda*), and of simultaneous, non-sequential immediacy as distinct from sequential progressiveness in verbal knowledge and in the meaning of a poem are familiar from Indian philosophical thought, the semantics of the *sphoṭa*-theory and the aesthetics of the *dhvani*-theory.[263] In the Vedānta as the *jñānakāṇḍa*, activity – the ritual works and duties (*karman*, *dharma*) of the *karmakāṇḍa* – has often been denied real soteriological value, gnosis (*jñāna*) alone being regarded as constitutive of deliverance; whereas by other authorities (e.g. Maṇḍanamiśra) the conjunction of gnosis and works (*jñānakarmasamuccaya*) has been recognized as conducive to deliverance. In the Vedānta too the direct instrumentality, for immediate intuitive gnosis (*aparokṣajñāna*) of *brahman*, of both mental reflection (*manana*) and meditative practice (*nididhyāsana*) in addition to *śravaṇa* – i.e. the

[263] In the 'resonance' (*dhvani*) theory of the Indian poeticians, for example, there is an opposition between the *asaṃlakṣyakramavyaṅgya* and the *saṃlakṣyakramavyaṅgya*, the two divisions of the *vivakṣitānyaparavācya* which is *abhidhāmūla*. As for progressiveness as opposed to sudden immediacy in the *sphoṭa*-theory of the philosopher-grammarians, see K. Kunjunni Raja, *Indian theories of meaning* (Adyar, 1969), p. 124 f.

'auditive assimilation' of the sense of the authorless and immemorial scriptural *mahāvākyas* inducing knowledge of *brahman* and immediate deliverance (*sadyomukti*, as opposed to *kramamukti*) – has been a subject of discussion. Repeated meditative practice (*prasaṃkhyāna*) subsequent to this *śravaṇa* has been held (by Sureśvara) to be superfluous in the face of *śābdajñāna* or Word-generated knowledge. Another notion germane to the present enquiry is immediate recognition (*pratyabhijñā*) – the 'recollection' as it were of reality[264] – to which may be added the soteriological concept of the abrupt onset of spiritual realisation (*sāhasa*). Mention may also be made of the state of *anupāya* 'absence of means' which – in so far as it corresponds to the ultimate state of the *turyātīta* where all means are excluded – is free from all mediacy, as opposed to the three successive levels involving means and mediacy of the *āṇava* (*kriyopāya*), the *śākta* (*jñānopāya*) and the *śāmbhava* (*icchopāya*). These terms and ideas – though not identical historically with the questions directly at issue in the Great Debate of bSam yas, and despite the basic difference between Buddhists and the Vedānta with regard to Word (*śabda*) and Word-induced knowledge (*śābdajñāna*) as constituting immediate intuitive gnosis (*aparokṣajñāna*) – nevertheless provide in their problematics a number of interesting parallels and points of comparison with the issues considered by Kamalaśīla and Mo-ho-yen and so merit the attention of the comparativist.

The fact that the authoritative sources cited by Kamalaśīla – mainly Mahāyāna Sūtras – have a direct or indirect bearing on this subject indicates at all events that the problems at issue go back a long way in the history of Buddhist thought. Kamalaśīla was clearly not dealing with issues that had arisen for the first time during the eighth century in the specific historical context of the encounter in Tibet between Indian and Chinese ways of thinking and of a confrontation between Indian and Chinese masters. That this was so seems moreover to have been recognized in the 'Alternative Tradition' of the *sBa bžed*,[265] where

[264] For some references see D. Seyfort Ruegg, *Le traité du tathāgatagarbha de Bu ston Rin chen grub* (Paris, 1973), p. 78 n. 1.

[265] See *sBa bžed*, G, p. 73.5–8.

Kamalaśīla's master Śāntarakṣita is shown referring to the understanding of Mind known as the Sovereign Remedy (*dkar po chig thub*) as a 'stain in theory' (*dṛṣṭikaṣāya*) that consists in taking pleasure in Emptiness (*stoṅ pa ñid la dga' ba*), and which was to be found not only in Tibet but also very widely among persons who are tainted by these 'stains' and take pleasure in the notion of Emptiness.[266]

Since the evidence available to us indicates that this complex of problems has repeatedly arisen in one form or the other in the history of the Buddhist traditions in South, Central and East Asia – none of which has been entirely homogeneous and monolithic and each of which has included various currents of theory and practice – contrary to what has been suggested in Demiéville's masterly study[267] it does not seem appropriate to see in Kamalaśīla's treatment of the issues merely a dehistoricization of the Great Debate. For Kamalaśīla the Great Debate was probably rather one more occasion when this set of religious and philosophical problems embedded in the history of Buddhist thought came once again to be focused upon and to raise acute difficulties. And it was then in the later Tibetan traditions, as already observed, that the expression 'teaching of the Hva šaṅ' was taken from its specific historical context and came to be employed as a dehistoricized *topos* and as a generic designation for a *type* of quietistic and innatist teaching.

What the comparativist has to study here are not so much abstract entities like 'Indian Buddhism', 'Chinese Buddhism' or 'Tibetan Buddhism' – which are to a certain degree merely convenient constructs for the scholar – but rather the structural and typological features subsumed under these designations. This is of course not to deny that certain features are, at particular times and places, predominant in a given geographically delimited form of Buddhism, and that they may characterize and

[266] On the *lta ba'i sñigs ma* = *dṛṣṭikaṣāya*, see Vasubandhu, *Abhidharmakośabhāṣya* iii. 94ab with Yaśomitra's *Vyākhyā*. It is one of the five *kaṣāyas*, on which see e.g. *Lalitavistara* p. 248.13; *Saddharmapuṇḍarīka* ii, p. 43.4, 56.8, 58.11; *Bodhisattvabhūmi* i.17 (p. 252); *Mahāvyutpatti* 2336–40. These stains characterize especially the last 500-year period of the Dharma (cf. *sBa bžed*, G, p. 66.8; S, p. 56.2–3). On the *dkar po chig thub* see above, pp. 88–89, 100 ff.

[267] Demiéville, *Concile*, p. 18.

constitute it: if there were no overarching structures and continuities, but only innumerable discrete features, the terms 'Buddhism', 'Indian Buddhism' and the like would be mere empty names of no use to an historian. But the richness and diversity within the Buddhist traditions militate against taking even such serviceable terms as names of single and homogeneous individual entities. In sum, such constructs can fulfil a useful and legitimate heuristic and descriptive purpose for an historian provided that he does not reify them in historical and comparative work.

In the following, several themes typical of the ideas at issue in the Great Debate, and ascribed either to the 'Gradualists' or the 'Simultaneeists', will be considered with a view to identifying earlier examples or prefigurations of these themes and to situating them in the Buddhist (and non-Buddhist) traditions of India.

1. The Giving Up of Activity and *Karman*

While it is recognized that Mo-ho-yen considered the activity of conceptual and discursive thinking (*rnam par rtog pa'i sems*, etc.) to be the root of involvement in the round of existence,[268] he is held by Tibetan authorities to have in addition advocated the total relinquishment – at least by all advanced practisers – of not only all unsalutary activity but of all religious and philosophical activity of a salutary kind also.[269] For according to him this kind of activity is inextricably bound up with dichotomizing construction (*rnam par rtog pa*) and unreal notions (*m[y]i bden pa'i 'du šes*) and thinking (*m[y]i bden pa'i sems*).[270]

[268] See *Stein 468* (cf. Gómez, *Studies*, p. 107); *Stein 709*, f. 28; *Cheng-li chüeh*, ff. 129b, 131b, 134a–b, 135b, 138a–b.

[269] On the giving up of the ten forms of Dharma-practice which was reputedly taught by the Hva šaṅ Mahāyāna, see *sBa bžed*, G, p. 68 (cf. p. 73–74); S, p. 58; *mKhas pa'i dga' ston*, ja, f. 117al; and Ňaṅ Ňi ma 'od zer, *Chos 'byuṅ Me tog sñiṅ po*, f. 430b2 (where the practice of the ten is compared with gradual ascent, *mas 'dzeg pa*). And for the Tibetan King's command that they should be practised, see *sBa bžed*, G, p. 75 and S, p. 62; *mKhas pa'i dga' ston*, ff. 119al; and *Chos 'byuṅ Me tog sñiṅ po*, f. 435b6. For a list of ten *dharmacaryās*, see *Mahāvyutpatti* 903–912.

[270] See *sBa bžed*, G, p. 64 (*lus ṅag gi chos bya mi dgos/ lus ṅag gi dge bas saṅs mi rgya*); S, p. 54 (*lus ṅag gi chos spyod dge ba byas pas saṅs mi rgya*); *mKhas pa'i dga' ston*, ja, f. 115al (*lus ṅag gi chos spyod mi dgos/ lus ṅag gi dge bas 'tshaṅ mi rgya*); G, p. 68 (*thams cad sems kyi rnam par rtog pas bskyed pas/ dge mi dge'i dbaṅ gis las dge mi dge mtho ris daṅ ṅan soṅ gi 'bras bu myoṅ žiṅ 'khor ba na 'khor ro*) ~ S, pp. 57–58; *mKhas pa'i dga' ston*, ja, f. 116b7–117al (... *gaṅ žig ci la yaṅ mi sems žiṅ ci yaṅ mi byed pa de 'khor ba las yoṅs su thar par 'gyur ro*); etc. But

In his third *Bhāvanākrama* Kamalaśīla has ascribed to an unnamed opponent the teaching that no salutary activity consisting in the virtues of generosity and the like should be accomplished, such activity having been taught solely for the foolish (*nâpi dānādikuśalacaryā kartavayā: kevalaṃ mūrkhajanam adhikṛtya danādi kuśalacaryā nirdiṣṭā*, ed. Tucci, p. 14). No action, salutary or otherwise, should be carried out (*na kiṃcit kuśalādikarma kartavyam*), for it would lead to the round of existences (*saṃsārāvāhaka*, pp. 20–21). That Kamalaśīla considered as ancient this idea that *karman*, salutary as well as non-salutary, should be abandoned is shown by the fact that he has ascribed to the old Śramaṇa-school of the Ājīvikas the doctrine that deliverance results from the exhaustion of deeds (*karmakṣayān muktiḥ*, p. 20).[271] And he has observed that no such doctrine is to be found in the teaching (*pravacana*) of the Buddha, who taught rather that liberation results from the exhaustion of the defilements/afflictions (*kleśakṣaya*, pp. 20–21).

Now, in some old Buddhist canonical texts also there are in fact found certain references to the idea that liberation from Ill (*duḥkha*) results from, and consists in, the non-production of any future *karman* at all and from the ending, often through austerities (*tapas*), of any existing bad *karman*. This idea is there usually ascribed to the Nigaṇṭha Nātaputta (Nirgrantha Jñātṛputra), in other words to Mahāvīra and the Jainas.[272] We also read that immobility of body and renunciation of speech bring Ease

compare *Cheng-li chüeh*, ff. 133b, 135b, 136b–138a, 140b, and 151b. See below, pp. 203–04.

[271] For *ājīvika*, the Tibetan translation reads *mu stegs can kun tu tshol ba*, although the usual Tibetan equivalent is *kun (tu) 'tsho (ba)*. The doctrine usually associated with the Ājīvikas, and with their reputed founder Makkhali Gosāla/Maskarin Gośāla, is that of determinism and 'destiny' (*niyati*); cf. A. L. Basham, *The Ājīvikas* (London, 1951), p. 224 f. However, the avoidance of action (*karman*) in favour of a kind of ataraxia (*śānti*) is already mentioned, in connexion with Maskarin, by Patañjali, *Mahābhāṣya* VI. i. 154 (*mā kṛta karmāṇi mā kṛta karmāṇi, śāntir vaḥ śreyasīty āha, ato maskarī parivrājakaḥ*); see also the *Kāśikā ad loc.* (and Basham, *op. cit.*, p. 79). (The commentators on the *Mahābhāṣya* consider that the actions to be avoided are the *kāmyakarman* alone; for even one desirous of liberation must, according to them, perform the *nitya* and *naimittika* actions [see Nāgeśa *ad loc.*].)

Another resemblance between Makkhali and Mo-ho-yen could then have been thought to lie in the former's denial of the usefulness of moral effort in view of his doctrine of *niyati*.

[272] See Majjhima Nikāya I 92–95 and II 214; Aṅguttara Nikāya I 220–1.

(*sukha*).[273] Moreover, in a couple of Buddhist canonical texts the idea that no new *karman* at all should be generated, and that any existing *karman* should be ended, has even been connected with the Buddha himself in a sermon he once addressed to a Nirgrantha and in another one he addressed to Vappa, a disciple of the Nirgranthas.[274]

The connexion of such a teaching with the Buddha himself seems nevertheless to be rare. When it does occur, it is evidently to be explained by the fact that his auditor was a Nirgrantha and that the teaching was thus intended as an introductory salvific device, a circumstance that would lend support to Kamalaśīla's statement denying that such relinquishment of all activity was the Buddha's own teaching. In the majority of other places where it has been mentioned in the Pali canon, this doctrine has in fact been severely criticized. It is patently inconsistent with such basic principles of Buddhist doctrine as the four correct efforts (*sammāppadhāna/ samyakprahāṇa*) whereby the exercitant seeks to generate an impulse (*chanda*) with a view both to the production of still non-present salutary *dharma*s and to the increase of already present ones, while also generating an impulse for the non-production only of non-present bad and non-salutary *dharma*s and for the elimination of already present ones.

Certain passages of the old canon have, however, referred to the idea that both good and bad *karman* binds one by leading respectively to good and evil states in the round of existence. And there are accordingly traces in it of the notion of a special kind of karmic intention (*cetanā*) that is neither good nor bad, and which would thus obviate any form of maturing *karman* binding one to Saṃsāra. It is thus said that *cetanā* having in view the elimination of black (*kaṇha*), white (*sukka*) and partially black and partially white (*kaṇhasukka*) acts constitutes a fourth kind of act that is neither wholly nor partially black or white (*akaṇhāsukka*) and which is indeed conducive to the exhaustion of acts (*kammakkhayāya saṃvattati*).[275]

[273] See Majjhima Nikāya I 94–95.

[274] See Aṅguttara Nikāya I 221 and II 196–8.

[275] See Aṅguttara Nikāya II 230–37; cf. Dīghanikāya III 230, and Majjhimanikāya I 389–91. The four kinds of *karman* are the black which has a *kaṇhavipāka*, the white which has a *sukkavipāka*, the black-and-white which has *kaṇhasukkavipāka*, and that which is

This last notion of what may be termed deconstructive, or counteractive, *karman* as the fourth variety in a tetralemmatic structure does not, however, appear to be identical with Mo-ho-yen's Mahāyānistically inspired idea of non-activity and quietism; nor indeed is it even totally incompatible with Kamalaśīla's own theory of spiritual practice. But the teaching ascribed to Mo-ho-yen concerning the relinquishment of all action is clearly comparable with the above-mentioned idea of deliverance through the exhaustion of all *karman*, wholesome as well as unwholesome, which Kamalaśīla has ascribed to the Ājīvikas, and which is found connected chiefly with the Nirgranthas in the old canon.

In this connexion attention may be called also to the interesting reference to the question whether exhaustion of action (*karmakṣaya*) can, alone, lead to liberation in the Pramāṇasiddhi chapter (ed. Miyasaka, 272c–280b) of Dharmakīrti's *Pramāṇavārttika* and in the commentaries on this passage. There – in the frame of a discussion of what has been taken by commentators to be the Nirgrantha doctrine of liberation, which may therefore be compared with the Devadahasutta of the Majjhimanikāya (II 214 ff.) cited above – Dharmakīrti has stated that, without a course of spiritual practices as a remedy (*vipakṣa* = *gñen po*) against desire (*tṛṣṇā*, and its associated *ātmagraha* or *ātmadṛṣṭi*), there can be no freedom from *karman*; and any effort (*yatna*) directed toward *karmakṣaya* is futile so long as *tṛṣṇā* remains. Indeed, faults (*doṣa*) do not result from *karman*, but it is the person who is 'defective' (*duṣṭa*) that acts; and without false conceptions (*mithyāvikalpa*) there is no craving (*abhilāṣa*) even because of pleasure (*sukha*). Manorathanandin has accordingly remarked that the cause of the *doṣas* is not *karman* but inexact mental activity (*ayoniśomanaskāra*).

Mo-ho-yen's teaching on the subject may be compared too with a doctrine such as that of the *Vajracchedikā* (§ 6, p. 32). There

neither black nor white and which has *akaṇhāsukkavipāka* and thus leads to the exhaustion of action (*kammakkhayāya saṃvattati*). Examples of this fourth kind are the eight factors of the Path, from *sammādiṭṭhi* to *sammāsamādhi*, and the seven factors of Awakening (*sambojjhaṅga*), from *sati* and *dhammavicaya* to *samādhi* and *upekhā* (Aṅguttaranikāya II 236–7). Concerning this kind of *karman*, see L. Schmithausen in R. W. Neufeldt (ed.), *Karma and rebirth: post-classical developments* (Albany, 1986), pp. 207, 222 n. 30.

we read that the Bodhisattva-Mahāsattva should not 'take up' (*udgrah-*) either *dharma* or *adharma*; hence, with this in mind (*saṃdhāya*), the Tathāgata has declared that those who fully understand the raft-like Dharma-text (*kolopama dharmaparyāya*) should abandon (*prahā-*) *dharmas* and *a fortiori adharmas*.[276] This text would, however, have been known to and recognized by Kamalaśīla, who composed a Ṭīkā on the *Vajracchedikā*. Besides, the comparison of the Dharma with a raft, which one abandons once one has used it to cross over to the further bank of a stream, is a classical one found in the old canon.[277] But as understood by Kamalaśīla – and as attested by passages of the *Cheng-li chüeh* – Mo-ho-yen went appreciably further than this classical view of the matter.

Nāgārjuna has furthermore analysed and deconstructed the notions of action (*karman*), its agent and its fruit in Chapter xvii of his *Madhyamakakārikās*. And the question of giving up both demerit and merit – in the wide sense as well as in the traditional, Vedic sense – is a topic discussed in the first chapter of the **Śataśāstra* ascribed to Ārya-Deva; in the same place also the progressive arising of the Way is mentioned.[278] This discussion has to do with the idea of merit and demerit as interconnected concepts in binary thinking (*vikalpa*), and as coimplicates (*pratidvandvin* 'contrapletes'), and with the fact that the postulation (*grāha*) of the happy and virtuous (*sukha*) and the pure (*śubha*, *śuci*) has to be eliminated together with that of the permanent (*nitya*) and self (*ātman*).[279]

In a verse of his *Catuḥśataka* (viii. 11) Āryadeva has furthermore written:

> *akurvāṇasya nirvāṇaṃ kurvāṇasya punarbhavaḥ/*
> *niścintena sukhaṃ prāptuṃ nirvāṇaṃ tena nêtaraḥ//*

'For one who is inactive [there is] Nirvāṇa [whilst] for one who is active [there is] renewed existence: for one free from concerns

[276] Cf. *Laṅkāvatārasūtra* i, p. 17; É. Lamotte, *Le traité de la Grande Vertu de Sagesse*, I (Louvain, 1944), p. 64.

[277] See the *kullūpama* parable applied to *dhamma* in the Majjhimanikāya I 134–5.

[278] See G. Tucci, *Pre-Diṅnāga Buddhist texts on logic* (Baroda, 1929), pp. 15–19.

[279] See e.g. Āryadeva, *Catuḥśataka*, Chap. i–iv.

(*niścinta* = *sems khral med pa*) Nirvāṇa is easy of achievement, [but] the other [viz. existences] not'. A doctrine of non-activity and ataraxia pure and simple could however be founded on this statement only if the total context of Āryadeva's treatise is left out of account. (In his comment Candrakīrti supposes that Āryadeva has formulated this (apparent) paradox in reply to those who point out how difficult – indeed how virtually impossible – it would be to achieve all the infinite wholesome factors which together constitute the means of achieving Nirvāṇa, the Best Ease (*bde ba dam pa*), whereas to achieve birth requires no effort at all.) It is true that 'participation' in the Tranquil can only exist when there has been produced a turning away in distaste from the here and now [i.e. Saṃsāra according to Candrakīrti] (viii. 12ab: *udvego yasya nâstîha bhaktis tasya kutaḥ śive*). In a teaching concerning the worldly level (*laukikī deśanā*) it is engagement (*pravṛtti*) that is spoken of, whereas disengagement (*nivṛtti*) is taught when speaking of ultimate reality (*paramārṭhakathā*) (viii. 8). And it is necessarily *dharma* as something involving activity (*pravartaka*) that the foolish practise, while fearing through lack of familiarity (*anabhyāsatā*) that very *dharma* which leads to the cessation of activity (*nivartaka*) (xii. 9). Āryadeva has also specified that for the least able generosity (*dāna*) and for the middling discipline (*śīla*) have been taught; for the best it is the Tranquil (*ži ba*) that has been indicated (viii. 14). Indeed, by somebody desiring the wholesome (*puṇyakāma*) no mention should be made of Emptiness, for as a medicine unsuitably used *śūnyatā* could become a poison (viii. 18). Still, the non-wholesome (*apuṇya*) has first to be eliminated, and the [dogma of a] self next; only then may all [postulation and positions relating to entities (cf. viii. 16, 20)] be eliminated (viii. 15).

It is only natural to consider Mo-ho-yen's devaluation of activity, ethical as well as mental, in the frame of Ch'an contemplation of Mind (*k'an-hsin* ~ *kuan-hsin*) and what Demiéville has termed anoetism (*wu-hsin*, *wu-nien*; *pu-kuan*; *wu-tso-i* 'not planning'), perhaps also of 'One-practice Samādhi' (*i-hsing san-mei*) understood as a quietistic development of *śamatha*, and of course of the Chinese idea of non-activity (*wu-wei*). And this has in fact been done by historians of Chinese

Buddhism.[280] It however needs to be recalled that, alongside the cases of rejection of karmic activity noted above from early Indian sources, the question of the combination of knowledge and activity (*jñānakarmasamuccaya*) was also a major problem and point of controversy in classical Vedānta. Thus, whereas Maṇḍanamiśra accepted in his *Brahmasiddhi* a particular conjunction of *karman* and *jñāna*, Śaṃkara and Sureśvara denied all soteriological value to *karman* and recognized only *jñāna* (or *vidyā*) for the achievement of this goal.[281] Moreover, in his comment on the *Bhagavadgītā* (iv. 21), Śaṃkara has gone so far as to write that, for one seeking liberation, even *dharma* constitutes a fault because it brings about bondage, so that freed from both *dharma* and its opposite (*pāpa* 'evil, sin') one is free from Saṃsāra (*dharmo 'pi mumukṣoḥ kilbiṣam eva bandhāpādakatvāt/ tasmāt tābhyām mukto bhavati, saṃsārān mukto bhavati*). These words of Śaṃkara's were written at a time that was probably not very far removed from that of the Great Debate of bSam yas; and they demonstrate that one of the points that Kamalaśīla has severely criticized in his opponent's teaching has a very close parallel in the thought of a leading Hindu authority of nearly the same time.

Hence, while the teachings of Kamalaśīla's opponents in the Great Debate may indeed have been strongly influenced and reinforced by the milieu in which the Dhyāna schools evolved in China, it is not necessary to account for rejection of activity solely by reference to Chinese developments.

2. Voluntary Death, Self-immolation and the *Samasīsi(n)*

The Pali *Paṭisambhidāmagga* and *Puggalapaññatti* recognize a category of persons (*puggala*) called *samasīsi(n)* 'equal-headed' because, for them, exhaustion of the impurities (*āsavapariyādāna*)

[280] See Demiéville, *Concile*, Index *s.v.* sans pensée. On 'One-practice Samādhi' see B. Faure in P. Gregory (ed.), *Traditions of meditation in Chinese Buddhism* (Honolulu, 1986), pp. 99–128.

[281] See Maṇḍanamiśra, *Brahmasiddhi* (ed. S. Kuppuswami Sastri, Madras, 1937), pp. 13, 26–26, 36, with Kuppuswami's Introduction, p. xxxi ff. On the relation between *karman* and *vidyā/jñāna* in Śaṃkara, see his *Brahmasūtrabhāṣya* III, iv. 5, 11, 13 (with reference especially to *Bṛhadāraṇyakopaniṣad* IV. iv. 2 and *Īśāvāsyopaniṣad* 2).

and of life (*jīvitapariyādāna*) are simultaneous.[282] This type of person is listed also in the *Nettippakaraṇa*, where he occupies a position after the types known as *saddhāvimutta*, *paññāvimutta*, *suññatavimutta* and *ubhatobhāgavimutta*, and before the *paccekabuddha* and the *sammāsambuddha*.[283] Such a *puggala* represents then a special case of simultaneousness that consists in the co-occurrence of spiritual realization and the end of life.

In several cases of accelerated or precipitate achievement of the state of an Ārya and Arhat alluded to in the Pali tradition, spiritual realization supervenes immediately on a self-inflicted death decided on as a result of a feeling of shock (*saṃvega*) springing from a person's sense of spiritual inadequacy or failure. Examples cited are Godhika Thera and Channa Thera – who cut their own throats because of dissatisfaction with their spiritual progress – and Mahānāma Thera, Sappadāsa Thera and Sīhā Therī – who in disgust prepared to kill themselves. However, in other cases the 'shock' in question is evidently one of pure rapture, resulting from a sense of the beauty of the environment, as in the case of Usabha Thera who was transported by the loveliness (*rāmaṇeyyaka*) of the season's fullness in forest and mountain.[284] In still other cases, spiritual realization is said to have been abruptly precipitated by a physical shock brought about by slipping and falling, as in the cases of Bhagu Thera or Dhammā Therī. The phenomenon in question is therefore not exclusively confined to cases of suicide, or near suicide, due to a feeling of inadequateness and depression.[285] A common factor in many if not all cases of shock suddenly precipitating (without

[282] *Paṭisambhidāmagga* I 101; *Puggalapaññatti*, pp. 2, 13. This category of person – connected with the *naivasaṃjñānāsaṃjñā* level – is not accepted by the Sarvāstivādins; cf. A. Bareau, *Les sectes bouddhiques du Petit Véhicule* (Paris, 1955), pp. 175, 184, 198, 262.

[283] *Nettippakaraṇa*, p. 190.

[284] *Theragāthā* 110 and *Aṭṭhakathā* I 217 f. (cited by G. Malalasekera, *Dictionary of Pali proper names* [London, 1937], p. 439, and W. Rahula, *Zen and the taming of the bull* [London, 1978], p. 22).

[285] Such cases have been studied by P.-A. Berglie and C. Suneson in E. Kahrs (ed.), *Kalyāṇamitrārāgaṇam* (Festschrift N. Simonsson, Oslo, 1986), pp. 13–47. To the bibliography cited by them one may add R. Fick, *Der indische Weise Kalanos und sein Flammentod*, Nachrichten von der Gesellschaft der Wissenschaften zu Göttingen, Philologisch-historische Klasse, Göttingen, 1938; and K. Bhattacharya, *L'ātman-brahman dans le bouddhisme ancien* (Paris, 1973), pp. 29, 113, 157–9.

exactly causing) spiritual realization seems to be a sense of impermanence (*anicca*), either as an immediately preceding condition in the case of Paṭācāra Therī (and perhaps Usabha Thera), or as a more remote condition.[286]

The case of Gautika (or: Bhautika) is known also to the Abhidharma. In his *Abhidharmakośabhāṣya* Vasubandhu has mentioned this Śaikṣa's killing himself because of the disgust he felt (*nirviṇṇa*) for having repeatedly fallen away (*parihīyamāṇa*) from conditional release (*sāmayikī vimuktiḥ*) owing to delectation (*āsvādana*) and the weakness of his faculties (*mṛdvindriyatva*).[287] The reference to his attaining Arhatship in these circumstances occurs in connexion with Vasubandhu's exegesis of the technical term *cetanādharman* (Tib. *'chi bar sems pa'i chos can*), which designates in the soteriology of the Abhidharma a category of Arhat interpreted by Yaśomitra as one having the quality of killing himself (*ātmamāraṇadharman*).[288]

Whether the self-immolation reported for a Ho-shang and his followers in Tibet after their defeat in debate could be even remotely linked with any of these cases of suicide coinciding with the achievement of spiritual realization is difficult to determine in the absence of clearer and more decisive evidence.[289] The cases reported from Tibet of self-immolation may ultimately be connected rather with a distinct set of ideas that go back to Mahāyāna Sūtras such as the *Saddharmapuṇḍarīka* (Ch. xxii) and the *Samādhirājasūtra* (Ch. xxxiii), where the Bodhisattvas Sarvasattvapriyadarśana and Kṣemadatta are related to have burnt an arm or the entire body as a mark of respect for a Tathāgata and his Caitya. These ideas seem then to have been reinterpreted, and to have been literally put into practice as an act of protest and moral pressure, mainly in the Buddhist traditions of East Asia including Vietnam. In its account of the events leading up to the

[286] The case of Vakkali Thera does not, however, easily fit this description. On these persons see G. Malalasekera, *op. cit.*, with references to the sources in which they are mentioned. See also É. Lamotte, *Traité de la Grande Vertu de Sagesse*, II (Louvain, 1949), p. 740 n. 1; Rahula, *op. cit.*, p. 22–23; and Bhattacharya, *op. cit.*, pp. 29, 157–9.

[287] *Abhidharmakośabhāṣya* vi. 58b.

[288] As though the word *cetanā* 'intention' were equivalent to *chedana* 'destruction' and derived, by a Prakritic development, from the root *chid-* rather than from *cit-* (?). See Yaśomitra, *Abhidharmakośavyākhyā* vi. 58b (p. 582).

[289] See above, pp. 86–88 with the references cited in n. 167.

Great Debate between the Ho-shang Mo-ho-yen and Kamalaśīla, the *sBa bžed* has actually cited the example of a certain sage (*draṅ sroṅ* = *ṛṣi*) bZod pa (Kṣānti?) who set fire to himself and thus made himself a living offering; however, it has done so not in connexion with the Ho-shang and the 'Simultaneist' *ston min pas* (or *cig car bas*) but with reference to a Tibetan folk-etymology, based on *brtse ba* 'compassion', of the term *brtse(n) min pa*, the word of Chinese origin denoting the 'Gradualist' (*rim gyis pa*) school of Kamalaśīla.[290]

3. The Gradual as Opposed to the Simultaneous/Instantaneous and the Procedure of Leaping

The Problem in Early 'Dhyāna' and 'Maitreya-traditions'

Mo-ho-yen's teaching concerning the ultimate irrelevance of good deeds and the virtues for the achievement of liberation and Awakening is evidently closely linked with the notion of an Immediate or Sudden Way either leaping over or simply suppressing stages of the Path that was developed by masters of India and Central Asian 'Dhyāna' and East Asian Ch'an. The contrast between the Gradual (Ch. *chien*) Way and the Immediate or Sudden (Ch. *tun*) Way in Indian, and in particular Kaśmīrian, Dhyāna traditions has been traced, on the basis of sources now available only in Chinese, at least as far back as the Mahāyānist supplement to Saṃgharakṣa's *Yogācārabhūmi*, and to Dharmatrāta and Buddhasena both of whom lived in Kaśmīr *c.* 400 CE.[291]

This Mahāyānist supplement to the *Yogācārabhūmi* (Taishō 606) by Saṃgharakṣa – a master of the Kaśmīrian Sarvāstivāda school who lived in the second century – which was translated into Chinese by Dharmarakṣa was touched on already in 1926 by J. Rahder;[292] and it has since been studied in detail by Demiéville

[290] *sBa bžed*, G, p. 64.19 and S, p. 54.13; *mKhas pa'i dga' ston*, ja, f. 115a3. The possibility of a link, however indirect, with the *tejodhātusamādhi* and associated ideas should probably also be borne in mind. On these ideas see J. Dantinne, *La splendeur de l'Inébranlable*, i (Louvain-la-Neuve, 1983), pp. 272–4.

[291] See P. Demiéville, 'La *Yogācārabhūmi* de Saṃgharakṣa', *Bulletin de l'École française d'Extrême-Orient* 44 (1954), pp. 339–436.

[292] J. Rahder, *Daśabhūmikasūtra* (Louvain, 1926), pp. xxi–xxiv.

in his substantial monograph of 1954.[293] Demiéville has dated the addition of this Supplement to the period between Dharmarakṣa's translation of the main text of the *Yogācārabhūmi* in 284 and Tao-an's Catalogue of 384.[294] And he has pointed out the relevance of the section of this Supplement on the Bodhisattva's practice to the history of Dhyāna in India and Serindia and to the question of 'Subitism' in China.[295] Moreover, in connexion with this same Supplement, Demiéville has studied the procedure of leaping (Ch. *ch'ao-hsing*: **vyutkrāntaka-caryā*) by which the Bodhisattva is enabled to skip over several stages of the Path,[296] the concept according to which the Bodhisattva achieves the stage of non-regression in virtue of his first production of the *bodhicitta*,[297] and the link between the technique of leaping and innate purity of mind (*prakṛtiprabhāsvaratā* of *citta*).[298] Demiéville has in addition investigated Saṃgharakṣa's own connexion with the Maitreya traditions.

As for Buddhasena (early fifth century),[299] he was in fact the author of the so-called *Dharmatāla-Dhyānasūtra (*Ta-mo-to-lo ch'an-ching*, Taishō 618) translated into Chinese by his disciple Buddhabhadra,[300] who also translated the *Mahāparinirvāṇasūtra* with Fa-hsien (Taishō 376)[301] and was himself connected with a Maitreya-tradition.[302] And from what is recorded in the Chinese sources, it appears that the teachings associated with the name of Dharmatrāta – identified as a Yogācāra who lived in Kasmīr *c.* 410 CE – were also closely linked with the idea of the immediate Sudden Way.[303]

[293] See also Z. Tsukamoto, *History of early Chinese Buddhism* (Tōkyō, 1985), p. 214.

[294] Demiéville, *loc. cit.*, p. 349. [295] Demiéville, *loc cit.*, pp. 340–1, 429 n. 1.

[296] Demiéville, *loc. cit.*, p. 429–31. [297] Demiéville, *loc. cit.*, p. 430.

[298] Demiéville, *loc. cit.*, p. 432. Compare the notions of the *tathāgatagarbha* and *prakṛtisthagotra*.

[299] Cf. Lin Li-kouang, *L'aide-mémoire de la vraie loi* (Paris, 1949), pp. 342–350.

[300] See Lin Li-kouang, *op. cit.*, pp. 341–51; Demiéville in M. Soymié (ed.), *Contributions aux études sur Touen-houang*, pp. 1 ff., and in Jao Tsong-yi, *Peintures monochromes de Dunhuang*, i, pp. 46–47; S. Yanagida in W. Lai and L. Lancaster (eds.), *Early Ch'an in China and Tibet*, p. 27. See further Z. Tsukamoto, *History of early Chinese Buddhism*, pp. 452–3, 814, 879–88, 893–4; R. Shih, *Biographies des moines éminents* (Louvain, 1968), pp. 90–98.

[301] See Tsukamoto, *History*, pp. 438–9.

[302] See Demiéville, *BEFEO* 44 (1954), pp. 377–8.

[303] See Lin Li-kouang, *op. cit.*, pp. 315–51 (esp. pp. 317, 347). — On Dharmatrāta, see P. Yampolsky, *The Platform Sutra of the Sixth Patriarch* (New York, 1967), pp. 6–8; S. Yanagida in W. Lai and L. Lancaster (eds.), *op. cit.*, pp. 27–28; P. Demiéville in Jao Tsong-yi et al., *Peintures monochromes de Dunhuang* I, p. 43.

In other words, questions concerning the immanent, immediate, spontaneous, and sudden were evidently already an issue in Kaśmīr and Serindia by the early fifth century. Indeed, differences between the *tun* and *chien* approaches have been noticed in the preface to Taishō 618 ascribed to Hui-yüan (334–416).[304]

Dharmatrāta, to whom the above-mentioned Taishō 618 was wrongly attributed, has often been conflated with a certain Dharmatāla (?), and also with the great Ch'an patriarch Bodhidharma/Bodhidharmatrāta.[305] In a Chinese tradition there is a curious record of the latter's leaving behind one of his shoes as a token of the future spread of his teaching,[306] a motif found also in the Tibetan traditions which relate *inter alia* that a certain Chinese Master (*rgya nag mkhan po*) – i.e. one of the Ho-shangs active in Tibet in the eighth century – left one of his boots behind in Tibet after being defeated in a controversy as a sign that his teaching would survive and later spread in that country.[307]

In the Tibetan iconographic and ritual traditions, moreover, the Upāsaka (*dge bsñen*) Dharmatāla/Dharmatrāta figures, together with a certain Hva šaṅ counted also as an Upāsaka, alongside the sixteen Arhats in a well-known group that thus consists of a total of eighteen figures.[308] The Hva šaṅ in this group is often identified with the Hva šaṅ Mahāyāna, even though the latter is usually regarded as a monk; and an identification is made in addition with Pu-tai/Mi-lo (Maitreya) of the Chinese tradition.[309] Dharmatāra/Dharmatāla/Bodhidharma figures in Tibetan sources as an authority of the *sTon min pa/Cig car ba* tradition, or of the *Tsuṅ men*, that originated with Kāśyapa,

[304] See Lin Li-kouang, *op. cit.*, pp. 342–3.

[305] On the *Ta-mo ch'an shih lun* discovered in Dunhuang, see P. Yampolsky, *op cit.*, p. 21, and in W. Lai and L. Lancaster, *Early Ch'an in China and Tibet*, p. 3; B. Faure, *Le traité de Bodhidharma* (Paris, 1986).

[306] See Yampolsky, *Platform Sutra*, p. 41.

[307] See *sBa bžed*, G, p. 75.8; G, p. 9 and S, p. 8; and the other sources cited above, n. 170.

[308] For the history, iconography and iconology, see S. Lévi and É. Chavannes, *Journal asiatique* 1916/ii, pp. 189–304, especially pp. 288–90, 297; G. Roerich, *Tibetan painting* (Paris, 1925), pp. 29, 31–32; F. Lessing, *Yung-ho-kung* (Stockholm, 1942), pp. 35–37; P. Demiéville, in Jao Tsong-yi, *op. cit.*, p. 45 f; Z. Yamaguchi, *Acta indologica* 6 (1984), pp. 393–422.

[309] For Pu-tai/Mi-lo (Maitreya), see Demiéville, *Concile*, p. 12 n.; R. Edwards, 'Pu-tai Maitreya', *Ars orientalis* 14 (1984), pp. 5–50.

passed through Nāgārjuna and Āryadeva and culminated, in the seventh generation of the Chinese lineage, with the Hva šaṅ Mahāyāna, i.e. the Ho-shang Mo-ho-yen.[310]

In the traditions outlined above we thus find mixed together reasonably tangible historical and doctrinal material and more or less vague associations or recollections. Tenuous though the latter may be, they still reflect connexions that have been made by the traditions in question; and they accordingly deserve mention beside the properly historical data.

Gradual Understanding and Single-moment Understanding according to the Abhisamayālaṃkāra

When considering the background to the controversy that opposed Kamalaśīla and the Ho-shang Mo-ho-yen, it is of the greatest interest to turn to Haribhadra – a contemporary of Kamalaśīla, and also a follower of Śāntarakṣita, who flourished in the latter part of the eighth century – to see what light he can throw on the question.[311]

[310] See *bSam gtan mig sgron*, f. 8a: *rgya nag por bdun brgyud tha ma ha šaṅ Ma hā ya na la thug*. Cf. *Blon po bka'i thaṅ yig* (in the *bKa' thaṅ sde lṅa*, lHa sa ed.), f. 19a: *rgya nag sprul bdun brgyud pa'i tha: hva šaṅ mahā yā na ñid la thug* (a passage quoted by Tshe dbaṅ nor bu, *rGya nag hva šaṅ gi byuṅ tshul grub mtha'i phyogs sṅa bcas sa bon tsam smos pa yid kyi dri ma dag byed dge ba'i chu rgyun* [collected works, Vol. V, Dalhousie, 1977], f. 7b4, as from the *Lo paṇ bka' yi thaṅ yig*). See also *Pelliot tibétain 116* (164), *121* (40), *813*; and compare *Pelliot tibétain 996* and *Stein 689, 710*.

For the seven Ch'an patriarchs in China, see Yampolsky, *Platform Sūtra*, p. 7, and B. Faure, *Cahiers d'Extrême-Asie* 2 (1986), p. 123 ff. In his *Grub mtha' šel gyi me loṅ* (rGya nag Chap., f. 12a), Blo bzaṅ Chos kyi ñi ma speaks of a line of 28 patriarchs from Kāśyapa to Bodhi-Dharmottāra, perhaps following mGon po skyabs, *rGya nag chos byuṅ*, p. 118–19, or a closely related source, which may be based on the *Pao lin chuan* (for which see Yampolsky, *op. cit.*, pp. 47–48, 51). For the number 28, see Yampolsky, *op. cit.*, pp. 9 and 48 ff., and H. Schmidt-Glintzer, *Die Identität der buddhistischen Schulen und die Kompilation buddhistischer Universalgeschichten* (Wiesbaden, 1982), p. 46; S. Yanagida in W. Lai and L. Lancaster (eds.), *Early Ch'an*, pp. 27–28. Tshe dbaṅ nor bu, *rGya nag hva šaṅ gi byuṅ tshul*, f. 8b, appears rather to speak of the *logia* or traditions of 25 Masters down to Mo-ho-yen.

[311] These masters have all been classified as Yogācāra-(Svātantrika-)Mādhyamikas by the Tibetan doxographers. By some doxographers Haribhadra is further described as an Alīkākāravādin; and his predecessor Ārya Vimuktisena (sixth century), whose Vṛtti is the earliest available commentary on the *Abhisamayālaṃkāra*, is further described as a Satyākāravādin. See for example, lCaṅ skya Rol pa'i rdo rje, *Grub mtha'*, kha, f. 115b–116a, p. 401; D. Seyfort Ruegg, *The literature of the Madhyamaka school of philosophy in India* (Wiesbaden, 1981), p. 101.

In his fundamental comments on the Prajñāpāramitā and on the *Abhisamayālaṃkāra-Prajñāpāramitopadeśa* contained both in his shorter *Sphuṭārthā Vṛttiḥ* and in his very extensive *Abhisamayālaṃkārālokā Prajñāpāramitāvyākhyā*, this master has discussed at length not only progressive activity (*anupūrvakriyā* = *mthar gyis pa'i bya ba*) – i.e. progressive intuition (*anupūrvābhisamaya*) – but also single-moment awareness (*ekakṣaṇāvabodha* = *skad cig ma gcig pa'i rtogs pa*) which is also known as *ekakṣaṇābhisambodha* and *ekakṣaṇābhisamaya*. This pair of understandings constitute the sixth and seventh main topics (*padārtha* = *dṅos po*) in Prajñāpāramitā philosophy as expounded in Chapters vi and vii of the *Abhisamayālaṃkāra* ascribed by tradition to Maitreya(nātha).

In the *Abhisamayālaṃkāra* (vi. 1) it has been specified that progressive activity is comprised of a series of good qualities extending from generosity (*dāna*) up to discriminative understanding (*prajñā*), as well as of 'commemoration' (*anusmṛti*) of the Buddha, etc., and lastly of a nature consisting in non-existence of the factors of existence as hypostatized entities (*dharmābhāvasvabhāva*).

This *anupūrvābhisamaya* has then been explicated as thirteenfold[312] inasmuch as it covers the six Perfections (*pāramitā*), set out in terms of non-attachment to all factors of existence (*sarvadharmāsaṅga*) mentioned in the *Aṣṭasāhasrikā Prajñāpāramitā* (p. 893); six 'commemorations' pertaining to the Buddha, Dharma and Saṃgha as well as to discipline (*śīla*), renunciation (*tyāga*) and deities (*devatā*), set out in terms of the non-differentiation of all factors of existence (*sarvadharmāsambheda*) in the same Sūtra (p. 893); and the non-substantial nature of all factors of existence, set out in terms of the Sūtra's teaching (p. 893) concerning the non-existence of all these factors (*sarvadharmāsambhava*).[313] At the outset Haribhadra has pointed out that, as Perfections (*pāramitā*), the qualities of generosity, discipline, energy, and receptive perseverance are comprised in the Perfec-

[312] See *Abhisamayālaṃkāra* i. 17; Ārya Vimuktisena, *Abhisamayālaṃkāra-Vṛtti*, P, f. 221b6.

[313] Cf. Ratnākaraśānti, *Sāratamā* (ed. P. S. Jaini) vi. i, pp. 163–5, referring to the *Aṣṭasāhasrikā Prajñāpāramitā* (ed. Wogihara), p. 893.

tion of discriminative understanding (*prajñāpāramitā*).[314] In consequence of this the three components of any of the relevant acts – viz. the agent, the intended beneficiary and the activity of giving, etc. – are relativized and cancelled as hypostatic entities through what is known as triaspectual purification (*trimaṇḍalaviśuddhi*).

Haribhadra has next explained that comprehension (*adhigama*) results, *inter alia*,

(i) from 'commemoration' (*anusmaraṇa*) of the Buddha finding expression progressively in the factors of the three Paths of preparation (*prayogamārga*, i.e. the four *nirvedhabhāgīyas*), vision (*darśanamārga*) and meditative realization (*bhāvanāmārga*);

(ii) from 'commemoration' bearing on Dharma, i.e. the factors that are categorized as wholesome (*kuśala*), unwholesome and undetermined (*avyākṛta*); and

(iii) from 'commemoration' bearing on the Saṃgha, which Haribhadra here understands as the community of non-retrogressing (*avaivartika*) Ārya-Bodhisattvas.

Now, very significantly for the purpose of this study, Haribhadra has specified that, in reality (*paramārthatas*), *buddhānusmaraṇa* is characterized precisely by non-recollection (*asmaraṇalakṣaṇa*). And comprehension (*adhigama*) has been stated by him to consist in understanding that the very nature of all *dharmas* is precisely their 'entitylessness' (*dharmābhāvasvabhāva*), i.e. their non-substantiality as hypostatized entities.[315]

Haribhadra has further explained that *anupūrvābhisamaya* consists in cultivation with a view to stabilization consequent on the progressive ordering of the matter, which is then understood both in disconnexion and in connexion (*vyastasamastatvenâdhigatān arthān anupūrvīkṛtya sthirīkaraṇāya vibhāvayati*).

Such then, according to Haribhadra, is progressive compre-

[314] It is to be noted that – unlike Ratnākaraśānti (*Sāratamā*, p. 163.19) – Haribhadra does not here refer to *dhyāna* as comprised in the *prajñāpāramitā*; and he speaks (vi. 1, p. 908) of *four* Perfections (*pāramitācatuṣṭaya*) being comprised in *prajñāpāramitā*. The significance of this restriction, which distinguishes Haribhadra from Kamalaśīla for example, remains to be clarified in detail.

[315] Cf. Bhadanta Vimuktisena, *Vārttika*, P. f. 180a–181a.

hension, the sixth main topic in the *Abhisamayālaṃkāra*'s exposition of Prajñāpāramitā philosophy.

The next main topic in Prajñāpāramitā philosophy, which makes up Chapter vii of the *Abhisamayālaṃkāra*, is known as single-moment awareness (*ekakṣaṇāvabodha*). As comprehension in a single moment (*kṣaṇenâikenâdhigamaḥ*), this awareness is known to Haribhadra in addition as *ekakṣaṇābhisambodha* and *ekakṣaṇābhisamaya*. Then, for one who has fully realized this *ekakṣaṇābhisambodha* there ultimately arises, in a second moment (*dvitīye kṣaṇe*), the eighth awareness relating to the *dharmakāya* as the culmination of Prajñāpāramitā philosophy and practice, i.e. the final main topic treated in Chapter viii of the *Abhisamayālaṃkāra*.[316]

In the philosophy of Prajñāpāramitā as expounded in the *Abhisamayālaṃkāra* and in Haribhadra's *Vṛtti* and *Ālokā* – works which are rightly regarded as veritable monuments of the 'Gradualist' current in Buddhist thought – what exactly is meant by single-moment awareness or understanding?

Following Chapter vii of the *Abhisamayālaṃkāra*, Haribhadra has explicated the concept under the following four headings.[317]

(i) *Ekakṣaṇābhisambodha* is to be understood first in terms of the fact that each pure factor (*anāsravadharma*) is included in the multitude of *dharmas*, and also of the fact that these *anāsravadharmas* are themselves all comprised in each single *dharma* extending from generosity (*dāna*) up to the eighty marks (*anuvyañjana*) of the Buddha. This is so in virtue of a particular Gnosis (*jñāna*) free from the error of grasping each object separately, and which is accordingly termed single-moment (*ekakṣaṇa*) Gnosis. The concept of a *jñāna* by which all is realized simultaneously and at once, in virtue of the Dharma-Sphere of totality (*dharmadhātu*),[318] has been illustrated in the *Abhisamayālaṃkāra* (vii. 2) by the image of the noria or Persian wheel (*araghaṭṭa* = *zo chun gyi rgyud* ~ *zo chun brgyud*) the entire mechanism of which is set in motion

[316] Compare also *Abhisamayālaṃkāra* i. 18.

[317] Haribhadra, *Abhisamayālaṃkārālokā* vii; cf. i. 17.

[318] The Sanskrit texts reads (p. 909): *pūrvapraṇidhānādhānāvedha-dharmadhātusāmarthyāt* (Tib. *sṅon gyi smon lam gyi 'phen pa'i šugs daṅ chos kyi dbyiṅs kyi mthus*).

simultaneously and at once (*sakṛt* = *cig car*, glossed as *ekavāram* = *dus gcig tu*) by a single impulse of energy. In this way, in the first form of *ekakṣaṇābhisambodha*, the single pure Gnosis (*anāsravajñāna*) 'presents' (*abhimukhīkārayati*), in one single moment, all that is in its scope as homogeneous (*sajātīya* = *ri[g]s mthun pa*). It is defined by Haribhadra as characterized by the single-moment comprehension of all pure, non-fruitional factors (*avipākānāsravadharma*).

(ii) The next aspect of *ekakṣaṇābhisambodha* is described as consisting in the fact that, once all obstacles have been removed in the Bodhisattva's meditative realization of the appropriate counteragents (*pratipakṣa*), there arises the state of 'reality of fruition' consisting in the aspect of total purification (*sakalavyavadānapakṣavipākadharmatāvasthā*). And through comprehension of all *anāsravadharmas* that have therewith reached, in one single moment, this state of fruition, there arises the Gnosis that corresponds to *prajñāpāramitā*. This second aspect of *ekakṣaṇābhisambodha* has accordingly been defined by Haribhadra as characterized by the single-moment comprehension of all pure factors in the state of reality of fruition. Haribhadra's forerunner Ārya Vimuktisena (sixth century) had earlier specified that fruition (*vipāka*) through understanding (*abhisamaya*) in a single moment arises and ceases all at once (*cig car du* = *sakṛt* or *yugapad*?).[319]

(iii) The following aspect of *ekakṣaṇābhisambodha* is defined as being characterized by the single-moment comprehension of all *dharmas* as devoid of characteristic marks (*alakṣaṇasarvadharmaikakṣaṇalakṣaṇa*), this marklessness also being known in one single moment. Indeed, as had been explained by Ārya Vimuktisena, were *dharmas* on the contrary differentiated from each other by distinct characteristic marks, their required inclusion within one single *dharma* would be impossible; and it would then wrongly follow that there could be no realization (*abhisamaya*) in a single moment.[320] According to the later commentator Ratnākaraśānti (*c.* 1000), because of the absence of characteristic mark,

[319] Ārya Vimuktisena, *Vṛtti*, f. 225a1. [320] Ārya Vimuktisena, *Vṛtti*, f. 225a3–4.

Gnosis at this level is of one value (*ekarasa*).[321] In this regard the *Abhisamayālaṃkāra* (vii. 4) refers to the Bodhisattva's taking his place in 'dream-like' *dharmas* through the practice of generosity and the associated series of other qualities.

(iv) Finally, the fourth aspect of *ekakṣaṇābhisambodha* is defined as being characterized by the single-moment comprehension of all *dharmas* as marked by non-duality (*advayalakṣaṇasarva-dharmaikakṣaṇalakṣaṇa*). With regard to this the *Abhisamayālaṃkāra* (vii. 5) compares the non-duality of what is dreamt (*svapna*) and its cognition in dream.

In all its many ramifications and applications this seventh topic is as important, and as complex, as any in the philosophy of Prajñāpāramitā; and a full explication and analysis of the above-mentioned four aspects of the *ekakṣaṇābhisambodha* on the basis of the Prajñāpāramitāsūtras and the extensive exegetical literature that relates to them could well fill a monograph. For our present purpose it will be sufficient to observe that single-moment comprehension here occupies a critical, and pivotal, position in the transition from the step-by-step cultivation of the Path by the Śaikṣa-practiser to the climactic comprehension of *dharmakāya* as a culminating awareness on the Aśaikṣa-level of a *buddha*.

At an even earlier stage of practice of the Path, following on the transition from the final moment of the mundane (*laukika*) Path of preparation (*prayogamārga*) of the worldling (*pṛthagjana*) – that is, from the *laukikāgradharmas* – to the supramundane Path of vision (*darśanamārga*) of the Ārya, mention has also been made in Haribhadra's *Ālokā* of this Darśanamārga as a single-moment understanding (*ekakṣaṇābhisamaya*).[322]

This concept is to be understood in the following way. The Darśanamārga is regularly represented as consisting of sixteen thought-moments (*citta*[-*kṣaṇa*]). In it the following four factors are then identified: (i) a preliminary externally objectified receptive perseverance in knowledge (*dharmajñānakṣānti*) and (ii) a full externally objectified knowledge (*dharmajñāna*) bearing on

321 Ratnākaraśānti, *Sāratamā* vii, 4, p. 171.1.

322 Haribhadra, *Abhisamayālaṃkārālokā* ii. 12 (ed. Wogihara, p. 171: =P, f. 120b).

the objective (*grāhya*) factors of existence, beside (iii) a preliminary consequent receptive perseverance in knowledge (*anvayajñānakṣānti*) and (iv) a full consequent knowledge (*anvayajñāna*) bearing on the subjective (*grāhaka*). This set of four factors is brought into relation with each of the four Principles or Realities of the Nobles (*āryasatya*).

Quoting one view of this matter in his *Ālokā*,[323] Haribhadra has explained that, in the exact moment when Ill (*duḥkha*, i.e. the first *āryasatya*) is eliminated following on its recognition, the other three *satyas* also are all simultaneously involved, viz. in the form of elimination of the origin of Ill (i.e. the second *āryasatya*), the realization of the cessation of Ill (i.e. the third *āryasatya*), and the practice of the Path (i.e. the fourth *āryasatya*). And the same applies *mutatis mutandis* in the case of each of the following three *satyas*. Hence, according to this view, the Mahāyānist intuition of the Darśanamārga is to be regarded in this respect as a single-moment intuition (*ekakṣaṇābhisamaya*) with respect to its intuition of a single effect (*ekakāryābhisamaya*).[324] According to another view of the matter also mentioned by Haribhadra, intuition of the Darśanamārga is an *ekakṣaṇābhisamaya* because there here arises a pure knowledge (*anāsravajñāna*) making known the nature of all modes (*sarvākārasvarūpaprativedhakārijñāna*); and this knowledge has within its scope the totality of all factors (*sarvadharmaviṣaya*), thus bearing a certain (at least formal) resemblance to the two aspects of the *ekakṣaṇābhisambodha* at the very end of the Path.

In sum, there are recognized in the tradition of Prajñāpāramitā philosophy to which Haribhadra belonged – a tradition very closely connected with the Yogācāra-Madhyamaka of Śāntarakṣita and Kamalaśīla and ultimately with a Maitreya-tradition – both a progressive, serial form of understanding involving *inter alia* forms of commemoration which are characterized as being in

[323] *Abhisamayālaṃkārālokā* ii. 12, p. 171 (=P, f. 120b).

[324] *Abhisamayālaṃkārālokā* ii. 12, p. 171: *ity ekakāryābhisamayād ekakṣaṇābhisamayo mahāyāne darśanamārge draṣṭavyaḥ* (Tib., P, f. 120b: *de ltar 'bras bu'i mṅon par rtogs pa la bltos nas theg pa chen po'i mthoṅ ba'i lam la mṅon par rtogs pa skad cig ma gcig yin no*). On the *kāryābhisamaya* see *Abhidharmakośabhāṣya* vi. 27 (below, pp. 177–8).

reality non-recollective (*asmaraṇalakṣaṇa*) and without mentation, and also a single-moment understanding aspects of which involve simultaneous (*sakṛt*) realization. This *ekakṣaṇābhisambodha* leads, in the following and culminating moment, to ultimate comprehension of the *dharmakāya*. In addition, at an even earlier stage of the Path, the pivotal transition from the mundane (*laukika*) Prayogamārga of the worldling (*pṛthagjana*) to the transmundane (*lokottara*) Darśanamārga of the Ārya, reference is made to a single-moment intuition (*ekakṣaṇābhisamaya*) on the Darśanamārga.

The above-mentioned transitions appear to parallel what has in the Vijñānavāda school been termed *mārgāśrayaparivṛtti* (so long as one remains a Śaikṣa) and *cittāśrayaparivṛtti* (when one attains the *aśaikṣamārga*).[325]

The notion of the momentary or instantaneous (*ekakṣaṇa*) as attaching to a crucial and pivotal point where a leap – a veritable *saut-de-plan* – is made from the conditioned level to the unconditioned – from the *saṃskṛta* level of the Bodhisattva under training (*śaikṣa*) to the *asaṃskṛta* level of the Aśaikṣa in Buddhahood (or Arhathood) – is thus a critical one. It is essential to underscore the fact that both these aspects, the Gradual and the Instantaneous/Simultaneous, have been recognized by the school that taught the progressive Path.

From the foregoing it therefore emerges that a classical school of Indian Prajñāpāramitā thought embraced a complex of typologically 'simultaneist' ideas and terms that figured also among the points at issue in the controversy that took place in Tibet at the end of the eighth century between the 'Gradualists' with Kamalaśīla at their head and the 'Simultaneists' with the Ho-shang Mo-ho-yen as one of their leading proponents. That the issues are even older in Prajñāpāramitā thought than the second half of the eighth century is demonstrated by the fact that the *Abhisamayālaṃkāra* (of uncertain date) and its early commentator Ārya Vimuktisena (sixth century) already clearly recognized both these forms of understanding or awareness as complementary, and also by the fact that several of the problems in question are implicitly or explicitly touched on in the canonical sources quoted by

[325] See *Abhidharmasamuccayabhāṣya* (ed. N. Tatia), p. 93.

Kamalaśīla in his *Bhāvanākramas* and in his commentary on the *Avikalpapraveśadhāraṇī*.

The Hva šaṅ Mahāyāna is recorded to have said that the simultaneous engagement (*gcig char 'jug pa*) he taught is like the tenth stage (*sa* = *bhūmi*).[326] It may be that he was thus referring to a state comparable to what we have just seen recognized for the *ekakṣaṇābhisambodha* in relation to *dharmakāyābhisambodha* in Prajñāpāramitā thought.

It is moreover in connexion with the *buddhabhūmi* that the Mādhyamika master Candrakīrti has evoked the instantaneousness of the *buddha*'s Gnosis (*jñāna*). In his *Madhyamakāvatāra* we read (xii. 2, p. 356):

> 'Just as space is not differentiated according to differences in the containers [in which it may be enclosed], so there is in reality no differentiation whatever caused by things (*bhāva*) [i.e. by the *skandhas* such as matter and feeling]. Therefore, when correctly comprehending [this reality] as being of one single value (*ekarasa*) – oh Thou of highest understanding! – Thou didst understand the knowable (*jñeya*) in one instant (*kṣaṇa*).'

In his autocommentary Candrakīrti has explained that, once he achieved Awakening in the Akaniṣṭha-sphere (see *Madhyamakāvatāra* xii. 1), Bhagavat attained the Gnosis of the Omniscient (*thams cad mkhyen pa ye šes*) in one instant. And it is by this understanding, in just a single knowledge-moment (*mkhyen pa'i skad cig gcig kho na*), that Bhagavat attained the Gnosis of the Omniscient in precisely that single knowledge-moment (*mkhyen pa'i skad cig gcig kho nar*).

Here then the single-moment character of Gnosis on the stage of the *buddha* is explained in terms of the one value (*ekarasatva*) of reality, that is, the fact that on the supreme and final level of Buddhahood all is understood to be of one single value only. This single value is liberation along with Emptiness (*śūnyatā*).

[326] See *sBa bžed*, G, p. 68.20 and S, p. 58.7; *mKhas pa'i dga' ston*, ja, f. 117a2; *Chos 'byuṅ Me tog sñiṅ po*, f. 430b5.

This theme has been alluded to also in the *Triśaraṇasaptati* ascribed to (a) Candrakīrti (verse 14):

> *chos rnams ñid kyi ṅo bo ni//thams cad yod pa ma yin te//*
> *de phyir skad cig gcig gis ni//bde gšegs thams cad mkhyen par 'dod//*
>
> 'A nature does not exist at all for the *dharmas*. Therefore it is held that, in one single moment, the Sugata knows all.'

This treatise was known to Haribhadra, who has quoted its verse 33 in his *Abhisamayālaṃkārālokā* (i. 3, pp. 8–9).

According to a much earlier source, the basic Commentary on the *Ratnagotravibhāga-Mahāyānottaratantraśāstra* (i. 25, pp. 21–22), the fact that stained Thusness (*samalā tathatā*) is simultaneously and at once (*yugapad ekakālam* = *cig car dus gcig*) both [naturally] pure (*viśuddhā*) and [adventitiously] Affected (*saṃkliṣṭā*), is to be regarded as an inconceivable matter (*acintyasthāna*), as is declared in the *Śrīmālādevīsiṃhanādasūtra*. And the further fact that stainless Thusness (*nirmalā tathatā*) is un-Affected by previous stains (*pūrvamalāsaṃkliṣṭā*), even though it is later purified (*paścād viśuddhā*), is also an inconceivable matter. Hence it is declared in the *Dhāraṇīśvararājasūtra* that Mind (*citta*) is by nature luminous (*prakṛtiprabhāsvara*), and is knowledge 'just so' (*tathaiva jñānam* = *de kho na bžin šes so*). As a consequence, it is also stated that Perfect Awakening (*samyaksambodhi*) is Awakened to (*abhisambuddhā*) in virtue of that understanding which is endowed with the characteristic of being a single-moment one (*ekakṣaṇalakṣaṇasamāyuktā prajñā*) (i. 25, p. 22).

A related idea is also expressed in another passage of the basic Commentary on the *Ratnagotravibhāga* (i. 15), where it is explained that the pair (*dvaya*) represented by what is termed 'natural luminosity of mind' (*cittasya prakṛtiprabhāsvaratā*) and its sub-defilement/affliction (*upakleśa*) is very hard to comprehend. For no second *citta* in fact intervenes (*anabhisaṃdhāna* = *mtshams sbyor ba med pa*) because of the single flow (*ekacaratva* = *gcig rgyu ba*) of both salutary and non-salutary *cittas* in the Pure Sphere (*anāsravadhātu*). Hence, as is declared in the *Śrīmālādevīsiṃhanādasūtra*, salutary thought (*kuśalacitta*) is instantaneous (*kṣaṇika*): it does not become Affected by defilements/afflictions (*na kleśaiḥ saṃkliśyate*). And non-salutary thought (*akuśalacitta*) is instantaneous: it is not in a state of Affection by the defilements/afflictions, and no defilements/afflictions touch this *citta*.

Still another 'inconceivable matter', as pointed out in the *Dhāraṇīśvararājasūtra*, is represented by the fact that Buddha-activity (*jinakriyā*) functions spontaneously (*anābhoga*) and without binary mental construction (*avikalpatas*) for sentient beings – in accordance with their predispositions and the way they are to be trained – simultaneously (*yugapat* = *cig car*), everywhere (*sarvatra* = *thams cad la*) and at all times (*sarvakālam* = *dus thams cad du*) (i. 25, p. 24; cf. *Ratnagotravibhāga* iv. 67).

Here in the *Ratnagotravibhāga*-Commentary and in its Sūtra sources, then, the notion of instantaneousness and simultaneity marks not exactly a critical and climactic transition from one stage of the Path to another (such as from the Prayogamārga to the Darśanamārga) or from the Path to the Fruit of Buddhahood (as in the cases from Prajñāpāramita philosophy studied above), but instead the so to speak non-rational 'co-relationship' of the *buddha*-level with the level of sentient beings. This co-relationship (if such it may be called) is in effect that of bondage and liberation in the classical Buddhist perspective of the ultimate non-duality of Saṃsāra and Nirvāṇa/Bodhi, or of *samalā tathatā* and *nirmalā tathatā*. And in view of the fundamental principles of non-substantiality (non-hypostatization) and non-duality (but *not* monistic identity), this 'relationship' is non-rational because, in reality, there exist no separate and opposed hypostatic entities, in other words no ultimately real relata. In the conventional discourse of philosophical analysis and of the description of the Path, the positions and sequences *sattva* : *buddha*, bondage: liberation, *saṃsāra* : *nirvāṇa*, *samalā tathatā* : *nirmalā tathatā* and so on no doubt all have their pedagogical and heuristic usefulness and legitimacy; but they lack any ontologically or gnoseologically real foundation as hypostatizable entities that could be related and opposed. This is why the ostensible terms of this non-rational 'relationship', which goes beyond the frames of space and time, are described as instantaneous, and also why the understanding that pertains to them is itself characterized as being a single-moment *prajñā*. Position in space and succession in time of the two levels are thus neutralized and cancelled in philosophical description by atemporal instantaneity and simultaneity.

That Kamalaśīla was not unfamiliar with these ideas expounded in the *Ratnagotravibhāga* and its Commentary and Sūtra-sources – and connected with the doctrines of the natural luminosity of Mind, the *tathāgatagarbha*, and the *prakṛtisthagotra* which is also a topic of Chapter i of the *Abhisamayālaṃkāra* – is suggested by the fact that in his *Madhyamakāloka* he incorporated the *tathāgatagarbha* doctrine in the Yogācāra-Madhyamaka.

Leaping and the Samāpatti *or* Samādhi *called* Avaskanda(ka), Viṣkanda(ka) *and* Vyutkrāntaka

Associated with various forms of rapid way and immediate access to Awakening, we find the Tibetan concepts of *thod rgal* and *khregs chod*.[327] The latter is known from the rDzogs chen tradition, where it is described as *ka dag*; and no Sanskrit original for this term has so far been identified.[328] On the other hand, the term *thod rgal*, well-known in rDzogs chen literature too, is amply attested elsewhere.[329] In rDzogs chen literature it is glossed as *lhun grub* 'spontaneous' (Skt. *anābhoga*),[330] but it actually means leaping or skipping. The Sanskrit words translated by *thod rgal* are *avaskanda(ka)* and *viṣkanda(ka)*, meaning jumping over, and *vyutkrānta(ka)*, used in the sense of striding over.[331]

[327] On these two terms, see H. V. Guenther, *Tibetan Buddhism in western perspective* (Emeryville, 1977), p. 151; G. Tucci, *Religions of Tibet* (London, 1980), pp. 85–87, 131; R. A. Stein, *Revue de l'Histoire des Religions* 179 (1971), pp. 23–28; and M. Broido, *Journal of the International Association of Buddhist Studies* 8 (1985), p. 35 (concerning the types of person known as *cig car ba, thod rgal ba* and *rim gyis pa*). *Thod rgal* has often been regarded as an essentially gradual, even though accelerated, process as opposed to *khregs gcod*. But in some cases *thod rgal* too can be extremely rapid and for all intents and purposes sudden.

[328] In the *Bod rgya tshig mdzod chen mo* (*Zang-Han daicidian*, Peking, 1985), *khregs chod* is defined as (1) *sṅa 'gyur ba'i lhag mthoṅ gi brda chad* (i.e. an expression used by the rÑiṅ ma pas for *lhag mthoṅ* = *vipaśyanā*), and (2) *ka dag khregs chod kyi bsdus tshig*.

[329] In Sakaki's edition of the *Mahāvyutpatti* the spelling *thod rgyal* is found under no. 1496.

[330] Cf. *Bod rgya tshig mdzod chen mo*, s.v.

[331] It should be noted that *ava-skand-* means not only 'to jump down' but also 'to assault, storm'. The latter meaning would be appropriate when the *avaskanda(ka)* technique designates an accelerated and very rapid process.

As for the term *viṣkanda(ka)*, the word *viṣkanda* is attested in the meaning of 'dispersing, moving away'.

In the *Mahāvyutpatti* (no. 1496), the *vyutkrāntakasamāpatti* (or *vyatikrāntakasamāpatti*) = *thod rgyal* (sic) *gyi sñoms par 'jug pa* follows on brief descriptions of the four Ārūpyas – i.e. the Samāpattis relating to the Ākāśānantyāyatana, the Vijñānānantyāyatana, the Ākiṃcanyāyatana and the Naivasaṃjñānāsaṃjñāyatana (nos. 1492–5) – and it precedes the *vyāskandaka-* or *vyatyasta-samāpatti* (= *snrel ži'i sñoms par 'jug pa*, no. 1497).[332] It is usually contrasted with the nine Samāpattis of progressive and sequential residence (*anupūrvavihārasamāpatti* = *mthar gyis gnas pa'i sñoms par 'jug pa*, no. 1498) consisting of the four Dhyānas (nos. 1478–81) and four Samāpattis (nos. 1492–5 already mentioned together with, in addition, the *saṃjñāvedayitanirodha*, no. 1500).

The notion of leaping or skipping stages of the graded Path is known in the Dhyāna-tradition of Buddhism.[333] And since it is relevant to the *ston mun pa* and *cig c(h)ar ba* techniques at issue in the Great Debate in Tibet, it will be of interest to see to what extent, and where, these ideas are attested in the main sources of the classical schools of Indian Buddhism and, especially, in those of Śāntarakṣita's and Kamalaśīla's school.

After briefly describing in both the forward (ascending, *anuloma*) and reverse (descending, *pratiloma*) directions the nine sequential Attainments in absorption (*anupūrvasamāpatti*) – i.e. the four Dhyānas relating to the *rūpadhātu* and the five Samāpattis relating to the four Āyatanas of the *ārūpyadhātu* and the Saṃjñāvedayitanirodha – the *Aṣṭādaśasāhasrikā Prajñāpāramitā* (ed. Conze, Ch. lxii, pp. 108–10) describes the Siṃhavijṛmbhita Samādhi, which is shown to consist in ascending through the four Dhyānas and four Āyatanas to the Nirodhasamāpatti and then descending from this high Samāpatti to the first Dhyāna in a progressive and sequential fashion. Next, this Sūtra takes up the Viṣkandaka ('jumping', or 'dispersing'?) Samādhi, which is practised once the Siṃhavijṛmbhita Samādhi has been worked

[332] On *vyatyasta/yamaka* see É. Lamotte, *Artibus asiae* 24 (1961), pp. 307–10, and *L'enseignement de Vimalakīrti* (Louvain, 1962), pp. 33–34. In the *samādhi*-list of the *Mahāvyutpatti* (no. 534), the *vyatyasta* follows the *siṃhavijṛmbhita*.

[333] See Demiéville, *BEFEO* 44 (1954), pp. 429–31; *Hōbōgirin*, s.v. *chōgyō*; above, p. 151.

through. This Concentration – otherwise referred to in the same Sūtra and elsewhere as the Avaskandaka ('jumping', and perhaps also 'storming'?) Samādhi – consists in the practiser's first ascending progressively through the Dhyānas and Āyatanas to the Nirodhasamāpatti, gaining (*samāpad-*) each stage in sequence. Then, from the Nirodhasamāpatti he jumps back to the second Dhyāna, thence again to the Nirodhasamāpatti and back down to the third Dhyāna, thence again to the Nirodhasamāpatti and back down to the fourth Dhyāna, thence again to the Nirodhasamāpatti and back down to the Ākāśānantyāyatana, thence again to the Nirodhasamāpatti and back down to the Vijñānānantyāyatana, thence again to the Nirodhasamāpatti and back down to the Ākiṃcanyāyatana, and thence again to the Nirodhasamāpatti and back down to the Naivasaṃjñānāsaṃjñāyatana. Then the practiser ascends once more to the Nirodhasamāpatti and descends back down to the Naivasaṃjñānāsaṃjñāyatana, from which he this time arises to remain in a state of non-concentration (*asamāhitacitte*[334] *'vatiṣṭhate*). Next, the practiser arises from the state of non-concentration and gains (*samāpadyate*) the Nirodhasamāpatti, from which he arises to remain in a state of non-concentration. The same procedure is followed by the practiser in descending order for each of the four Āyatanas of the *ārūpyadhātu* and for each of the four Dhyānas of the *rūpadhātu*, so that having finally arisen from the first Dhyāna he remains in a state of non-concentration. This Sūtra-passage concludes by stating that standing (*sthita*) in the Avaskandaka Samādhi one thus achieves (progressively) the Equality of all factors of existence (*sarvadharmasamatām anuprāpnoti*), and that it is in this way that a Bodhisattva-Mahāsattva standing in the *prajñāpāramitā* takes up (*parigṛhṇāti*) the Perfection of *dhyāna*.

The *Śatasāhasrikā Prajñāpāramitā* (ed. Ghoṣa, i, pp. 272–3), using the expression *viṣkadya samāpadyate*, describes a process by which Bodhisattva-Mahāsattvas cross (*saṃkrāmanti*) to a Buddha-field (*buddhakṣetra*) in virtue of their very first production of the Thought of Awakening (*prathamacittotpāda*). This procedure consists in such Bodhisattvas who achieve the four Dhyānas and

[334] In his edition of the *Aṣṭādaśasāhasrikā prajñāpāramitā* (Rome, 1962), Conze prints *asamahitacitta* throughout. But the *Aṣṭasāharikā* and other texts have *asamāhita*°.

Ārūpyasamāpattis attaining the first Dhyāna and then, having arisen from it, the Nirodhasamāpatti. Thence the practiser attains the second Dhyāna, thence again the Nirodhasamāpatti, thence the third Dhyāna, thence again the Nirodhasamāpatti, thence the fourth Dhyāna, and thence again the Nirodhasamāpatti. Next, attaining once again the Nirodhasamāpatti, and following a similar procedure, the practiser ascends through the four Āyatanas. And arising from the fourth Āyatana – the Naivasaṃjñānāsaṃjñā – the practiser attains the Nirodhasamāpatti finally. The description of this procedure of jumping in the *Śatasāhasrikā* follows a statement (p. 272) as to how Bodhisattva-Mahāsattvas awaken to supreme and perfect Awakening (*anuttarasamyaksambodhi*) in virtue of their very first *cittotpāda*.

A similar procedure is also described in the version of the *Pañcaviṃśatisāhasrikā* published by N. Dutt (pp. 70–71), where it is stated that Bodhisattva-Mahāsattvas attain *samādhi* by jumping (*avaskandaka*) and then awaken to supreme and perfect Awakening in the various Buddha-fields. One who proceeds thus is then referred to as a *kāyasākṣin* (p. 71).[335]

Pertinent to this matter too is the statement in the version of the *Pañcaviṃśatisāhasrikā* published by Dutt that the Bodhisattva-Mahāsattva, having attained the Diamond-like Concentration (*vajropamasamādhi*)[336] immediately after the Bodhicitta, acquires the Omnimodal Gnosis of a *buddha* by means of discriminative knowledge conjoined with a single thought moment (*ekacittakṣaṇasamāyuktayā prajñayā sarvākārajñatām anuprāpnoti*, p. 82).

Concerning the *kāyasākṣin* (Pali *kāyasakkhi[n]*), he is one of several kinds of psychological and spiritual types recognized in

[335] See below, pp. 168–70.

[336] On the *vajropamasamādhi*, see *Abhidharmakośa* vi. 44d (= *ānantaryamārga*, on the level of the *bhavāgra*, for a candidate for Arhatship, followed by the *vimuktimārga* and *āsravakṣayajñāna*), and Yaśomitra's *Vyākhyā* ii. 16c (where the *bhāvanāmārga* is described as extending from the *anvayajñāna* relating to *mārga* to the *vajropamasamādhi*, where the Fruit of Arhatship is attained). See also *Śrāvakabhūmi* iv, p. 506 f. (cf. L. Schmithausen's ed. in: L. Hercus et al. (eds.), *Indological and Buddhist studies* [Festschrift J. W. de Jong], Canberra, 1982, p. 460 f.), where (p. 510 [= p. 472]) the *vajropamasamādhi* consists in the *prayoganiṣṭha manaskāra*, one of the seven forms of the 'act of mentation' listed in the *Śrāvakabhūmi*. Cf. also L. de La Vallée Poussin, *L'Abhidharmakośa*, vi, pp. 227–9, and *Vijñaptimātratāsiddhi* (Louvain, 1929), p. 667; below, p. 200.

the Buddhist traditions as being worthy of honour (*dakkhiṇeyya*);[337] he is characterized by the faculty of concentration (*samādhindriya*).[338] By extension (*pariyāyena*) the name Kāyasākṣin is used for one who has 'contacted' the four Dhyānas and the four Ārūpyas; and strictly (*nippariyāyena*) this designation applies to one who has attained the Saṃjñāvedayitanirodha, in which case the impurities (*āsava*) are exhausted by discriminative knowledge (*paññā*, which is to say that the Kāyasākṣin is then an Arhat).[339] When his mental attention (*manasikāra*) focuses on Ill (*dukkha*) the *samādhindriya* predominates in him; and his realization, or 'attestation' (*sacchikar-*), is described as being by bodily contact, for he first 'contacts' Dhyāna and then Stoppage and Nirvāṇa (*jhānaphassaṃ paṭhamaṃ phusati, pacchā nirodhaṃ nibbānaṃ sacchikaroti*).[340] Moreover, the designation Kāyasākṣin applies both to a person who attains the *sotāpattimagga* by the power of the *samādhindriya* and to the persons who by the power of this faculty of concentration attain the *sotāpattiphala*, the Paths and Fruits of the Sakadāgāmin and the Anāgāmin, the Path of Arhathood and the Fruit of Arhathood; while the *samādhindriya* predominates in this type, the other four faculties (*saddhā*, *paññā*, etc.) nevertheless play a subordinate part in his spiritual constitution.[341] The Kāyasākṣin is described as one who abides having contacted 'in the body' the tranquil Vimokṣas – the Ārūpyas beyond the Rūpas – and *some* of whose *āsava*s are exhausted by discriminative knowledge; the restriction 'some' (*ekacce*) is also applied to the *āsava*s in the cases of the spiritual types of the Dṛṣṭiprāpta, the Śraddhāvimukta and the Dharmānusārin, but significantly it is not so applied in the cases of the Ubhayatobhāgavimukta (who also abides in bodily contact with the tranquil Ārūpya Vimokṣas) and the Prajñāvimukta (who however does not abide in bodily contact with the Ārūpya Vimokṣas).[342] In the

[337] Dīghanikāya III 105; 253–4; Majjhimanikāya I 439, 477–8; etc.

[338] Aṅguttaranikāya I 119. [339] Aṅguttaranikāya IV 451–2.

[340] *Paṭisambhidāmagga* II 51–52. [341] *Paṭisambhidāmagga* II 54.

[342] Majjhimanikāya I 478. (In the Nālandā edition, the negative *na* is missing before *kāyena phussitvā/phassitvā* in the case of the *paññāvimutta*.) On this and parallel passages, and on the relationship between *saṃjñāvedayitanirodha* and *prajñā*, see L. Schmithausen in K. Bruhn and A. Wezler (eds.), *Studien zum Jainismus und Buddhismus* (Gedenkschrift L. Alsdorf, Wiesbaden, 1981), p. 216 f.

Puggalapaññatti, the Kāyasākṣin is clearly connected with the eight Vimokṣas.[343]

The Kāyasākṣin thus figures alongside the person released through confidence (*śraddhāvimukta, saddhāvimutta*), the person released through discriminative knowledge (*prajñāvimukta, paññāvimutta*) and the Dṛṣṭiprāpta (*diṭṭhippatta*). And in the Aṅguttaranikāya there is found an interesting discussion as to which of three psychological and spiritual types is superior; Saviṭṭha/Samiddha – who figures as the interlocutor of Musīla and Nārada in a comparable context (see pp. 191–2) – holds that the *saddhāvimutta* is best because of the predominance in him of the faculty of confidence (*saddhindriya*), Mahākoṭṭhita/Mahākoṭṭhika – a monk known elsewhere for his skill in *paṭisambhidā* – holds that the *kāyasakkhi(n)* is best because of the predominance of the faculty of concentration, and Sāriputta holds that the *diṭṭhippatta* is best because of the predominance of the faculty of discriminative knowledge (*paññindriya*). When approached to resolve this difference of opinion the Buddha is said, however, to have remarked that it is not possible to decide unilaterally (*ekaṃsena*); for any one of these three types may become not only a Sakadāgāmin and Anāgāmin but also an Arhat.[344]

In the *Abhidharmakośa* (vi. 43cd), the Kāyāsākṣin has been defined as an Anāgāmin who reaches *nirodha*; and Yaśomitra has specified that the Anāgāmin in question may be either *śraddhādhimukta* or *dṛṣṭiprāpta*. According to the Vaibhāṣika theory summarized here by Vasubandhu, the Kāyasākṣin attests 'in the body' a *dharma* that is a simulacrum of Nirvāṇa; and he does this because the body serves him as his *āśraya* in the absence of mind (*citta*) in the state of *nirodha* (*Bhāṣya* vi. 43cd). According to Vasubandhu's own (Sautrāntika) view, however, on arising from concentration the Kāyasākṣin attains a previously unattained conscious bodily tranquillity (*tasmād vyutthāyâpratilabdhapūrvāṃ savijñānakāṃ kāyaśāntiṃ pratilabhate*), thinking: 'Tranquil is the Nirodhasamāpatti, Nirvāṇa-like is the Nirodhasamāpatti'.[345] It is in this way, then,

[343] *Puggalapaññatti*, pp. 14–15, 29, 72.

[344] Aṅguttaranikāya I 118–20.

[345] Cf. *Abhidharmakośabhāṣya* ii. 44d (p. 72) and 61d (pp. 98–100) on the *samantarapratyaya* for the *vyutthānacitta* when a meditator arises from the *nirodhasamāpatti*.

that tranquillity (*śāntatva*) is 'attested'. 'Attestation' has been defined (*Bhāṣya* vi. 43cd) as immediate perception by the attestation of 'connexion' or 'knowledge' (*prāptijñānasākṣātkriyābhyāṃ pratyakṣīkāro hi sākṣātkriyā*). According to Yaśomitra, at the time of *samādhi* there is attestation through *prāpti* of a suitable *āśraya*, and on arising from *samādhi* there is attestation through *jñāna* that is awareness of the preceding. Alternatively, it is through having attained conscious 'bodily tranquility' that *prāpti* 'connexion' with this state is understood in the state of unconscious bodily tranquillity (*savijñānakakāyaśāntipratilambhena vā avijñānakakāya-śāntyavasthāyāṃ tatprāptir gamyata iti*).[346]

In Asaṅga's *Abhidharmasamuccaya* (p. 88), the Kāyasākṣin has been defined as a Learner (*śaikṣa*) who meditates in the eight Vimokṣas.

The process of jumping stages is further treated in the *Abhisamayālaṃkāra* (v. 24–25) and its commentaries just after the Siṃhavijṛmbhita Samādhi. These texts have not hitherto been examined in connexion with the notion of skipping stages of the Path, presumably because these works are not included among the sources of the Sino-Japanese Buddhist tradition on which discussion has so far been mainly concentrated.

In *Abhisamayālaṃkāra* v. 23, the Siṃhavijṛmbhita Samādhi is mentioned in connexion with the Darśanamārga that involves the vision of the twelve members of the chain of origination in dependence (*pratītyasamutpāda*) in both the forward direction (*anulomam*), beginning with nescience (*avidyā*) as the condition for the arising of the constructions (*saṃskāra*), and in the reverse direction (*pratilomam*), beginning with the cessation of ageing and death as a consequence of the cessation of birth.[347]

Then, on the level of the highest supramundane Path of meditative realization (*bhāvanāmārga*), mention is made first of the nine successive Attainments in absorption (*anupūrvasamā-*

[346] As noted by Vasubandhu (*Abhidharmakośabhāṣya* viii. 34), *sākṣātkaraṇa* 'attestation, realization' is connected specifically with the third Vimokṣa (of *śubha*) and the eighth Vimokṣa (of *saṃjñāvedayitanirodha*).

[347] In the *samādhi*-list of the *Mahāvyutpatti* (no. 533), the *siṃhavijṛmbhita* immediately precedes the *vyatyasta* (*snrel ži*).

patti = *mthar gyis gnas pa'i sñoms par 'jug pa*) and then of the Avaskanda-Samāpatti (v. 24–25):

> *kāmāptam avadhīkṛtya vijñānam asamāhitam/*
> *sanirodhāḥ samāpattīr gatvâgamya nava dvidhā//*
> *ekadvitricatuḥpañcaṣaṭsaptāṣṭavyatikramāt/*
> *avaskandasamāpattīr ā nirodham atulyagā//*
>
> 'Having taken as a terminal the unconcentrated consciousness belonging to [the level of] desire, and having gone [upwards] and returned [downwards], doubly, through the nine attainments including the Nirodha[samāpatti], by passing over one, two, three, four, five, six, seven, and [finally] eight [stages in the series of the nine successive Samāpattis] the Attainment of Jumping, without even(ness), proceeds up to Cessation.'

According to Haribhadra, the Avaskanda-Samāpatti comprises the nine successive Samāpattis that make up the Bhāvanāmārga. The procedure of jumping consists to begin with in ascending in sequence from the first Dhyāna to the Nirodha and then descending in sequence back to the first Dhyāna, thus describing a forwards and backwards sequence (*anulomapratiloma-krama*) through the four Dhyānas, the four Ārūpyas and the Nirodha(samāpatti). Next, the practiser attains (*samāpadyate*) the first Dhyāna and then, arising from it, he attains the Nirodha. And he follows this method through the Dhyānas and Āyatanas until from the Naivasaṃjñānāsaṃjñāyatana he at last attains the Nirodha once again. Next, after arising from the latter, he takes as his support (*ālambya*) the 'adjacent attainment'[348] and, fixing (*avasthāpya*) as his terminal (*maryāda*) the consciousness in the sphere of desire (*kāmāvacāraṃ vijñānam*) and then arising from Samāpatti through the strength of his expertness in means (*upāyakauśalya*), the practiser 'faces' (*āmukhīkṛ-*) the unconcentrated consciousness (*vijñānam asamāhitam*). Then, from this state of non-concentration he attains the Nirodha, thence again the non-concentrated state, and thence – leaving out (*parityajya*) only the Nirodha – the Naivasaṃjñānāsaṃjñāyatana. Thence he again

[348] *anantarasamāpatti* = Tib. *de ma thag pa'i sñoms par 'jug* pa (P, f. 382b).

reaches non-concentration and – leaving out this time two stages – he attains the Ākiṃcanyāyatana, and thence non-concentration once again. Finally, leaving out eight stages, he attains the first Dhyāna, and thence non-concentration once more. Thus, by the leaving out (*parityāga*) of from one to eight stages, the practiser proceeds as far as the Nirodha. And it is in this way that one wishing to take up the Avaskanda-Samāpatti which is without even progression (*atulyagā*) – and which is characterized by the practiser's mastery (*vaśitva*) and has as its nature the Bhāvanā-mārga and expertness in means – should course in *prajñāpāramitā*. Haribhadra cites the *Pañcaviṃśatisāhasrikā* with regard to this procedure.[349]

Haribhadra then compares and contrasts the related theory of the *Abhidharmakośa* where, instead of *avaskanda(ka)samāpatti*, the term used is *vyutkrāntakasamāpatti* (viii. 18c–19b):

> *gatvâgamya dvidhā bhūmīr aṣṭau śliṣṭaikalaṅghitāḥ//*
> *vyutkrāntakasamāpattir visabhāgatṛtīyagā/*
> 'Having gone [upwards] and returned [downwards], doubly, through the eight stages, [either] consecutively [or] jumping one [at a time], the Vyutkrāntaka-Samāpatti proceeds to a third [stage from the starting one] of a heterogeneous kind.'

According to Vasubandhu's *Abhidharmakoṣabhāṣya*, the word 'doubly' relates to the stages that are either impure (*sāsrava*) or pure (*anāsrava*). The word 'consecutively' (*śliṣṭa*) refers to a progressive sequence (*anukrama*), whilst the word 'jumping one' (*ekalaṅghita*) refers to the skipping of one stage in each movement. The meditator who proceeds thus has been called a *vyutkrāntakasamāpattṛ*.[350]

The procedure (*prayoga*) in question consists, according to the *Bhāṣya*, in the practiser's first passing over in ascending and descending sequence eight *sāsrava* stages, and then seven *anāsrava* stages.[351] Next, he attains the third *sāsrava* Dhyāna from the first,

[349] Cf. the analysis of the *Pañcaviṃśatisāhasrikā Prajñāpāramitā* in *Hōbōgirin*, pp. 356–7.

[350] *Abhidharmakośabhāṣya* viii. 15ac (p. 444.2).

[351] According to La Vallée Poussin, *L'Abhidharmakośa*, viii, pp. 145 and 175, the *naivasaṃjñānāsaṃjñā* (*bhavāgra*) level is never *anāsrava*, so that only the seven preceding

and thence the Ākāśānantyāyatana (i.e. the first Samāpatti), and thence the Ākiṃcanyāyatana (i.e. the third Samāpatti), thus skipping one stage in each movement. And having next passed over these stages in a backwards and downwards direction (*pratilomam*), the practiser goes on to attain the *anāsrava* stages first in a forwards and then in a backwards movement, skipping one stage in each movement. But when, starting from the first *sāsrava* Dhyāna, he gains the third *anāsrava* Dhyāna, thence the *sāsrava* Ākāśānantyāyatana, and thence the *anāsrava* Ākiṃcanyāyatana, and then descends once more, owing to the fact that one proceeds to a third stage from the starting point which is of a heterogeneous kind (*visabhāgatṛtīyadravya*), the attainment is complete (*abhiniṣpannā*). One does not, according to the *Bhāṣya*, attain a fourth stage from the starting point (thus skipping two stages instead of one), for it is too distant. It is, moreover, only the Asamayavimukta – i.e. the Arhat who is unconditionally released[352] – who proceeds in this way; for he is without defilements/afflictions (*kleśa*), and he has mastery over concentration (*samādhau vaśitvam*). Sequentiality as opposed to skipping is on the contrary the rule (*niyama*) that applies for the beginner (*prāthamakalpika*); and only those who have acquired mastery at will (*prāptakāmavaśitvāḥ*) can gain the stages by skipping one.[353]

In the Pali tradition, the technique of skipping one stage at a time in the sequence of Concentrations and Attainments is attested under the name of *jhānukkantika* in Buddhaghosa's *Visuddhimagga* (xii. 2 and 5) and in the *Aṭṭhasālinī* (§ 3.388, p. 187), which also mention the *jhānānuloma* and the *jhānapaṭiloma*. The technique of skipping one stage only is known in addition from a number of further Śrāvakayānist sources, and also from the *Yogācārabhūmi*.[354]

levels may be counted as *anāsrava*; see below, pp. 195, 200.

In the *bhavāgra* the *bodhimārgāṅgas* are lacking (*Abhidharmakośa* vi. 73a). In the *Abhidharmasamuccaya* (p. 69) and its *Bhāṣya* (p. 81), this level is stated to be exclusively mundane (*laukika*) and not to belong therefore to the *āryamārga*; the reason given is that the Buddha has declared that there is *ājñāprativedha* only so long as there is *saṃjñāsamāpatti* (see below, pp. 199–200).

352 *Abhidharmakośa* vi. 57a.

353 *Abhidharmakośabhāṣya* ii. 44d (p. 72), a passage which also mentions the *vyutkrāntasamāpattis*.

354 See *Hōbōgirin* s.v. *chōjō* and *chōotsushō*.

The *Vyutkrāntaka-Samādhi has been discussed in the *Ta-chih tu-lun* ascribed to Nāgārjuna in the context of the Perfection of *dhyāna*.[355] Since in this treatise the practiser is not a Śrāvakayānist but a Bodhisattva-Mahāsattva of the Mahāyāna, he is considered able to skip not only from the first to the third Dhyāna-level for example, but from the first to the fourth Dhyāna-level or to one of the last five Samāpattis including the Saṃjñāvedayitanirodha. In other words, unlike the Śrāvakayānist, the Mahāyānist is not restricted to skipping only one stage at a time as is prescribed in the *Abhidharmakośa* (*ekalaṅghita*, viii. 18d).[356]

In sum, in the Mahāyāna the notion of leaping over a large number of stages of the Path can be followed fairly far back in the Vijñānavāda school and even further in the Madhyamaka. As already noted, the concept is attested also in the Mahāyānist supplement to Saṃgharakṣa's *Yogācārabhūmi* (Taishō 606) dealing with the practice of the Bodhisattva. And very interestingly the **Vimuttimagga* (Taishō 1648) also recognizes the possibility of skipping more than one stage at a time.[357]

It thus appears that a standard Śrāvakayānist method of skipping differs in an important respect from the Mahāyānist ones in so far as the technique taught in the *Abhidharmakośa* as well as in the Pali tradition allows a practiser each time to jump over only one stage in the sequence of stages, whereas the technique mentioned in the *Abhisamayālaṃkāra* for example allows for up to eight stages to be skipped at a time. This possibility that exists for the Bodhisattva-Mahāsattva may be connected with his ability, mentioned in the *Śatasāhasrikā Prajñāpāramitā*, to awaken to *anuttarasamyaksambodhi* in virtue of his very first production of the Thought of Awakening (*prathamacittotpāda*). However, the Mahāyānist methods noted above differ among themselves in certain significant respects. Not only are some clearly more rapid

[355] See Lamotte, *Le traité de la Grande Perfection de Sagesse*, II, p. 1048. Cf. La Vallée Poussin, *Vijñaptimātratāsiddhi*, pp. 733 and 779 f.; May, *Hōbōgirin*, p. 358.

[356] This important difference has been discussed in the *Hōbōgirin*, in the articles *chōjō* and *chōotsushō*, by J. May, who has also pointed out (pp. 358, 369) that the leap over several stages is attested in the *Abhidharmasamuccayavyākhyā*. May considers that the notion of the attestation of the Fruits by leaping prefigures the idea of Sudden Awakening (*tongo* = *tun wu*) in Ch'an (pp. 356 and 371).

[357] See N. R. M. Ehara, Soma Thera and Kheminda Thera, *The path of freedom of the Arahant Upatissa* (Colombo, 1961), pp. 130–31; cf. *Hōbōgirin*, p. 356.

than others, but one involves the Bodhisattva's returning, in a final series of movements, to a state of non-concentration (*asamāhitacitta*) while the other does not. The former method of leaping – known sometimes also as Viṣkandaka Samādhi – appears to emphasize the Bodhisattva's resolve to remain in an ordinary, unconcentrated state of consciousness in Saṃsāra (compare the Bodhisattva who refrains from entering Nirvāṇa, *apratiṣṭhitanirvāṇa*);[358] whereas the latter method is directed toward the highest Samāpattis culminating in the cessation of notions and feelings (*saṃjñāved*[*ay*]*itanirodha*). The Mahāyānist method of leaping moreover differs from that of the Śrāvakayāna by including this ninth stage of *saṃjñāvedayitanirodha*, which the Śrāvakayānist technique has left aside.

It has furthermore to be noted that in Haribhadra's comment on the *Abhisamayālaṃkāra*, as well as in Vasubandu's *Abhidharmakośa*, the procedure of leaping seems to have less to do with a way of instantaneous and immediate access to the highest than with a particular technique in meditation. In the *Śatasāhasrikā Prajñāpāramitā* on the contrary, the notion of rapidity and instantaneous access seems to be implicit in what is said about the Bodhisattva's very first *cittotpāda* bringing on *anuttarasamyaksambodhi*.

The comprehension (*abhisamaya*) of the four Principles or Realities of the Nobles (*āryasatya*) and the acquisition of the four Fruits (*phalaprāpti*) of the Noble's religious life – viz. those of the Stream-winner (*srotaāpanna*), the Once-returner (*sakṛdāgāmin*), the Non-returner (*anāgāmin*), and the Arhat – are said by some Buddhist schools to be sequential and by others to be simultaneous.

In many passages of the old canon, the gradualness of training (*anupubbasikkhā*), spiritual activity (*anupubbakiriyā*) and of the Path of insight (*anupubbapaṭipadā*) has been affirmed.[359] And it is stated that the wise person proceeds gradually and little by little

[358] On the question of dispersal beside concentration, compare Demieville, *BEFEO* 44 (1954), pp. 397 n. 3 and p. 429 n. 1; *Hōbōgirin*, pp. 357 and 359.

[359] See *Cullavagga*, Vinaya II 238; *Udāna*, p. 54; Majjhimanikāya I 479–80, III 1; and Aṅguttaranikāya IV 198, 201, 207; cf. below, p. 180.

in each moment, in the same way that a metal-worker would remove impurities from silver-ore.[360] The comprehension of the *āryasatyas* is furthermore compared with the gradual construction, storey by storey, of a lofty mansion (*kūṭāgāra*).[361]

A theory of both the gradual development and then the final instantaneousness of the Path of preparation (*prayogamārga*) has been set out in Chapter vi of Vasubandhu's *Abhidharmakośa*. There mention has specifically been made of the gradualness of the Salutary Root (*kuśalamūla*) of Heat (*uṣmagata*) – i.e. the first of the four factors of penetration (*nirvedhabhāgīya*) – which is said to be nurtured in progressive stages (*kramābhivṛddha*) in its three degrees, viz. the slight (*mṛdu*), the middling (*madhya*), and the superior (*adhimātra*);[362] and the *uṣmagata* is further described in terms of serial prolongation (*prākarṣikatva* = *prābandhikatva*) when having as its object the four *satyas*.[363] A similar gradualness is stated to apply to all three degrees of the Head-stage (*mūrdhan*), the second of the four *nirvedhabhāgīyas*.[364] As for the third *nirvedhabhāgīya*, receptive perseverance (*kṣānti*), in contradistinction to its middling degree where Ill (*duḥkha*) is the object of mental attention lasting through two moments (*kṣaṇa*), its superior degree is stated to comprise one single moment only (*kṣaṇikā*) and not to be serially prolonged (*prākarṣikī*).[365] Finally, the fourth factor of penetration, the *laukikāgradharmas*, are all described as momentary (*kṣaṇika*).[366]

In the section of Vasubandu's *Abhidharmakośabhāṣya* treating of the sequential process of comprehension (*abhisamayakrama*) of the four *āryasatyas* – each of which has four aspects (*ākāra*) making a total of sixteen mind-moments (*ṣoḍaśacittaka*) – this *abhisamaya* has been specifically described as taking place gradually (*krameṇa*). Accordingly it is stated that a Sūtra-reference to single-

[360] See *Dhammapada* 239; cf. *Suttanipāta* 962cd.

[361] See Saṃyuttanikāya V 452. For the Sanskrit version, see Yaśomitra, *Abhidharmakośavyākhyā* vi. 27, where two further relevant Sūtras from the Saṃyuktāgama are also cited.

[362] *Abhidharmakośabhāṣya* vi. 15b–17.

[363] *Abhidharmakośabhāṣya* vi. 17b.

[364] *Abhidharmakośabhāṣya* vi. 18b.

[365] *Abhidharmakośabhāṣya* vi. 19ab; *duḥkham dvābhyāṃ kṣaṇābhyāṃ manasi karoty eṣā sarvâiva madhyā, kṣāntir yadâikam eva kṣaṇaṃ tad adhimātrêti/ kṣaṇikā câsau, na prākarṣikī.*

[366] *Abhidharmakośabhāṣya* vi. 19c. Compare Vasumitra's view mentioned below, p. 179.

comprehension (*ekābhisamaya*)[367] will need to be understood with regard to an (unexpressed) intention (*abhiprāya*) of the Buddha.[368] Such a mention of *ekābhisamaya* may then have to be interpreted by taking this comprehension to concern the effect (*kāryābhisamaya*) of the four *satyas* – viz. *parijñāna*, *prahāṇa*, *sākṣātkaraṇa* and *bhāvana* – in contrast to comprehension as vision (*darśanābhisamaya*) achieved through pure discriminative knowledge (*anāsravā prajñā*);[369] for when it is stated in a Sūtra that *abhisamaya* is gradual this is what was really aimed at (*lakṣyate*) in respect to *darśanābhisamaya*. (Yet another Sūtra-reference to *ekābhisamaya* might according to some involve an allusive utterance (*abhisaṃdhivacana*)[370] to singleness, as when absence of uncertainty concerning *duḥkha* is stated to include absence of uncertainty in respect to the Buddha.[371])

The transition from the stage of a worldling (*pṛthagjana*) on the mundane (*laukika*) level of the Prayogamārga to that of a Noble (*ārya*) on the transmundane Darśanamārga depends on receptive perseverance with a view to *dharma*-knowledge concerning Ill (*duḥkhe dharmajñānakṣāntiḥ*) – that is, the stage of entry into determination (*niyāmāvakrānti*) in view of Exactness (*samyaktva* = *nirvāṇa*) – in association with the *laukikāgradharmas* at the culminating point of the Prayogamārga. Here the *laukikāgradharmas* may be seen as fulfilling the function of an *ānantaryamārga*, the *anāsrava dharmajñānakṣānti* having then the function of a *vimuktimārga*.[372]

The Darśanamārga proper has been described by Vasubandhu as consisting in fifteen moments (*kṣaṇa*) beginning with this *dharmajñānakṣānti* concerning Ill and culminating in the *anvayajñānakṣānti* concerning the Path (*mārga*). For the sixteenth and final moment – i.e. consequent knowledge concerning the Path

[367] As with the Dharmaguptas, according to Yaśomitra.

[368] *Abhidharmakośabhāṣya* vi. 27a. On the notion of *abhiprāya*, see D. Seyfort Ruegg, *Journal of Indian Philosophy* 13 (1985), pp. 309–25, and 16 (1988), pp. 1–4, with the literature cited there.

[369] *Abhidharmakośabhāṣya* vi. 27bc.

[370] On the notion of *abhisaṃdhi*, see D. Seyfort Ruegg, 'Allusiveness and obliqueness in Buddhist texts', in C. Caillat *et al.* (ed.), *Formes dialectales dans les littératures indo-âryennes* (Paris, 1989), p. 299 ff.

[371] *Abhidharmakośabhāṣya*, vi. 27bc.

[372] *Abhidharmakośabhāṣya* vi. 26a.

(*mārge 'nvayajñānam*) – represents the pivotal instant of transition from the Darśanamārga to the Bhāvanāmārga.[373] And it is reckoned to belong to the Bhāvanāmārga because, *inter alia*, it cultivates (*bhāvanāt*) the eight *jñānas* of the Darśanamārga and the sixteen aspects (*ākāra*) of the *satyas*, and because it pertains to continuation (*prābandhikatvāt*).[374]

Vasubandhu has specified that the Bhāvanāmārga is like the Darśanamārga in respect to the gradualness of reflection on the sixteen aspects of the *satyas*.[375] Nevertheless, a reference has been made by both Vasubandhu and Yaśomitra to acquisition by single attainment (*ekaprāptilābha*) of the total elimination of all that is to be eliminated by vision (*darśana*) when the Srotaāpanna achieves the Fruit of entry into the stream; and to the acquisition simultaneously (*yugapad*) of the eight *jñānas* – viz. the four *dharmajñānas* pertaining to the Kāmadhātu and the four *anvayajñānas* pertaining to the Rūpa and Ārūpya levels – when the Fruit of the Once-returner (*sakṛdāgāmiphala*) is achieved by eliminating what is to be eliminated by *darśana* as well as all that is to be eliminated by the Bhāvanāmārga.[376]

In his comment on the *Abhisamayālaṃkāra* Haribhadra has also explained how, by force of proper method (*nyāyabalāt*) in virtue of a specific intention (*abhiprāya*), the Darśanamārga, even though it consists in single-moment *abhisamaya*, has nevertheless been stated to consist of sixteen discrete moments from the point of view of the Candidates for and the Achievers of the Fruits of the Ārya (*pratipannakādi*), in contrast to comprehension as effect (*kāryābhisamaya*).[377]

As was observed by Vasubandhu in his *Abhidharmakośabhāṣya* (vi. 27), opinions have differed in the Śrāvaka schools (*nikāya*)

373 *Abhidharmakośabhāṣya* vi. 28–29. The eight *kṣāntis* have the function of *ānantaryamārgas*, and the eight *jñānas* that of *vimuktimārgas*, according to *Abhidharmakośabhāṣya* vi. 28a.

374 *Abhidharmakośabhāṣya* vi. 28cd. Compare *prākarṣikī* as the antonym of *kṣaṇikā* in vi. 19b (above, p. 176).

375 *Abhidharmakośabhāṣya* vi. 27bc.

376 *Abhidharmakośabhāṣya* and *Vyākhyā* vi. 52–53c. Cf. vii. 22.

377 Haribhadra, *Abhisamayālaṃkārālokā* ii. 12–16 (p. 171 = P, f. 121a4): *prativedhābhisamayād ekakṣaṇābhisamayo darśanamārga ity apare* (see above, p. 159).

concerning the gradualness as against the simultaneity of comprehension. These differences figure prominently among the doctrines the doxographers of these schools have ascribed in particular to the Mahāsāṃghikas and their branches, the Lokottaravādins and the Ekavyāvahārikas.[378] And a connexion between the Mahāsāṃghikas (*phal chen sde*) and the Simultaneous Engagement (*cig car 'jug pa*) of Kāśyapa as transmitted by the school of (Bodhi-)Dharmottārala (*sic*) is seemingly suggested in a chapter of the *bKa' thaṅ sde lṅa*, the *Blon po bka'i thaṅ yig*.[379]

According to Vasumitra's *Samayabhedoparacanacakra*, in the view of the Mahāsāṃghikas it is by a single thought that [a *buddha*] knows all (*sems gcig gis chos thams cad rnam par mkhyen to*); and it is through discriminative knowledge (*prajñā*) conjoined with single thought-moment that [a *buddha*] fully knows all *dharmas* (*sems kyi skad cig ma gcig daṅ mtshuṅs par ldan pa'i śes rab kyis chos thams cad yoṅs su mkyen to*).[380] A branch of the Mahāsāṃghikas, the Ekavyāvahārikas, are so named according to Bhavya's *Nikāyabhedavibhaṅgavyākhyāna* because they have in this way accepted one single procedure (*ekavyavahāra*).[381]

According to Vinītadeva's **Samayabhedoparacanacakre Nikāyabhedopadarśananāma-saṃgraha*, moreover, in the view of the Lokottaravādin-Mahāsāṃghikas, the four Principles of the Nobles (*āryasatya*) are realized all at once (*bden pa ni cig car mthoṅ ṅo*).[382] And in the view of the two subschools of the Mahāsāṃghikas in

[378] Cf. Lamotte, *Le traité de la Grande Vertu de Sagesse*, V (Louvain, 1980), pp. 2328–35.

[379] lHa sa edition of the *bKa' thaṅ sde lṅa*, f. 19a: *'od sruṅs cig car 'jug pa phal chen sde: mkhan po dharmottā ra la'i brgyud pa ni* ... 'the Simultaneous Entry of Kāśyapa, Mahāsāṃghika: the line of the Master Dharmottārala ...'. The standard Tibetan equivalent of Mahāsāṃghika is *dge 'dun phal chen po('i sde)*, and Tucci's translation in his *Minor Buddhist texts* (II, p. 81) differs from the one offered here. There is no correspondence in the parallel passage of the *bSam gtan mig sgron*, f. 8.

[380] Vasumitra, *Samayabhedoparacanacakra* (Tibetan translation ed. E. Teramoto and T. Hiramatsu, Kyōto, 1935), p. 5. For *ekacittakṣaṇasamāyuktā prajñā*, see *Mahāvastu* (ed. É. Senart), I, p. 229 and II, p. 133, 285, 416. Cf. *Lalitavistara* (ed. Lefmann), p. 350.13–14; *Śikṣāsamuccaya*, p. 278.12.

[381] Bhavya, *Nikāyabhedavibhaṅgavyākhyāna* (Tibetan transl., ed. E. Teramoto and T. Hiramatsu), p. 19: *saṅs rgyas bcom ldan 'das rnams kyi chos thams cad thugs gcig gis rnam par mkhyen ciṅ skad cig gcig daṅ ldan pa'i ~~śes rab~~ kyis chos thams cad yoṅs su mkhyen to žes tha sñad 'dogs te| des na tha sñad gcig gis pa žes bya'o*. On the interpretation of the term *ekavyavahāra* see A. Bareau, *Les sectes bouddhiques du Petit Véhicule* (Saigon, 1955), p. 78.

[382] Vinītadeva, **Samayabhedoparacanacakre Nikāyabhedopadarśana-nāma-saṃgraha* (Tibetan translation, ed. E. Teramoto and T. Hiramatsu), p. 41.

Bhavya's account – the Ekavyāvahārikas and Gokulikas – the Bodhisattva fully knows the four *āryasatyas* by a single *jñāna* (*ye šes gcig gis bden pa bži rnams yoṅs su šes so*).[383]

According to Vinītadeva's account of the doctrine of the Mahīśāsakas (an offshoot of the Vibhajyavādin Sthaviras and the Sarvāstivādins), too, the *satyas* are realized all at once (*bden pa cig car mthoṅ ṅo*).[384] But according to Bhavya this view was rejected by the Sarvāstivādins, who taught that the four *āryasatyas* are known gradually (*rim gyis rtogs par 'gyur ro*); and the Sūtra-reference to simultaneous comprehension may then be non-definitive and require further elicitation (*draṅ ba'i don* = *neyārtha*).[385] For the Sarvāstivādins, the *laukikāgradharmas* belong, however, to a single thought-moment.[386]

Controversy concerning simultaneousness as against gradualness is reported in the *Kathāvatthu* also. There (ii. 9) we find a lengthy discussion as to whether comprehension is gradual (*anupubbābhisamaya*) or not. According to the Aṭṭhakathā, the Andhakas, Sabbatthikas, Sammitiyas and Bhadrayānikas maintained the thesis of the *anupubbābhisamaya* by Candidates for the four Fruits in virtue of their seeing the four Principles of the Nobles, etc. These schools are said to have done so on the basis of canonical texts such as the *Dhammapada* (239), *Udāna* (p. 54), *Cullavagga* (II 238), Saṃyuttanikāya (V 452), Majjhimanikāya (III 1), and Aṅguttaranikāya (I 162).[387] On the contrary, according to the Theravādins – and notwithstanding what is stated in the canonical passages cited above – this comprehension is not gradual. Indeed, as is said in *Suttanipāta* 231, because of the attainment of vision (*dassanasampadā*) the three fetters (*saṃyojana*, namely *sakkāyadiṭṭhi*, *vicikicchita* and *sīlabbata*[*parāmāsa*]) are all simultaneously (*saha*) eliminated, a text corroborated by others that declare that the three fetters are all simultaneously (*saha*) eliminated by the Noble Śrāvaka with the arising in him of the

[383] Bhavya, *op. cit.*, p. 24

[384] Vinītadeva, *op. cit.*, p. 43. See Bareau, *op. cit.*, p. 183.

[385] Bhavya, *op. cit.*, p. 27. See above, p. 177, for Vasubandhu's references to *abhiprāya* and *abhisaṃdhi* in Sūtra-statements.

[386] Vasumitra, *op. cit.*, p. 10. See *Abhidharmakośabhāṣya* vi. 19c (above, p. 176).

[387] See also the *Paṭisambhidāmagga* II 105–07; and A. K. Warder's introduction to Ñaṇamoli's translation, *The guide* (London, 1977), p. xxv.

'Dharma-eye', i.e. the knowledge that whatever originates (*samudayadhamma*) ceases (*nirodhadhamma*).[388] A closely related point is made in *Kathāvatthu* i. 4, where there is a discussion as to whether Candidates for the four Fruits of the Nobles eliminate defilement (*kilesa*) piecemeal (*odhisodhiso*), through their vision of the *āryasatyas*. (According to the Aṭṭhakathā [p. 43] the doctrine discussed in i. 4 was that of the Sammitiyas and some others.) And according to another section of the *Kathāvatthu* (xxii. 8) and its Aṭṭhakathā, two branches of the Mahāsāṃghikas – the Pubbaseliyas and the Aparaseliyas – maintained that all *dhammas* belong to a single mental moment (*ekacittakkhaṇika*). The same two sources further mention (xi. 6) the opinion – ascribed to the Sabbatthivāda and Uttarāpathaka – that *samādhi* pertains to a single mind-moment (*ekacittakkhaṇiko samādhi*).[389]

According to Asaṅga's *Abhidharmasamuccaya*,[390] the Stream-winner (*srotaāpanna*) – that is, the first of the four Nobles (*ārya*) at the pivotal point of the sixteenth moment of the Darśanamārga and the first of the Bhāvanāmārga – may be either one who obtains release gradually (*rim gyis pa*) or one who obtains release all at once (*sakṛnnairyāṇika* = *cig car ṅes par 'byin pa*). The first type is said to be of the kind described earlier (p. 89). The *sakṛnnairyāṇika* is on the contrary defined as one who, having achieved the comprehension of the four *satyas*, takes the threshold-meditation (*anāgamya* = *mi lcogs pa med pa*)[391] as his base and eliminates all at once (*sakṛt* = *cig car*) all the defilements/afflictions of the three

388 Saṃyuttanikāya IV 47, 107; Aṅguttaranikāya IV 186.

389 Compare also the discussion in the *Kathāvatthu-Aṭṭhakathā* v. 9 (p. 86).

390 *Abhidharmasamuccaya* (ed. Pradhan), p. 92 (Tibetan translation, D, f. 110a).

391 Pradhan reads *aprāptasamāpatti*. The four Dhyānas and the four Ārūpyas each have a threshold called *sāmantaka* (*ñes bsdogs*), the one before the first Dhyāna being known specifically as the *anāgamya*. The *anāgamya* is deficient in *śamatha*, while the Ārūpyas are deficient in *vipaśyanā* according to *Abhidharmakośabhāṣya* vi. 66b.

On the *anāgamya* see *Abhidharmakośa* iv. 18, v. 66, vi. 20, 47; viii. 22, as well as La Vallée Poussin, *L'Abhidharmakośa* vi. p. 235 n. 3, and viii, pp. 166–7, 179 n. 6; P. Jaini, *Abhidharmadīpa*, p. 415 note; E. Lamotte, *Le traité de la Grande Vertu de Sagesse*, II, p. 1036 ff.; E. Frauwallner, 'Abhidharma-Studien iii', *WZKS* 15 (1971), p. 100; L. Schmithausen in K. Bruhn and A. Wezler (eds.), *Studien zum Jainismus und Buddhismus*, pp. 240, 246. Cf. below, p. 190.

levels (*traidhātukāvacarāḥ sarvakleśāḥ*) by means of the transmundane Path (*lokottaramārga*). In his case only two (rather than the usual four sequential) Fruits are achieved, namely those of the Stream-winner and the Arhat. The person in question is then stated mainly to reach full liberating knowledge (*ājñā*, of the Arhat) in the present existence (*dṛṣṭa-dharma*) or at the time of his death.[392]

It thus emerges clearly that the *sakṛnnairyāṇika* type of Srotaāpanna can achieve his goal rapidly, without acquiring successively all four Fruits of the *āryamārga*.

4. The Conjunction of Quieting and Insight and of Means and Discriminative Knowledge

One of the most important points repeatedly made by Kamalaśīla in his *Bhāvanākramas* is that Quieting (*śamatha*) and Insight (*vipaśyanā*) should be conjoined (*yuganaddha*), that they must operate so to speak in conjunction like a pair of oxen teamed together (*yuganaddhavāhibalīvardadvayavat*). The perfect Path is accordingly described as operating as a syzygy of Quieting and Insight (*śamathavipaśyanāyuganaddhavāhī mārgo niṣpannaḥ*).[393]

Quieting, defined as one-pointedness of mind (*cittaikāgratā*),[394] involves observing the nine 'positions' or 'stations' of mind (*cittasthiti*) which are known from a number of sources such as the *Śrāvakabhūmi* and the *Abhidharmasamuccaya*.[395] As for *vipaśyanā*, it is defined as exact analytical investigation [of the real] (*bhūtapratyavekṣā*, *Bhāvanākrama*, III pp. 3, 5). This *bhūtapratyavekṣā* consists in the analysis of the factors of existence (*dharmapravicaya*), which is otherwise known as discriminative knowledge (*prajñā*) (III pp. 14–15). The *bhūta* is here explained as the non-

392 When this is not so, the reason is one's resolve (*praṇidhānavaśena*); in that case, being born in the Kāmadhātu because of this resolve, one becomes a *pratyekajina* at a time when there is no *buddha*.

393 Kamalaśīla, *Bhāvanākrama* III (ed. G. Tucci), pp. 1, 9–10. Compare the discussion in G. Bugault, *La notion de 'Prajñā' ou de sapience selon les perspectives du 'Mahāyāna'*[2] (Paris, 1982), pp. 56 ff., 75 ff.

394 *Bhāvanākrama* III, p. 3.

395 *Śrāvakabhūmi* (ed. Shukla), pp. 363–5; Asaṅga, *Abhidharmasamuccya*, p. 75; cf. *Peṭakopadesa*, p. 122, for an expanded list.

substantiality or essencelessness of both an individual self and the factors of existence (*pudgaladharmanairātmya*, III, p. 5).

The process of analytical investigation is no doubt associated with recollective attention (*smṛti*) and mentation (*manasikāra*) (cf. III, p. 16); but when brought to its highest point, *bhūtapratyavekṣā* is the necessary condition for the absence of both recollection (*asmṛti*) and mentation (*amanasikāra*) in the sense of non-constructive Gnosis (*nirvikalpaṃ jñānam*) and the ceasing of all mental and verbal proliferation (*prapañcopaśama*).[396]

If *śamatha* is in excess, the mind of the meditator will be blunted and dull and *prajñā* will then have to be especially cultivated. But if *prajñā* is in excess, his mind will be agitated and *śamatha* will then have to be cultivated in particular. When *śamatha* and *vipaśyanā* are on the contrary in balance, the mind is in equilibrium (*samapravṛtta*). And in view of the absence then of both dullness (*laya*) and agitation (*auddhatya*) *citta* proceeds naturally of itself (*svarasavāhin*). It is then also stated to be in its natural state.[397]

It cannot therefore be maintained that the Perfections (*pāramitā*) are all comprised in *dhyāna*, and that by cultivating the latter all of them are cultivated (III, p. 25). All the Bodhisattva's virtues inclusive of *dhyāna* are in fact to be controlled by *prajñā*, and it is because of this *prajñā* that these qualities become true *pāramitās*. To proceed in accordance with this principle is referred to by Kamalaśīla as being *prajñottaradhyāyin*.[398] Such *dhyāna* in which *prajñā* is supreme is opposed to the 'Dhyāna' which is said to subsume all *pāramitās* in itself (III, pp. 25–26) – in other words, apparently, the 'Dhyāna' of Kamalaśīla's opponent Mo-ho-yen. And the exclusive observance of non-recollection (*asmṛti*) and non-mentation (*amanasikāra*) – i.e. the method advocated by Mo-ho-yen – would merely lead to a state like that of the cataleptic cessation of thinking (*cittanirodha*) by the worldling (*pṛthagjana*) on the level of the fourth Dhyāna (III, pp. 16–17) – i.e. the attainment of unconsciousness (*asaṃjñisamāpatti*) which is, how-

[396] *Bhāvanākrama* III, pp. 15–17; cf. pp. 94–95.

[397] *Bhāvanākrama* III, p. 9–10. Here Skt. *praśaṭhavāhin* is translated by Tib. *mnal du 'jug pa*.

[398] Tib. *śes rab mchog gi bsam gtan (pa)*. See *Bhāvanākrama* II (ed. K. Goshima), p. 47; III, p. 8; above, p. 95.

ever, not to be practised by the Buddhist Ārya.[399]

Kamalaśīla has supported his teaching concerning the co-ordination of *śamatha* and *vipaśyanā* by quoting a large number of Mahāyānasūtras. Among them is the *Saṃdhinirmocana*, Chapter viii of which is devoted to a detailed discussion of the subject. It was this Sūtra that the Hva šaṅ Mahāyāna cast aside according to a Tibetan tradition recorded in the *sBa bžed*.[400]

Beside this syzygy of *śamatha* and *vipaśyanā* (or *dhyāna* and *prajñā*), and in a position of no less importance, Kamalaśīla has placed the conjunction of Emptiness (*śūnyatā*) and Means (*upāya*) and of discriminative knowledge (*prajñā*) and practice (*caryā*) through means. Practice (*caryā*) is stated to consist in generosity (*dāna*) and the other virtues, as does salvific means (*upāya*).[401]

Now, when *śūnyatā* is thus correctly and indissolubly bonded with *upāya*, it is known to Kamalaśīla as Emptiness endowed with all excellent modes (*sarvākāravaropeta-śūnyatā*). This notion is contrasted with an isolated emptiness, that is, an 'emptiness-method' (*śūnyatānaya*) that makes of *śūnyatā* something that is a self-sufficient and independent principle (*ekanaya*).[402] Because of such a method of isolation, however, practice (*caryā*) would no longer be purified; and those who thus cultivate *śūnyatā* in isolation 'fall' in Nirvāṇa, like an Auditor (*kevalaṃ śūnyatām eva sevamanaḥ śrāvakavan nirvāṇe patanti*).[403] When the need for conjoining *prajñā* and *dhyāna* is not appreciated and *dhyāna* is overemphasized, the meditator's practice would, moreover, be like that of a Śrāvaka who attains the concentration of cessation (*nirodhasamādhi*)[404]

The correct method for a practiser involves then a gradual (*krameṇa*) procedure of purification (*viśuddhi*, III, p. 2), one in which the mind-continuum (*cittasaṃtati*) is purified in a way compared with the purification of gold by a metal-worker (III,

[399] See below, p. 202–03. Compare *sBa bžed*, G, p. 69; S, p. 58–59; Ñaṅ Ñi ma 'od zer, *Chos 'byuṅ Me tog sñiṅ po*, f. 431a–b; dPa' bo gTsug lag phreṅ ba, *mKhas pa'i dga' ston*, f. 117a.

[400] See above, pp. 114–15.

[401] *Bhāvanākrama* III, pp. 14, 27–29.

[402] *Bhāvanākrama* I (ed. G. Tucci), p. 196; II, pp. 59–61; III, pp. 27–28.

[403] *Bhāvanākrama* III, p. 27.

[404] *Bhāvanākrama* III, p. 26.

p. 25). In this way one enters the *buddha*-stage (*tathāgatabhūmi*) after having progressively cleansed the preceding stages (*pūrva-bhūmi*) (III, p. 25), each of which is purified (*pariśuddh-*) in a way similar to gold (III, p. 30). It has been noted above that the idea of the gradualness of the process of spiritual development is well attested in texts from the old canon, where it is sometimes compared with the metalworker's treatment of his material.[405]

The idea of the yoking together of Quiet (*samatha*) and Insight (*vipassanā*) is also well attested in texts of the old canon,[406] and in Pali treatises such as Buddhaghosa's *Visuddhimagga* (xxiii. 43).

Thus, in its description of the practiser who perfects the eight-fold path, the constituents of Awakening, etc., the Majjhimanikāya (III 289) states that for him *samatha* and *vipassanā* are yoked (*yuganaddhā*).[406a] And in his comment on this passage in the *Papañcasūdanī* Buddhaghosa has defined this pair as yoked in a single-moment syzygy (*ekakkhaṇikayuganaddhā*), for concentration (*samāpatti*) and insight belong on the *ariyamagga* to one single moment (*ekakkhaṇikā*). This case he contrasts with the one where the two belong to different moments (*nānākkhaṇikā*).[406b] In the same commentary Buddhaghosa has also spoken of the serial (*paṭipātiyā*) attainment of the three marks (viz. *dukkha*, *anicca* and *anattā*) and production of *vipassanā* whereby the practiser attains the path of Stream-winning; at this moment, he then adds, the practiser penetrates the four *sacca*s by a single penetration (*ekapaṭi-vedha*) and comprehends by a single comprehension (*ekābhisama-ya*).[406c]

405 See above, pp. 175–6, 180.

406 See for example Dīghanikāya III 213 and 273; Majjhimanikāya I 494 and 289. For Aṅguttaranikāya II 156–7, see below, pp. 187–8.

406a So read, instead of 'yuganandhā' in the Pali Text Society edition.

406b *Papañcasūdanī* V 104: *'yuganaddhā' ti ekakkhaṇikayuganaddhā. ete hi aññasmiṃ khaṇe samāpatti aññasmiṃ vipassanā ti evaṃ nānākkhaṇikā pi honti, ariyamagge pana ekakkhaṇikā.* For *nānākkhaṇa* and *nānārammaṇa* opposed to *ekakkhaṇa* and *ekārammaṇa*, see also Buddhaghosa's commentary on the Saṃyuttanikāya (*Sāratthappakāsinī* I 158), and Dhammapāla's on the *Itivuttaka* (*Paramatthadīpanī* [II], I 132). The *Paramatthadīpanī II* also deals with *samatha* and *vipassanā* as *yuganaddhā* (II 29).

406c *Papañcasūdanī* I 73: *evaṃ tīṇi lakkhaṇāni āropetvā paṭipātiyā vipassanaṃ pavattento sotāpattimaggaṃ pāpuṇāti. tasmiṃ khaṇe cattāri saccāni ekapaṭivedhen' eva paṭivijjhati, ekābhisamayena abhisameti.* For *ekābhisamaya* see also pp. 176–7.

The Peṭakopadesa has defined (p. 122) *samatha* in terms of *samādhi*, non-distraction and non-dispersal of thought, as well as of calming and one-pointedness of *citta*. And *vipassanā* has been defined there as analysis bearing on the *dhammas*, analytical reflection (*vīmaṃsā*), weighing, *ñāṇa*, *vijjā* and *paññā* as well as various forms of illumination (*obhāsa*, *āloka*, *ābhā*, *pabhā*). This text then goes on to remark (pp. 123–4) that by developing *samatha* one comprehends the material (*rūpa*), thereby eliminating desire (*taṇhā*) and so realizing *cetovimutti* by detachment from passions (*rāgavirāga*). And by developing *vipassanā* one comprehends the 'mental' (*nāma*), thereby eliminating nescience (*avijjā*) and so realizing *paññāvimutti* by detachment from *avijjā*. Correlations on the one hand between Quieting, cultivation of *citta*, elimination of the passions, *rāgavirāga* and *cetovimutti*, and on the other between Insight, cultivation of *paññā*, elimination of *avijjā* and *paññāvimutti* are also to be found in the Aṅguttaranikāya (I 61), where both *samatha* and *vipassanā* are described as pertaining to knowledge (*vijjābhāgiya*). In the *Visuddhimagga*, *nāma* is associated with the person whose Vehicle is Quieting (*samathayānika*, xviii. 3–4); and *rūpa* is linked with the person whose Vehicle is pure Insight (*suddhavipassanāyānika*), this correlation being however possible also for the *samathayānika* (xviii. 5). It is further stated in the *Peṭakopadesa* (pp. 134–5) that *samatha* and *vipassanā* together constitute the fourth *ariyasacca*, the Path. And the *Nettippakaraṇa* (pp. 110–11) has specified that *samatha* consists in both the *sīlakkhandha* and the *samādhikkhandha* of the Eightfold Path, whilst *vipassanā* is made up of its *paññākkhandha*.

It is also explained in the *Peṭakopadesa* (pp. 133–5) that the intuition (*abhisamaya*) of the four *ariyasacca*s takes place in a single time (*ekakāla*), a single moment (*ekakkhaṇa*) and a single thought (*ekacitta*). In a single time, moment and thought, too, the syzygy of *samatha* and *vipassanā* accomplishes four functions, namely comprehension of Ill (by *pariññābhisamaya*), comprehension of its origin (by *pahānābhisamaya*), comprehension of its stoppage (by *sacchikiriyābhisamaya*), and comprehension of the Path (by *bhāvanābhisamaya*). This is followed by the stage of vision (*dassanabhūmi*) where the Stream-winner (*srotāpanna*) does not fall back (*avinipātadhamma*) and is fixed (*niyata*, in Rightness).

In the *Peṭakopadesa* (p. 249) it is moreover explained that *vipassanā* preceded by *samatha* is for one who understands through a mere mention (*ugghaṭitaññu*) – i.e. for the person receiving the 'soft' (*mudukā*) teaching and training in higher discriminative knowledge (*adhipaññāsikkhā*); that *samatha* preceded by *vipassanā* is for one to be trained gradually (*neyya*) – i.e. for the person receiving the 'sharp' (*tikkhā*) teaching and higher training pertaining to *citta* (*adhicittasikkhā*); and that the conjunction of *samatha* and *vipassanā* is for one who understands through expatiation (*vipañcitaññu*) – i.e. for the person receiving a teaching that is both 'sharp' and 'soft' (*tikkhamudukā*) and training in higher ethics (*adhisīlasikkhā*).

The correlations thus made of *samatha* with *rūpa* and the *adhipaññāsikkhā* and of *vipassanā* with *nāma* and the *adhicittasikkhā* are noteworthy.

The *Nettippakaraṇa* confirms (p. 125) the correlation of *samatha* with the *ugghaṭitaññu* and of *vipassanā* with the *neyya* type of person. And it specifies (p. 100–01) that *samatha* was taught by Bhagavat to the person of sharp faculties (*tikkhindriya*, who receives the *adhipaññāsikkhā*), *vipassanā* to the person of dull faculties (*mudindriya*, who receives the *adhisīlasikkhā*), and both *samatha* and *vipassanā* to the person whose faculties are middling (*majjhindriya*, who receives the *adhicittasikkhā*). The three teachings in question are perhaps to be understood here as serving as antidotes for the use of the three types of person mentioned. However this may be, the question arises as to how these correlations might relate to Mo-ho-yen's view that his teaching of understanding Mind, with its quietistic and non-analytical tendency, is especially suited to advanced disciples whose faculties are sharp.

In its typology of persons (*puggala*) the *Puggalapaññatti* has proposed a fourfold categorization according to which some persons achieve *cetosamatha* without achieving *adhipaññādhammavipassanā*, some do the reverse, some achieve both together, and others achieve neither.[407]

An interesting classification in the present context is the one found in the *Yuganaddhasutta* of the Aṅguttaranikāya.[408] There Ānanda says that whenever a monk or nun declares having

[407] *Puggalapaññatti* iv, pp. 61–62. [408] Aṅguttaranikāya II 156–7.

achieved Arhathood, he or she is endowed with one of four Paths (*magga*), namely the Path cultivating *vipassanā* preceded (*pubbaṅgama*) by *samatha*, the Path cultivating *samatha* preceded by *vipassanā*, the Path cultivating *samatha* and *vipassanā* yoked together (*yuganaddha*), and the Path where the monk's 'mental' is seized by agitation with respect to the *dhammas*.[409] In his translation of the *Visuddhimagga* Ñaṇamoli has translated: 'A bhikkhu's mind is seized by agitation about highest states';[410] but in his translation of the *Paṭisambhidāmagga* the same writer has rendered this by 'A bhikkhu's mind is agitated by overestimation of ideas [manifested in contemplation]'.[411] While the first three *maggas* are obviously based on the principle that Quieting and Insight are cultivated either successively or together, the last *magga* poses a problem. Yet, with regard to this fourth Path too, the text continues by saying that there exists a time when (the meditator's) mind internally comes to rest, settles, becomes one-pointed and is concentrated.[412] For him the Path is then produced. And (just as with the first three Paths) for the person who observes, cultivates and practices this fourth Path, the fetters (*saṃyojana*) are thrown off and the traces (*anusaya*) cease.

These four Paths are reproduced and explained in the *Paṭisambhidāmagga* (II 92–103), and then commented on in the *Saddhammappakāsinī* (pp. 585, 589 f.) and Buddhaghosa's *Visuddhimagga* (xx. 105–12). According to the *Paṭisambhidāmagga* (II 101–03), in the description of the fourth Path the word *dhamma* refers to an illumination that arises when one reflects on things as impermanent (*aniccato manasikaroto obhāso uppajjati*), Ill (*dukkhato*) and not-self (*anattato*). And in each case agitation (*uddhacca*) – that is, distraction (*vikkhepa*) – results from adverting to this illumination. Hence, a 'mental' that is thus seized, or 'seduced', by agitation does not correctly know what is presented (*upaṭṭhāna*) as impermanent, Ill and not-self. This 'illumination' is counted as

409 The PTS ed. reads *dhammuddhaccaviggahītamanā*, and the Nālandā ed. reads *dhammuddhaccaviggahitaṃ mānasam*.

410 Ñaṇamoli, *The path of purification* (Colombo, 1964), p. 739 n. 33.

411 Ñaṇamoli, *The path of discrimination* (London, 1982), pp. 287, 294.

412 Aṅguttaranikāya II 157: *taṃ cittaṃ ajjhattam eva santiṭṭhati sannisīdati ekodi hoti samādhiyati*. Compare for example *Mahāsuññatasutta* and *Cūḷasuññatasutta* (Majjhimanikāya III, pp. 105 ff., 111 f.).

one of the ten 'Sub-Afflictions of Vipassanā' that are said to affect an inexperienced meditator. Buddhaghosa has explained this *obhāsa* as *vipassanobhāsa* 'illumination from Insight'.[413]

Although the full implications of this fourth Path are perhaps not altogether clear, the obstacle formed by agitation with respect to the *dhammas* (*dhammuddhacca*) may be relatable to the case where, in meditation, discriminative knowledge (*prajñā*) becomes excessive and overwhelms *śamatha*. This situation – which could affect the person described as *dhammayoga* in the Aṅguttaranikāya (III 355), as opposed to the *jhāyi(n)*, and also the *sukkhavipassaka* or 'dry inspector'[414] – has of course been fully and explicitly recognized by Kamalaśīla, for example in his *Bhāvanākrama* III (pp. 9–10). Nevertheless, Mo-ho-yen's depreciation of analytical investigation may be a later example of the attitude just mentioned of meditators who were especially on their guard against the mental agitation that can arise in a person given to analysis of the *dharmas*. Although this danger has been noted in the Pali texts just cited, there is in them no rejection or condemnation of analysis and inspection in favour of *dhyāna* and Quieting alone.[415]

This yoking together of Quieting and Insight is known equally from Vasubandhu's *Abhidharmakośa* (viii. 1d; cf. v. 59). And in the four *(maula)dhyānas* the Path (*pratipad*) is described as being easy (*sukhā*) owing to the effortless procedure (*ayatnavāhitvāt*) that is due to equilibrium of *śamatha* and *vipaśyanā*; but it is

[413] *Visuddhimagga* xx. 107.

It is possible that it is such a light-experience that was criticized by the Hva šaṅ Mahāyāna, quoted in the *bSam gtan mig sgron*, as being characteristic of the Śrāvaka and Pratyekabuddha, and as being linked with a condition of notionlessness (*asaṃjñā*) that a practiser should *not* fall into through his practice of non-objectification (f. 83a: *mi dmigs bžin du snaṅ žiṅ/ gsal bar šes pas ñaṅ thos daṅ/ raṅ saṅs rgyas ži ba phyogs par mi lhuṅ/ ci yaṅ šes pa mi dmigs pas 'du šes med par mi ltuṅ/ mi g-yo žiṅ yoṅs su gsal lo sñam pa'i rtog pa med pas rtag par mi 'gyur/*).

[414] See *Visuddhimagga* xxxiii. 18.

On the *sukkhavipassaka* (and *suddhavipassanāyānika*), see *Visuddhimagga* viii. 237 and xviii. 5; *Saddhammappakāsinī*, pp. 563, 584. Cf. Nyanatiloka-Nyanaponika, *Buddhist dictionary*[4] (Colombo, 1980), p. 215; and S. Z. Aung, *Compendium of philosophy* (London, 1910), pp. 55, 75. On *vipassanā* as 'rough' or 'brittle' (*lūkhabhūta*), in contradistinction to *samatha* as 'soft' or 'malleable' (*siniddhabhūta*), see *Saddhammappakāsinī*, p. 281.

[415] On *samatha* and *vipassanā* in Pali sources, see L. Cousins in *Buddhist studies in honour of H. Saddhatissa* (Nuregoda, 1984), pp. 56–68.

difficult (*duḥkhā*) on the threshold-stage (*anāgamya*) preliminary to the first *dhyāna*, on the interval-stages (*dhyānāntara*) between *dhyānas*, and, very significantly, in the (three) *ārūpyas* also (vi. 66).[416] In the *anāgamya* and the *dhyānāntaras*, procedure requires effort because *śamatha* is deficient there; conversely, in the *ārūpyas* the need for effort is due to deficiency in *vipaśyanā* (vi. 66).[417]

A related theory is found in the *Abhidharmasamuccayabhāṣya* (p. 84) in connexion with the *viśuddhinairyāṇika mārga*, where a link is established between a deficiency in either *śamatha* or *vipaśyanā* and the difficulty of the Path based on either the *anāgamya* or the *ārūpyas*. On the contrary, the Path based on *dhyāna* is easy owing to the fact that there *śamatha* and *vipaśyanā* proceed in a syzygy (*yuganaddhavāhitvāt*).

The yoking of *śamatha* and *vipaśyanā* is similarly known from a number of further Mahāyānist treatises such as the *Mahāyānasūtrālaṃkāra* (xiv. 8–10) and its *Bhāṣya* (iv. 19, xi. 8–12 and 67, xviii. 49 and 66), the *Bodhisattvabhūmi* (xiii, p. 207), and Prajñākaramati's *Bodhicaryāvatārapañjikā* (viii. 4).

The conjunction of Emptiness and Means is furthermore known under the name of *sarvākāravaropetā śūnyatā* to Śāntideva, who has quoted the *Ratnacūḍāsūtra* on the subject in his *Śikṣāsamuccaya* (xv, pp. 272–3). This Sūtra – which is quoted in this connexion also by Kamalaśīla (*Bhāvanākrama* II, p. 59, and III, p. 27) – emphasizes that *dhyāna* is to be accompanied by all modes – such as generosity and the other virtues and salvific means – and is realized through the mode of Emptiness (*sarvākāravaropetaṃ śūnyatākārābhinirhṛtaṃ dhyānaṃ dhyāyati*, p. 272.11).[418] In the Sūtra the *sarvākaravaropetā śūnyatā* is described as lacking neither in generosity (*dāna*) nor salvific means (*upāya*), etc.

This Emptiness endowed with all excellent modes is thus the opposite of the isolated emptiness-principle mentioned above (p. 184).

416 See also the *Abhidharmadīpa* (ed. P. S. Jaini, Patna, 1959) vi. 4, n. 440.

417 Or *vidarśanā: Abhidharmadīpa* vi. 4, no. 440, with the *Vibhāṣāprabhāvṛtti*.

For one whose faculties are sharp (*tīkṣṇendriya*), furthermore, super-knowledge (*abhijñā*) too is rapid (*kṣiprā*) since there is no procedure with effort (*ayatnavāhitvāt*). But when a person's faculties are weak (*mṛdvindriya*) super-knowledge is slow (*dhandhā*). See *Vibhāṣāprabhāvṛtti* on *Abhidharmadīpa* vi. 4, no. 440.

418 For the parallel notion of *sarvākāradhyāna*, see *Bodhisattvabhūmi* i. 13, p. 209.

The theoretical contrast and the tension in practice between a scholar-philosopher who concerns himself with the analysis of the factors of existence – the *dhammayoga* – and the pure concentrated meditator – the *jhāyi(n)* – is one that has been made clear in a Sūtra of the Aṅguttaranikāya (III 355–6). It is parallel to, and at least in certain cases closely linked with, the distinctions made in the Buddhist tradition between a person concerned principally with philosophical and religious learning and teaching (Pāli *pariyatti*; cf. Tib. *bšad pa*) and a person who devotes himself above all else to spiritual practice and realization (Pāli *paṭipatti* and *paṭivedha*; cf. Tib. *sgrub pa*, etc.), between the teacher (*dhammakathika*) and the ascetic (*paṃsukūlika, tapassi(n)*), or even between the cenobitic monk dwelling in or near a village (*gāmavāsi(n)*; compare the *vargacārin*), and ministering also to the religious needs of laymen, and the reclusive and perhaps idiorhythmic forest-dwelling anchorite (*āraññaka*; cf. the type of the *khaḍgaviṣāṇakalpa*). (In one place, furthermore, the Aṭṭhakathā on the Aṅguttaranikāya has recorded a difference between Paṃsukūlikas and Dhammakathikas, in which the latter prevailed.[419])

Such contrasts reflect the antithesis, well known in Indian thought, between analytical thinking (*pratisaṃkhyāna, sāṃkhya*) and spiritual exercise (*yoga, bhāvanā*). It is related to the pair of spiritual types – identified by La Vallée Poussin after the Saṃyuttanikāya (II 115–18) – of on the one side the monk Musīla (Musila, Mūsila) who silently assented to being regarded as an Arhat all of whose impurities are exhaused (*khīṇāsava*) after he had declared that he 'knew' and 'saw' that the cessation of existence (*bhavanirodha*) and Nirvāṇa are equivalent, and on the other side the monk Nārada who, even though he knew this equivalence, still did not agree to being regarded as an Arhat because he did not reside in actual and immediate 'bodily contact' (*kāyena phusitvā vihar-*) with the highest state of spiritual realization.[420] The distinction between knowing *about* the highest and

[419] Cf. W. Geiger, *Culture of Ceylon in Mediaeval times* (Wiesbaden, 1960), pp. 201–03; W. Rahula, *History of Buddhism in Ceylon* (Colombo, 1956), pp. 158–61.

[420] L. de La Vallee Poussin, *Mélanges chinois et bouddhiques* 5 (1937), pp. 189–222. For the sense of 'in the body' (*kāyena*), see *Cūḷasuññatasutta*, Majjhimanikāya III 107–08 on the *animitto cetosamādhi*. Cf. L. Schmithausen in K. Bruhn and A. Wezler (eds.), *Studien*

directly realizing it is compared in this Sūtra with the difference between a traveller in a wasteland who, when seeing a well, identifies what is in it as 'water' (that is, a concept or word) and a traveller who drinks the water.

A comparable tension and contrast (but not necessarily contradiction) between meditative enstasis and intellectual analysis is to be found in the discussion reported in the Aṅguttaranikāya between Mahākoṭṭhita/Mahākoṭṭhika, who held that the *kāyasākṣin* is best because of the predominance in him of the faculty of concentration (*samādhi*), and Sāriputta, who held that the *dṛṣṭiprāpta* is best because of the predominance in him of the faculty of discriminative knowledge (*prajñā*).[421]

5. Absence of Notion (*saṃjñā*) and Non-mentation (*amanasikāra*)

Another fundamental teaching ascribed by Kamalaśīla to an unnamed opponent in the passage of the third *Bhāvanākrama* quoted above,[422] namely that nothing at all should be thought on and that there should be neither recollective attention (*smṛti*) nor mentation (*manasikāra*) – a teaching attributed to Mo-ho-yen/Mahāyāna in the Chinese and Tibetan documents from Dunhuang and in the later Tibetan historical and doxographical tradition –, cannot fail to evoke types of meditation in the form of the Samāpattis and Vimokṣas that are well known from the Buddhist tradition. Some aspects of this topic have already been touched on above in connexion with the method of leaping with respect especially to the *naivasaṃjñānāsaṃjñāyatana* and the *saṃjñāved[ay]itanirodha*, the last two of nine sequential stages in meditation.[423]

zum Jainismus und Buddhismus, pp. 214, 223, 236; above, p. 168 f.; below, pp. 194, 198.

For the notion of 'contact' in connexion with religious 'wellness' (sometimes free of *vedanā* or *citta*), and the spiritual achievement of salvation (e.g. in *cetosamādhi* or *amata* 'immortality') in the context of the expression *phāsuvihāra* (= Skt. *sparśavihāra*), etc., see C. Caillat, *Journal asiatique*, 1960, pp. 41–55, and 1961, pp. 497–502 (cf. R. L. Turner, *Collected papers* (London, 1975), p. 430 ff.).

In the Majjhimanikāya I 480 we find a juxtaposition of direct realization of supreme reality by the 'body' and the penetrative seeing of it by discriminative knowledge (*kāyena c'eva paramaṃ saccaṃ saccikaroti paññāya ca naṃ ativijjha passati*).

421 Aṅguttaranikāya I, pp. 118–20. See also above, p. 169.

422 *Bhāvanākrama* III, p. 14–15 (above, p. 93).

423 The factors *saṃjñā*, *smṛti* and *manas(i)kāra* are classified as mental (*caitta* or *cetasika*),

In the first Ārūpya-attainment (*samāpatti*) corresponding to the fourth Liberation (*vimokṣa*) and the seventh Sovereignty-sphere (*abhibhvāyatana*), the meditator – who at this stage has transcended all apperceptive notions relating to the visible-material (*rūpasaṃjñāḥ*) and has ceased to take as his object of mentation (*manasikāra*) the apperceptive notions of multiplicity (*nānātva-saṃjñāḥ*) – reaches the sphere of the infinity of space (*ākāśānantyā-yatana*).[424] Later, in the fourth Ārūpya-Samāpatti corresponding to the seventh Vimokṣa, the meditator reaches the sphere described as comprising neither (distinct) notions nor total absence of (indistinct) notions (*naivasaṃjñānāsaṃjñāyatana*) at the 'peak of existence' (*bhavāgra*).[425] Finally – and of particular importance in the present context – the meditator reaches the Attainment of

along with e.g. *vedanā*; see *Abhidharmakośa* ii. 24.

An association of *manas(i)kāra* with *saññā/saṃjñā* is to be found in the old canon, as is also the *amanasikāra* of sets of *saññā* (e.g. *Cūḷasuññatasutta*, Majjhimanikāya III 104–09). *Amanasikāra* of the notion of the multiple (*nānattasaññā*) is set forth as a goal in the *ākāsānañcāyatana* in the Majjhimanikāya (I 436) and Aṅguttaranikāya (IV 425). In the Upasīva section of the *Suttanipāta* (1070–2), the person endowed with attention (*satīmā*) is associated with both *ākiñcañña* and *saññāvimokkha*; and in the Tuvaṭakasutta of the *Suttanipāta* (916, 933), the *sato* is associated on the one hand with the eradication of *papañcasaṅkhā* (on which see 874) and on the other with examination (*vicinaṃ*) and knowledge (*aññāya*) of *dhamma*. Compare *Udānavarga* xxix. 3 for *mati* and *saññā*. The Sūtra quoted in the *Abhidharmakośavyākhyā* iii. 12 (p. 273) places *manasikāra* in *dhyāna*; compare L. Schmithausen in *Studien zum Jainismus und Buddhismus*, p. 226.

On the seven forms of *manaskāra*, see *Śrāvakabhūmi* (ed. Shukla), iv, pp. 439–510; ed. Schmithausen, in: L. Hercus *et al.* (ed.), *Indological and Buddhist studies* (Felicitation vol. for J. W. de Jong, Canberra, 1982), p. 460 ff. *Abhidharmasamuccaya* (ed. Pradhan), p. 68; *Abhidharmasamuccayabhāṣya* (ed. Tatia), p. 80.

The *Suttanipāta* contains much that is relevant to the problem of *saṃjñā*, *smṛti* and understanding (*prajñā*). In addition to the passage from the Upasīva section just cited, see the Māgandiyasutta which associates the *saññāviratta*, who is free from the *ganthas*, and the *paññāvimutta*, who is free from *mohas* (: *diṭṭhi*) (*Suttanipāta* 847); and the Kalahavivādasutta (especially 874, on *saññānidānā papañcasaṅkhā* and the avoidance not only of *saññā* but also of its negative). Some aspects of the question have been interestingly discussed, with reference to 'proto-Mādhyamaka' and Ch'an, by L. Gómez, *Philosophy East and West* 26 (1976), pp. 137–65.

424 While Ratnākaraśānti, *Sāratamā* viii. 2–6, describes (the first) three *vimokṣas* as *rūpin*, he characterizes (the last) five as *arūpin* (ed. Jaini, p. 175). The same author also states that while the first three are Liberations from the *nirmāṇāvaraṇa*, the last five are Liberations from the *śāntavihārasamāpattyāvaraṇa*. (On the *samāpattyāvaraṇa*, cf. *Ratna-gotravibhāga* ii. 45 with iii. 29.)

On the eight *vimokṣas*, see L. Hurvitz in: A. K. Narain (ed.), *Studies in Pali and Buddhism* (Delhi, 1979), pp. 121–69.

425 This stage is sometimes described as involving *saññā*, as in the compound *nevasaññānāsaññāyatanasaññā*; see Aṅguttaranikāya IV 414 and Majjhimanikāya III 107. Compare L. Schmithausen in: K. Bruhn and A. Wezler (eds.), *Studien zum Jainismus und Buddhismus*, pp. 224 n. 87, 225 n. 95, 229–32, 235 n. 130.

Stoppage or Cessation (*nirodhasamāpatti*), i.e. the ninth and final consecutive stage (*anupūrvavihāra*) in meditation corresponding to the eighth Vimokṣa,[426] where he transcends that stage which was still bound up with notions, however subtle and indistinct, and realizes immediately – 'in the body-aggregate' (*kāyena*)[427] – the stoppage of all notions and feelings (*saṃjñāved[ay]itanirodha*).[428] In this final stage, then, the exercitant is regarded as one who has achieved a simulacrum of Nirvāṇa (*nirvāṇasadṛśa, Bhāṣya* vi. 43).[429]

Now it is of very considerable significance that the *saṃjñāvedayitanirodha*, together with the four preceding Samāpattis which make up the non-material (*ārūpya*) levels of the Bhāvanāmārga and follow on the four Dhyānas making up the material levels, is nòt regarded in the whole of the Buddhist tradition as leading directly to supreme and perfect Awakening and Nirvāṇa. Thus, in some standard accounts of his Awakening, the Buddha is stated to descend from the Ārūpya-Samāpattis (when he is even said to have attained them at all) and to achieve Awakening directly from the fourth Dhyāna belonging to the *rūpadhātu*.[430] And according to the Mahāyāna and Mantrayāna, *anuttarasamyaksambodhi* is attained by a *buddha* on the level of the Akaniṣṭha-sphere (or Ghanavyūha) of the Śuddhāvāsa, the highest of the *rūpāvacāra*, where he then abides in his *sambhogakāya*, that is, in one of the two *rūpakāyas*. It is thus clear that the final five (or four) successive Ārūpya-Samāpattis – the last of the nine (or eight) consecutive stages – occupy a place somewhat apart in the plan of meditative exercises leading to the attainment of Nirvāṇa and the supreme and perfect Awakening of a *buddha*.

[426] Cf. *Abhidharmakośa* viii. 33. For the *anupubbavihāras*, see Dīghanikāya III 265 f., 290; Aṅguttaranikāya IV 410 f.; Saṃyuttanikāya, II 210–12; III 235–8. Cf. F. Heiler, *Die buddhistiche Versenkung* (München, 1922), p. 27 f.; É. Lamotte, *Le traité de la Grande Vertu de Sagesse*, iii (Louvain, 1970), p. 1308 ff.; L. Schmithausen, *loc. cit.*, p. 215.

[427] For the meaning of *kāyena* see pp. 168, 191–2, 198.

[428] For the meaning of *saṃjñā* see D. Seyfort Ruegg, *Le traité du tathāgatagarbha de Bu ston Rin chen grub* (Paris, 1973), pp. 76 n. and 116 n. ('notion différenciatrice, apperception'); L. Schmithausen, *loc. cit*, p. 214 n. 51 ('ideation').

On the place of *saṃjñāvedayitanirodha* in Buddhist soteriology and gnoseology, see L. Schmithausen, *loc. cit.*, pp. 214–19, 230–9.

[429] See L. Schmithausen, *loc. cit.*, p. 214 f.

[430] Cf. L. Schmithausen, *loc. cit.*, pp. 203–04 (on the 'stereotyped detailed description' of the Path of liberation).

The supreme degree of Samāpatti and Vimokṣa, the *saṃjñāvedayitanirodha* which is recognized in classical Buddhist literature as belonging to the Ārya alone,[431] is moreover very clearly distinguished both from the attainment of unconsciousness (*asaṃjñisamāpatti, asaṃjñāsamāpatti*) and from the unconsciousness of the *āsaṃjñika* state, that is, from two states that are not counted as Vimokṣas forming part of the *āryamārga* and which are not cultivated by the Buddhist Ārya as components of his consecutive stages (*anupūrvavihāra*) of spiritual practice.[432]

As for the Bhāvanāmārga, in Buddhist soteriology it may be either mundane (*laukika*) or transmundane (*lokottara*), quite unlike the Darśanamārga which is always transmundane and pure.[433] The transmundane Bhāvanāmārga is of course the pure (*anāsrava*) one practised by the Ārya, which includes the four Ārūpya Samāpattis culminating in the 'peak of existence' (*bhavāgra*) and then issuing in the *nirodhasamāpatti*. On the contrary, for the practiser of the mundane Bhāvanāmārga, detachment from the *bhavāgra* is not possible because he has no access to a state higher than it on the basis of which he could so detach himself.[434] This mundane and impure (*sāsrava*) Bhāvanāmārga is accordingly one that is not specific to the Ārya, though it may once have been practised by him too; it can precede the Ārya's Darśanamārga and does not have as its object the four Noble Principles (*āryasatya*) as such (Bhāṣya, vi. 1). An Ārya may have acquired detachment (*vairāgya*) previously by means of this *laukikamārga*, but the acquisition of such detachment is then a mundane one (vi. 46ab). The fruits of asceticism (*śrāmaṇyaphala*) of a Sakṛdāgāmin and an Anāgāmin can even be obtained by this *laukikamārga* (vi. 53cd).

According to Yaśomitra, Quieting (*śamatha*) is characteristic of this *laukikamārga*, full liberating knowledge (*ājñā*) being on the

[431] *Abhidharmakośa* ii. 43.

[432] See *Abhidharmakośa* ii. 41–42; cf. É. Lamotte, *Le traité de la Grande Vertu de Sagesse*, iii, p. 1299; below, p. 196 f.

[433] *Abhidharmakośabhāṣya* vi.1, 45c; and vii. 22. Cf. Asaṅga, *Abhidharmasamuccaya*, pp. 68–69; L. de La Vallée Poussin, *L'Abhidharmakośa*, ii, p. 117; viii, pp. 144–6; Lamotte, *Le traité de la Grande Vertu de Sagesse*, ii, p. 1027; iii, p. 1274. See however *Kathāvatthu* i. 5, which denies that the worldling (*puthujjana*) eliminates *kāmarāgavyāpāda*. It is to be recalled also that the *naivasaṃjñānāsaṃjñāyatana* is not counted as *anāsrava* and *lokottara*; see above, note 351 and below, p. 200.

[434] *Abhidharmakośabhāṣya* and *Vyākhyā* vi. 45; cf. viii. 20.

contrary a distinctive feature of the supreme transmundane Path.[435]

The practiser of the Path then either acquires its fruits consecutively in the manner of the *ānupūrvika*, attaining in order (*kramāt*) the Srotaāpattiphala (when the Darśanamārga turns into the transmundane Bhāvanāmārga) and the Sakṛdāgāmiphala (on the Bhāvanāmārga).[436] Alternatively, before entering the Darśanamārga, he may have practised a mundane Bhāvanāmārga in the condition of a worldling (*pṛthagjanāvasthā*) and have thus freed himself from the defilements/afflictions (*kleśa*) of the Kāmadhātu, becoming either a Bhūyovītarāga or a (Kāma-)Vītarāga.[437] The Buddha himself is cited as an example of one who has followed the latter procedure.[438]

In Buddhism three distinct states are characterized by the absence of notions, or unconsciousness.

The factor termed 'the notionless' (*āsaṃjñika*) is classified in the *dharma*-theory of the Vaibhāṣika-Abhidharma as a *cittaviprayukta-saṃskāra* that brings to a stop both mind (*citta*) and the mental factors (*caitta*) for beings known as *asaṃjñisattva*s (*Abhidharmakośa* ii. 41bc).[439] Its fruition (*vipāka*) is located in the sphere of the Bṛhatphala-deities (ii. 41d) – i.e. on the level of the fourth Dhyāna (*Bhāṣya* iii. 2cd and 6c) – and it is described as one of the nine residences of beings (*sattvāvāsa*, iii. 6d). Another factor, also classified as a *cittaviprayuktasaṃskāra* and located on the level of the fourth Dhyāna (iii. 6c), is the *asaṃjñisamāpatti*; and it too has

[435] *Abhidharmakośavyākhyā* ii. 16d and vi. 46ab. For *śamatha* and *manaskāra* on the *laukika* level according to Asaṅga, see *Abhidharmasamuccaya*, p. 68.

[436] *Abhidharmakośabhāṣya* vi. 33; cf. 11.16 and viii. 14 on the *ānupūrvika*.

[437] *Abhidharmakośabhāṣya* ii. 16cd, vi. 30cd, 55. Cf. L. de La Vallée Poussin, *L'Abhidharmakośa*, ii, pp. 117, 134–6, 180, 205; iii, p. 196 note 3; v/vi, pp. vi–ix, 119, 194, 233, 243, 266, 288; *Mélanges chinois et bouddhiques* 5 (1937); p. 192 ff.; *Vibhāṣāprabhāvṛtti* on *Abhidharmadīpa* ii. 2 [92] (ed. Jaini, pp. 57–58).

[438] Cf. L. de La Vallée Poussin, *Mélanges chinois et bouddhiques* 5, pp. 197 note 1, 219–22; Lamotte, *Le traité de la Grande Vertu de Sagesse*, ii, p. 1035 n. 1.

[439] In the *Mahāvyutpatti* (Sakaki's ed., § 104, nos. 1987–9), the *āsaṃjñika*, together with the *asaṃjñisamāpatti* and the *nirodhasamāpatti*, appears in the list of *caitasika-dharmas*. This may be an error of redaction, for they are preceded by the *viprayuktasaṃskāras prāpti* and *aprāpti* and followed by *jīvita* and *nikāyasabhāga*, etc. However, the question as to what

the function of stopping both *citta* and the *caittas* (ii. 42). The difference between these two forms of unconsciousness is that the *āsaṃjñika*, as fruition (*vipāka*), is neutral (*avyākṛta*), whereas the *asaṃjñisamāpatti* is wholesome (*śubha* = *kuśala*, ii. 42). The latter is cultivated by ordinary worldlings (*pṛthagjana*), who take it to be release (*niḥsaraṇa*) and liberation (*mokṣa*), whereas the Āryas consider it a *vinipātasthāna* (ii. 42d). It is furthermore described as being the product of great mental effort (*mahābhisaṃskārasādhya*, ii. 42d). These two states are in the Buddhist tradition clearly not thought of as being characteristic of the Buddhist Path.

These two forms of notionlessness are accordingly carefully distinguished from the *cittaviprayuktasaṃskāra* already mentioned above termed 'attainment of cessation of notions and feelings' ([*saṃjñāved(ay)ita*]*nirodha-samāpatti*) – the ninth of the Samāpattis which follows on the four Ārūpyas after the 'peak of existence' (*bhavāgra*) and the eighth Vimokṣa – which also has the function of stopping both *citta* and the *caittas*.[440] It differs from the two forms of notionlessness just mentioned by being cultivated only by the Ārya. Following on the fourth Ārūpya – the *naivasaṃjñā-nāsaṃjñāyatana* sphere where notions are so subtle that it can be described as neither with nor without notions – it is defined as 'born of the peak of existence' (*bhavāgrajā*), and as good (*śubhā* = *kuśalā*, ii. 43bc). This stage is attained through a mental act relying on the notion of residence in quietude (*śāntavihārasaṃjñā-pūrvaka manasikāra*, ii. 43b). However, even though it is described as a simulacrum of Nirvāṇa (*nirvāṇasadṛśa*, vi. 43cd),[441] one can still fall away from the *nirodhasamāpatti* (ii. 44d); for it is acquired by effort (*prayogalabhyā*) rather than by pure dispassion (*vairāgya*,

kind of consciousness may subsist in the *nirodhasamāpatti* is an old one (see n. 440).

The *Mahāvyutpatti* also evidently counts (no. 2297) the *asaṃjñisattvas* in the ninth *sattvāvāsa* – i.e., apparently, on the level of the *saṃjñāvedayitanirodha* – rather than in the fifth *sattvāvāsa* pertaining to the fourth Dhyāna of the Rūpāvacāra (cf. Dīghanikāya III 263). See also *Abhidharmakośa* iii. 6. (The *Mahāvastu* (I, p. 127.5) seems in addition to imply a criticism of the *saṃjñāvedayitanirodha*. See Edgerton, *Buddhist Hybrid Sanskrit Dictionary*, s.v.)

440 *Abhidharmakośa* ii. 43a; cf. ii. 44d, vi. 43cd, 64a and viii. 33. On the persistence of subtle thought in this *nirodhasamāpatti*, see L. de La Vallée Poussin, *L'Abhidharmakośa* viii, p. 207 n. 6, and ii, p. 211 n. 3; *Vijñaptimātratāsiddhi*, *La Siddhi de Hiuan-tsang*, pp. 204 ff., 400 ff.

441 Cf. *Vibhāṣāprabhāvṛtti* on *Abhidharmadīpa*, p. 93.5.

ii. 44a).[442] And only in the case of a *buddha* – for whom there is nothing produced through effort (*prāyogika*) – is the *nirodhasamāpatti* acquired in virtue of Awakening (*bodhilabhyā*, ii. 44a). According to the Vaibhāṣikas, furthermore, because in the *nirodhasamāpatti* there is no *citta*, the Non-returner (*anāgāmin*) Ārya who attains this Samāpatti takes a 'body-aggregate' (*kāya*) as support; and he is then termed a *kāyasākṣin* in so far as he realizes this Nirvāṇa-like factor through a 'body-aggregate' (*kāyena*, vi. 43cd).[443]

The *nirodhasamāpatti* has also been defined in Asaṅga's *Abhidharmasamuccaya* (pp. 10–11), where it is distinguished from the *asaṃjñisamāpatti* on the ground that the latter issues from a mental act relying on the notion of release (*niḥsaraṇasaṃjñāpūrvaka manasikāra*) on the part of one free from passion (*vītarāga*) on the Śubhakṛtsna level of the third Dhyāna, but not yet free from passion above this level; whereas the *nirodhasamāpatti* issues from a mental act relying on the notion of residence in quietude (*śāntavihārasaṃjñāpūrvaka manasikāra*) for a Vītarāga on the level of the Ākiṃcanyāyatana. As for the *āsaṃjñika*, it differs according to the *Abhidharmasamuccayabhāṣya* (p. 9) from both the *asaṃjñisamāpatti* and the *nirodhasamāpatti* in so far as it lacks *manaskāra*; whereas the latter are both specified with respect to several factors one of which is *manaskāra*.[444]

[442] In the *Cūḷasuññatasutta* (Majjhimanikāya III 107–08), the *animitto cetosamādhi* – which (like the *nirodhasamāpatti*) follows on the *nevasaññānāsaññāyatana* and is the object of *manasikāra* – is said to be deliberately constructed (*abhisaṅkhata*) and intentionally formed (*abhisañcetayita*), so that it is impermanent (*anicca*) and subject to cessation (*nirodhadhamma*). But it nevertheless leads to pacification and stabilization of *citta*, and finally to the freedom of *citta* from the *kāmāsava*, *bhavāsava* and *avijjāsava*, and thus to liberation. Compare the *Aṭṭhakanāgarakasutta* (Majjhimanikāya I 350–2) on the contemplation of the successive stages up to and including the *ākiñcaññāyatana* as *abhisaṅkhata* and *abhisañcetita*, and accordingly as *anicca* and *nirodhadhamma*.

The *Mahāmāluṅkyasutta* (Majjhimanikāya I 436–7) lists neither the *nevasaññānāsaññāyatana* nor the *saññāvedayitanirodha* as a basis for liberating knowledge; and it mentions the *amatā dhātu* as the final goal.

In Majjhimanikāya I 333, one who has entered this state of *saññāvedayitanirodha* is said to look like one who is dead (*kālakato*). Cf. N. Hakamaya, *Journal of Indian and Buddhist Studies (IBK)*, 23/2 (1975), p. 1083.

[443] See above, pp. 168–70, 191–2, 194.

[444] On the *nirodhasamāpatti* in the Vijñānavāda, see Hakamaya, *loc. cit.*, pp. 1081–1074, where attention is called (following Asaṅga's *Mahāyānasaṃgraha* i. 7) to the absence of the *manovijñāna* and the *kliṣṭamanas*, and to the presence of the *ālayavijñāna*, in this *samāpatti*.

In a Sūtra of the old canon found in the Anussativagga of the Aṅguttaranikāya, it is furthermore stated that the expert, 'thoroughbred' person (*purisājānīya*) does not rely in his meditation on the elements earth, water, air and fire and on the four Ārūpya-spheres. For such a meditator, each notion (*saṃjñā*) – beginning with that of earth and extending to the *nevasasaññānāsaññāyatana* – is dissolved (*vibhūtā*) in earth and so forth.[445]

It is worthy of notice that although the Samāpatti and Vimokṣa attainments have been accepted by Mahāyānasūtras in their treatment of Dhyāna,[446] they are in no way specifically linked with the Mahāyāna. They are also acknowledged in such Mahāyānist treatises as the *Ratnagotravibhāga* – where the tranquil Dhyānas and Samāpattis are mentioned in passing (i. 73) – and in the *Abhisamayālaṃkāra* – for example in the section (viii. 2) dealing with the qualities of the *advayajñānātmaka dharmakāya* (where it is specified that the nine Samāpattis are successive) and in the commentaries on Chapter ii.

In certain respects the final Samāpatti of the Stoppage of notions and feelings (*saṃjñāvedayitanirodha*), not to speak of the lower states of 'notionlessness' known in the Buddhist tradition as the *asaṃjñisamāpatti* and the *āsaṃjñika*, seems to correspond to what is known in Pātañjalayoga as *cittavṛttinirodha* (*Yogasūtra* i. 2), in other words to what Erich Frauwallner termed the Yoga of suppression (Unterdrückungsyoga) in contradistinction to the eight-membered (*aṣṭāṅga*) Yogic path described in other parts of the *Yogasūtras*.[447]

Now it is to be observed that in the old canon it has been explicitly stated that penetration with full liberating knowledge is

[445] Aṅguttaranikāya V 353–5; cf. *Bodhisattvabhūmi* i. 4, pp. 49–50. Compare also Saṃyuttanikāya II 153–4.

[446] See for example *Pañcaviṃśatisāhasrikā Prajñāpāramitā* (ed. N. Dutt), p. 19; *Śatasāhasrikā Prajñāpāramitā* (ed. Ghoṣa), pp. 58, 1445.

[447] See E. Frauwallner, *Geschichte der indischen Philosophie*, i (Salzburg, 1953), p. 436 f. On connexions between Pātañjalayoga and Buddhism, see L. de La Vallée Poussin, *Mélanges chinois et bouddhiques* 5 (1937), pp. 223–42.

achieved only to the extent that there is meditative absorption involving an apperceptive notion (*yāvatā saññāsamāpatti tāvatā aññāpaṭivedho*).[448]

This principle has been specifically invoked in Asaṅga's *Abhidharmasamuccaya* and its *Bhāṣya*, where it is concluded that the *naivasaṃjñānāsaṃjñāyatana* – viz. the fourth Ārūpya described as neither involving the total absence of all notions nor as comprising (distinct) notions – is mundane (*laukika*) rather than transmundane (*lokottara*), and that the *āryamārga* is not to be found at its level. While the *naivasaṃjñānāsaṃjñāyatana* is thus not regarded as transmundane, the *saṃjñāvedayitanirodha* is classified as *lokottara* in so far as it is the outcome of the *āryamārga* involving liberating knowledge.[449]

According to the *Abhidharmasamuccaya*, the Ārūpya-attainments are totally infused with Quieting (*śamathaikarasa*). Yet, according to this same source and its commentary, a set of seven mental acts (*manaskāra*) makes for the attainment not only of the four Rūpa-Dhyānas but also of the four Ārūpyas up to and including the sphere where ideation subsists in a form that can be described as neither total absence of notions or as containing (distinct) notions (*naivasaṃjñānāsaṃjñāyatana*). The *Abhidharmasamuccayabhāṣya* moreover specifies that the second of these seven forms of mental act, the *ādhimokṣika manaskāra*, transcends learning (*śruta*) and reflection (*cintā*) and realizes both Quieting (*śamatha*) and Insight (*vipaśyanā*) having as object the phenomenal sign of the characteristic of gross quiet (*audārikaśāntalakṣaṇanimittālambanā*).[450] In the relevant summary verse (*uddāna*) of the *Śrāvakabhūmi*, the Dhyānas and Ārūpyas are connected with mental acts; and the *vajropama-samādhi* is identified as the sixth kind of mental act, the *prayoganiṣṭha manaskāra*.[451] This placing of *vipaśyanā* as well as *śamatha* in the four Ārūpyas is noteworthy.

[448] Aṅguttaranikāya IV 426. For the Sanskrit version of this Sūtra-text, see Asaṅga, *Abhidharmasamuccaya*, p. 69, and *Abhidharmasamuccayabhāṣya*, p. 81. And for a discussion of this, and of the meaning of the compound *aññāpaṭivedha*, see L. Schmithausen, *loc. cit.*, p. 224 and p. 229.

[449] See Asaṅga, *Abhidharmasamuccaya*, p. 69; *Abhidharmasamuccayabhāṣya*, p. 81.

[450] See *Abhidharmasamuccaya*, p. 68; *Abhidharmasamuccayabhāṣya*, p. 80.

[451] *Śrāvakabhūmi*, ed. Shukla, p. 510; ed. Schmithausen in: L. Hercus *et al.* (ed.), *Indological and Buddhist studies* (J. W. de Jong Felicitation vol., Canberra, 1982), p. 472.

As mentioned above, the state of *saṃjñāvedayitanirodha* has been described as being perceived as a simulacrum of Nirvāṇa (*nirvāṇa-sadṛśa*) and as tranquil (*śānta*) on the level of the Anāgāmin and Kāyasākṣin. Now Buddhist tradition knows of a path which, independently and taken all by itself, leads exclusively to quietude (*śamaikāyana*).

In the old canon, the *ekāyano maggo* was of course the way of the four Applictions of mindfulness (*satipaṭṭhāna* = *smṛtyupasthāna*) that, uniquely, leads to the realization of Nirvāṇa.[452] In some places, however, the term *śamaikāyana* came to be used in connexion with a class of persons who seek a more or less cataleptic calm, that is, with persons attached, in terms of the Three-Vehicle (*triyāna*) theory, to the *śrāvakagotra* considered as a 'genus' fundamentally different from the *bodhisattvagotra*. A Śrāvaka of this particular class would therefore be unable ever to attain the supreme Awakening (*anuttarasamyaksambodhi*) of a *buddha*, unlike the type of Śrāvaka who on the contrary turns towards *bodhi*.[453]

Now, according to the *Ratnagotravibhāga* (ii. 58–59), those persons who, being established on the path of calm, conceive the notion that they have achieved Nirvāṇa (*prāptanirvāṇasaṃjñin* = *myaṅ 'das thob 'du šes can*) are deflected from their earlier postulation (*pūrvagraha*) by the teachings of the *Saddharmapuṇḍarīkasūtra*; and being thus made to mature in the supreme Vehicle (*uttama yāna*, *viz.* the Mahāyāna), they receive the prophecy (*vyākaraṇa*) that they are to achieve supreme *bodhi*. Furthermore, according to a text quoted by Haribhadra in his commentary on the section of the *Abhisamayālaṃkāra* that treats of the Single Vehicle (*ekayāna*) – a text close to the *Bodhicittavivaraṇa* ascribed to Nāgārjuna – those persons whose minds are tormented by Saṃsāric existence (*bhavād uttrastamānasāḥ*), and who conceive the notion that they have achieved Nirvāṇa (*prāptanirvāṇasaṃjñin*) once their life-span is spent, have in fact not really achieved Nirvāṇa but merely the cessation of birth in the three realms of

[452] See for example Dīghanikāya II 290; Saṃyuttanikāya V 167, 185.

[453] See *Saṃdhinirmocanasūtra* (ed. Lamotte) vii. 14–15.

existence. They therefore require to be awakened by the *buddhas* so that they may eliminate undefiled nescience (*akliṣṭājñāna*) and thus also finally become *buddhas*.[454]

Mo-ho-yen's teaching, which lays so much emphasis on the elimination of discursive thinking (*sems pa*), recollective attention (*dran pa*) and mentation (*yid la byed pa*), presents some very noteworthy parallels to what a practiser achieves in the Samāpattis and Vimokṣas, and in particular in the Samāpatti where notions and feelings have come to a stop (*saṃjñāvedayitanirodha*). For clarifying the background to his teachings, and in order to appreciate the criticisms that Kamalaśīla and his school have directed against what they considered to be an unbalanced and disproportionate stress on eradicating any and every trace of analytical thinking, the above-mentioned theories of meditative practice need to be borne in mind.

Kamalaśīla and his school may in addition have feared that the Hva šaṅ's meditative methods approached perilously closely the cataleptic state of notionlessness (*asaṃjñisamāpatti*) that arises for a worldling (*pṛthagjana*) on the level of the fourth Dhyāna, as a result of his desire for deliverance (*mokṣakāmatā*) when he conceives the idea of release (*niḥsaraṇasaṃjñin*), but which (as already noted) has not been accepted by Buddhist tradition as forming an integral part of the Ārya's Path of meditative realization.[455] What Kamalaśīla has stated in his *Bhāvanākrama* regarding the resemblance between his unnamed opponent's view concerning the absence of recollective attention (*asmṛti*) and mentation (*amanasikāra*) and the suppression of thinking (*cittanirodha*) which a worldling can achieve on the level of the fourth Dhyāna seems indeed to have to be understood in this way.[456] Kamalaśīla has furthermore called attention to the resemblance

[454] Haribhadra, *Abhisamayālaṃkārālokā* ii. 1 (ed. Wogihara, p. 134). See D. Seyfort Ruegg, *La théorie du tathāgatagarbha et du gotra* (Paris, 1969), pp. 178, 189 ff., 194, 242.

[455] See above, p. 195 f.

[456] *Bhāvanākrama* III, pp. 15–17. This can refer to the state of the Bṛhatphala-gods of *Abhidharmakośabhāṣya* ii. 41 and iii. 2 (cf. above, p. 196). See also *Abhidharmakośabhāṣya* ii. 41bc on the *āsaṃjñika* as cessation of *citta* and the *caittas* among the *asaṃjñisattva* (cf. i. 28 and iv. 84) gods.

that would apparently arise between a Śrāvaka absorbed in the meditation of cessation (*nirodhasamādhisamāpanna*), where no phenomenal signs (*nimitta*) are present, and a Bodhisattva who would accomplish together all six Perfections (*pāramitā*) without cultivating generosity (*dāna*) and the like when undue emphasis is placed on *dhyāna* alone as embracing in itself all other *pāramitās*.[457]

In the account of the Great Debate given in the *sBa bžed* and related sources, moreover, Kamalaśīla is reported to have objected against the Hva šaṅ's teaching the argument that if one were entirely to eliminate thinking, etc., one would not differ from a person who has fainted or fallen into senselessness, or from certain gods of the higher spheres (*khams goṅ ma'i lha*), so that it would be necessary to conclude that, if not thinking really were to lead to Awakening, beings in these states of unconsciousness would equally have to be considered as liberated.[458]

In one respect this question of *nirodha* and the suppression of all notions recalls the distinction made in the Abhidharma between *nirvāṇa* as *pratisaṃkhyānirodha* – that is, liberation consciously achieved through knowledge defined as a specific *prajñā* (cf. *Abhidharmakośabhāṣya* i. 6a) – and *apratisaṃkhyānirodha*, which is mere cessation due to the absence of the necessary conditions (*pratyaya*). This point arises in the theory of meditation of the *ānimittānimittasamādhi* with respect to *apratisaṃkhyānirodha* in the aspect of quietude (*śāntākāra*, *Abhidharmakośabhāṣya* viii. 26cd).

A further basic teaching of Mo-ho-yen, frequently mentioned in the *Cheng-li chüeh* as well as in the Tibetan Dunhuang documents, was that all (false) notions (*hsiang*, *wang hsiang*) should be abolished.[459] The expression '(false) notion' is explained in the *Cheng-li chüeh* as designating all movements of

[457] *Bhāvanākrama* III, p. 26.

[458] See *sBa bžed*, G, p. 69; S, p. 59; *mKhas pa'i dga' ston*, ja, f. 117a–b. Compare Ñaṅ Ñi ma 'od zer, *Chos 'byuṅ Me tog sñiṅ po*, f. 431a–b (with variants). Cf. for example Vasubandhu, *Triṃśikā* 16.

[459] *Cheng-li chüeh*, ff. 131a, 131a–132a, 133b–134b, 148a–149a, 150a (P. Demiéville, *Concile*, pp. 62, 66–71, 75–77, 130–41, 158). For *myi bden pa'i sems*, *myi bden pa'i 'du šes*, etc., see *Pelliot tibétain 21* (1), *116* (245), *117*, *812r*; *Stein 709* (14b), *710* (24a–25a, 33a, 35b, 52a). See also *Pelliot tibétain 823* (cited by Y. Imaeda, *Journal asiatique* 1975, pp. 142–3), an old Tibetan text from Tun-huang closely related to the *Cheng-li chüeh*. Cf. L. Gómez in: R. M. Gimello and P. Gregory (eds.), *Studies in Ch'an and Hua-yen*, p. 125.

thinking that grasp objects; while 'all' is explained as covering everything from infernal existences up to just below the level of a *buddha*.[460] But by 'watching Mind' (*k'an hsin*), which eliminates the Impregnations, these notions are made to disappear according to Mo-ho-yen.[461]

Apart from the scriptural sources cited in the *Cheng-li chüeh*, this doctrine could of course find support for example in a passage from the *Kāśyapaparivarta* (§ 144): 'For the monk absorbed in the attainment of the stoppage of notions and feelings, there is nothing further that needs to be accomplished'.[462]

Parallels to Mo-ho-yen's teaching are to be found in particular when a Sūtra is referring to the level of ultimate reality (*paramārtha*) and to non-duality (*advaya*). Thus, in Chapter viii of the *Vimalakīrtinirdeśa*, the Bodhisattva *Bhadrajyotis proposes a description of entry into non-duality in terms of the absence of both movement (of thinking, *g-yo ba*) and of (false) mentation (*rlom sems* : *manyanā*), and also in terms of the absence of any (karmic?) qualification/entitlement (*lhag par bya ba* : *adhikāra*?) and freedom from the same (*lhag par bya ba daṅ bral ba*). And further on in the same chapter the Bodhisattva *Siṃhamati proposes a description of entry into non-duality in terms of the non-production of any notion (*saṃjñā*), pure or impure, and even of the non-arising of absence-of-notion (*'du śes med par gyur pa*).

In reply to a question as to whether Auditors fond of quietistic cessation can have access to the Mahāyāna, Mo-ho-yen is nevertheless stated in the *Cheng-li chüeh* to have said that, for a person residing in the notionless, there is no seeing of the Mahāyāna, so that one should keep from attaching oneself to absorption without notions.[463]

[460] Demiéville, *Concile*, p. 75 and n. 7.

[461] *Cheng-li chüeh*, ff. 129a, 135a f., 150a f. On *k'an hsin*, see P. Demiéville, *Concile*, pp. 43, 51, n. 52, 78, 125, 158. The corresponding Tibetan expressions are *sems la blta* (attested in the Tibetan Dunhuang documents, e.g. *Pelliot tibétain 823r* (1); *Stein 468* (1b), *689*), *sems rtogs pa*, and *sems ṅo 'phrod pa* (attested in dPa' bo gtsug lag phreṅ ba's *mKhas pa'i dga' ston*, ja. f. 120b6). See above, p. 100.

[462] *saṃjñāvedayitanirodhasamāpattisamāpannasya bhikṣor nâsty uttarīkaraṇīyam* (quoted e.g. in Candrakīrti's *Prasannapadā* i., p. 48).

[463] *Cheng-li chüeh*, f. 132a (Demiéville, *Concile*, p. 71).

It is furthermore to be noted that the *bSam gtan mig sgron* has also ascribed to the Hva śaṅ Mahā yan the teaching that notions (*saṃjñā*) are *not* to be stopped (*'du śes dgag par yaṅ mi bya*, f. 83a4). In the same context, the recognition through awareness of the nescience-related mental factors that (mental) instability is faulty and the stoppage of the latter are both described as the 'Śrāvaka's *nirodha*' (*ma rig pa'i sems byuṅ ba tshor bas g-yo ba skyon tu rig ste bkag na ñan thos 'gog pa'o*, f. 83a2). Hence one should not fall into notionlessness through objectification of the anoetic (*ci yaṅ śes pa mi dmigs pas 'du śes med par mi ltuṅ*, f. 83a5–6). In a parallel passage from *Pelliot tibétain 117* the restriction 'of the Śrāvaka' is also to be found.[464] According to statements reproduced in *Stein 709* (f. 4a–b), the Mahāyānist way of no-mind is said to be like that of neither the non-Buddhist nor the Śrāvaka.[465]

Wang Hsi's *Cheng-li chüeh* has moreover repudiated the suggestion that the state of not thinking taught by Mo-ho-yen could be legitimately equated with either the unconscious state of the Bṛhatphala-gods, who are placed immediately below the Śuddhāvāsa level in the fourth Dhyāna, or with any unconscious state reached by a worldling by means of a mundane, non-*lokottara* path.[466]

It is finally of special importance to observe that for Mo-ho-yen – and indeed for so much of the classical tradition of later Buddhism (whether or not it postulates either an *ālayavijñāna* or an *amalavijñāna*) – the Bhāvanāmārga and the state of cessation of notions and feelings (*saṃjñāvedayitanirodha*) is not strictly speaking entirely 'mind-less': the discursive and proliferating activity of thinking has indeed been brought to a stop at the highest level of the Path, but Mind (*sems* [*ñid*] = *citta*[*tā*]; Chinese *hsin*) subsists in some more or less fine form. According to Mo-ho-yen it is then discursive thinking (*sems pa*), as connected with recollective attention (*dran pa*) and mentation (*yid la byed pa*), that is to be relinquished; but (innate) Mind is to be recognized in face-to-face confrontation (*sems la blta ba* = Ch. *k'an hsin*; *sems rtogs pa*, *sems ṅo 'phrod pa*).

[464] Cf. Gómez in *Studies*, p. 112.

[465] Cf. *Stein 710*, f. 5b.

[466] *Cheng-li chüeh*, ff. 131a–b, 148a–b (Demiéville, *Concile*, pp. 62 ff., 130 ff.).

6. On a *Bhāvanākrama* in Bhavya's *Madhyamakaratnapradīpa*

After considering *śamathavipaśyanā-yoga* in Chapter vii of his *Madhyamakaratnapradīpa* (P, f. 351a) which is described as a *bhāvanākrama* – and in connexion with the statement taken from the *Bhavasaṃkrānti* ascribed to Nāgārjuna that the world proceeds from conceptual construction (*vikalpa*) which in its turn issues from mind (*citta*), and that mind proceeds from bodily-structure (*lus* = *kāya*) which has therefore to be analysed[467] – Bhavya has observed (f. 352a–353a) that knowledge (*śes pa* = *jñāna*) rests nowhere, that [in reality] there is no mental construction as anything at all (*cir yaṅ mi rtog*), no thinking on anything (*ci la yaṅ sems pa med pa*), no dwelling in any extreme positions, no arising of cognition in the form of anything whatever (*śes pa ci'i ṅo bor yaṅ ma skyes pa*), and that non-predication as anything at all is to be realized in meditation (*ci yaṅ ma yin par bsgom par bya'o*). This text specifies that analytical *prajñā* (*so sor rtog pa'i śes rab*) is itself free from appearance (*snaṅ ba med pa* : *nirābhāsa*).

To illustrate the point that at this level knowledge itself no longer exists (*śes pa raṅ ñid kyaṅ med par gyur pa*), the *Madhyamakaratnapradīpa* (f. 352b) refers to the *Kāśyapaparivarta*'s comparison of analytical investigation (*pratyavekṣā*) and the faculty of transcending discriminative understanding (*prajñendriya*) with fire produced from rubbing together two pieces of wood which both consumes the wood from which it is produced and is thus itself extinguished, a comparison cited also by Kamalaśīla. So the 'fuel' of philosophical theory (*lta ba* = *darśana, dṛṣṭi*) is declared to be consumed; and when theory thus comes to a stop, the fire of knowledge itself no longer arises, while all afflictions/defilements (*kleśa*) are then consumed.[468] The *Madhyamakaratnapradīpa* describes this process as a Gross Yoga (*rags pa'i rnal 'byor*) that it

[467] *Bhavasaṃkrānti* 7. Compare Section ii of the *Ṭīkā* ascribed to Maitreyanātha (ed. N. Aiyaswami Sastri, Adyar, 1938, p. 89 f.). Cf. C. Lindtner, *Nāgārjuniana* (Copenhagen, 1982), p. 13. On the relation between *citta* and *kāya*, see *Abhidharmakośabhāsya* ii. 44d (p. 72), as well as the sources on the *nāma-rūpa* concept.

[468] *Kāśyapaparivarta* § 69, cited by Kamalaśīla in his *Bhāvanākrama* (III, p. 20). Also cited are the *Ghanavyūha* and *Mahāsukhanātha (on whom see C. Lindtner, *Wiener Zeitschrift für die Kunde Südasiens* 26 (1982), p. 176 and *Indologica taurinensia* 12 (1984), p. 178). Cf. above, pp. 94–95 note, 114.

contrasts with the Subtle Yoga based on *nirābhāsa* and *māyā*-like Mind, for which it refers to the *Laṅkāvatarasūtra* (Sagāthaka 256–7).

Later the *Madhyamakaratnapradīpa* takes up again the themes of non-mentation (*amanasikāra*, f. 354b7), single-moment Awakening (*ekakṣaṇābhisaṃbodhi*, f. 355a2) and single-moment understanding (ff. 358b–359a, 360a6), and refers as well to Awakening in the *vajropamasamādhi* (ff. 356a4, 359a1) and progressive engagement (*kramavṛtti*) on the Path of the Bodhisattva (f. 358a6, following the *Dharmadhātustava* ascribed to Nāgārjuna, verse 91). In particular, it is stated that *bhāvanā* should be cultivated by freeing oneself from both *smṛti* and *manasikāra* (f. 354b7). Consideration is given also to the question as to how one avoids becoming a person exclusively given to quiet (*ži ba phyogs gcig pa*) by taking recourse in the complete *rūpakāya* and in the *apratiṣṭhitanirvāṇa* (f. 360a, by which the Bodhisattva does not enter into Nirvāṇa in order to be able to work for the benefit of living beings by making use of salvific means or *upāyas*).

It thus appears that the *Madhyamakaratnapradīpa* belongs to the long line of treatises concerned with the question of *amanasikāra* and *asmṛti*, and that in its treatment of a Mādhyamika's *bhāvanā-krama* it addresses certain problems also discussed in Tibet at the time of the Great Debate of bSam yas.

The question thus arises of the date and exact authorship of the *Madhyamakaratnapradīpa*. In the bsTan 'gyur catalogues, this work has been attributed implicitly to Bhāvaviveka/Bhavya, the (sixth-century) Mādhyamika author of the *Prajñāpradīpa* and *Madhyamakahṛdayakārikās*; and this ascription has been explicitly made by some modern scholars.[469] This attribution is however far from being certain. In the first place, the *Madhyamakaratnapradīpa* mentions favourably, and cites as authorities, Dharmakīrti and Candrakīrti – two masters who have usually been placed in the seventh century – even though the latter was the chief

[469] See C. Lindtner, *Wiener Zeitschrift für die Kunde Südasiens* 26 (1982), pp. 172–84; *Indologica taurinensia* 12 (1984), pp. 163–84; *Adyar Library Bulletin* 50 (1986), p. 84 n. 65. See however the contrary opinion of Y. Ejima, *Journal of Indian and Buddhist Studies (IBK)*, 28/2 (1980), pp. 37–43, and *Chūgan-shisō no tenkai – Bhāvaviveka kenkyū* (Tōkyō, 1980); D. Seyfort Ruegg, *The literature of the Madhyamaka school of philosophy in India*, p. 66, and 'Towards a chronology of the Madhyamaka school', in L. A. Hercus et al. (eds.), *Indological and Buddhist studies* (Felicitation vol. for J. W. de Jong, Canberra, 1982), p. 513.

opponent and critic of Bhāvaviveka, the author of the *Prajñāpradīpa*. Moreover, it quotes a verse (f. 354a3–4) to be found in the Apabhramśa *Dohākoṣa* of Saraha, and it describes the author of this *dohā* as 'teacher's teacher' (*bla ma'i bla ma*);[470] in other words, the author of the *Madhyamakaratnapradīpa* may have been the grand-pupil of Saraha, the teacher (also known as Rāhulabhadra) of Ārya-Nāgārjunapāda, who lived perhaps in the seventh century.[471] Finally, beside many other texts often placed at the earliest in the seventh century such as the *Bodhicittavivaraṇa* (also ascribed to Nāgārjuna), it quotes (f. 361b) a 'prophecy' on Nāgārjuna from the *Mañjuśrīmūlatantra*, whereas the Rājavyākaraṇaparivarta of the *Mañjuśrīmūlakalpa* in its form now known to us contains – in addition to a differently worded *vyākaraṇa* on Nāgārjuna – another 'prophecy' relating to King Gopāla who founded the Pāla dynasty in Bengal (*rg. c.* 770–810 or 775–812).[472] In other words, it is possible that the *Madhyamakaratnapradīpa* was composed by an author who lived after the seventh century, and perhaps as late as the ninth century, and that he was either a contemporary or perhaps even a successor of Śāntarakṣita and Kamalaśīla.[473] It was indeed in the eighth century that the *bhāvanākrama*-theme attracted special attention among Mādhyamikas, as is demonstrated not only by Kamala-

[470] P, mi, f. 77a2. This has been noted too by Lindtner, *Wiener Zeitschrift* ... 26 (1982), p. 175.

[471] See Seyfort Ruegg, in *Indological and Buddhist studies*, p. 511. If this is so, the author of the *Madhyamakaratnapradīpa* could have been a disciple of the Deutero-Nāgārjunapāda since the latter was a disciple of Saraha = Rāhulabhadra.

[472] *Mañjuśrīmūlakalpa* (ed. T. Gaṇapati Śāstri), liii. 628, 816 (= ed. Rāhula Sāmkṛtyāyana, verses 683 and 883, in K. P. Jayaswal, *An imperial history of India*, Lahore, 1934). The *Mañjuśrīmūlakalpa* was translated into Chinese by T'ien hsi tsai at the end of the tenth century, and into Tibetan in the eleventh century by Kumārakalaśa and Śākya blo gros at the command of Byaṅ chub 'od at Tho liṅ. On the date of the *Mañjuśrīmūlakalpa*, and on earlier Chinese versions, see Y. Matsunaga, *Mélanges chinois et bouddhiques* 20 (Mélanges R. A. Stein, iii, Brussels 1985), pp. 882–93.

It is of course possible that the version of the Tantra quoted in Bhavya's *Madhyamakaratnapradīpa* did not contain the *vyākaraṇa* relating to King Gopāla, which could be a later interpolation; and the date of Gopāla is not therefore *necessarily* a *terminus a quo* for dating the *Madhyamakaratnapradīpa*. But the references to other texts, such as Saraha's *Dohā* and the *Bodhicittavivaraṇa*, as well as the citation of both Dharmakīrti and Candrakīrti as authorities would seem to suggest a very late seventh-century date at the earliest, and more probably a date in the eighth or even ninth century.

[473] This is the opinion of Y. Ejima, as quoted by Lindtner in *Wiener Zeitschrift für die Kunde Südasiens* 26 (1982), p. 183.

śīla's three *Bhāvanākramas* but also by the **Bhāvanāyogamārga* (or **Yogabhāvanāmārga*?) of Jñānagarbha which insists too on the need to examine Mind alone (*raṅ gi sems kho na la brtag par bya'o*).[474]

Hence, although our knowledge of the history of Madhyamaka thought is admittedly fragmentary and partly based on hypothetical reconstruction, the *Madhyamakaratnapradīpa* might be thought to fit especially well into a period later than the sixth century when Bhāvaviveka, the author of the *Prajñāprādīpa* and *Madhyamakahṛdayakārikās*, in all likelihood lived. (On the contrary, were it possible to demonstrate that this text belongs to the sixth century too, this would show that important points at issue in the Great Debate were being discussed in *bhāvanākrama*-form by Indian Mādhyamikas two or three centuries earlier than the time of Kamalaśīla and Mo-ho-yen.) Thus the *bhāvanākrama* section of the *Madhyamakaratnapradīpa* is of very considerable interest in considering Indian views on the points being discussed at the Great Debate of bSam yas.

7. Silence

Following the example of Vimalakīrti to which he has explicitly referred,[475] Mo-ho-yen was an advocate of the philosopher's silence: 'Tout ce que j'ai dit, avant comme après, n'était conçu que pour répondre aux questions, en me référant aux textes de *sūtra*; et ce n'était nullement le vrai système de ma méthode de Dhyāna. Mon système est sans attribut de parole, sans attribut de différenciation due à notre propre esprit; c'est la vérité vraie, qui ne se transmet et ne se confère que par le silence, le chemin du langage étant coupé. Si l'on se met à débattre du pour et du contre, du juste et du faux, il n'en résulte que dispute. Le recueillement est comme une eau de saveur unique, mais les vues de chacun sont différentes ...'[476]

According to the Mahāyāna as a whole, ultimate reality is in

[474] D, f. 4a3. A *Bhāvanākrama* is also ascribed in the bsTan 'gyur to (a) Nāgārjuna. A *Yogabhāvanāmārga*, or *Bhāvanāyogamārga*, by Kamalaśīla is included in the bsTan 'gyur.

[475] See *Cheng-li chüeh*, f. 143b (Demiéville, *Concile*, pp. 113–14). Cf. *Vimalakīrtinirdeśa*, Chap. viii.

[476] *Cheng-li chüeh*, ff. 154b–155a (Demiéville, *Concile*, p. 156).

itself inexpressible discursively (*anabhilāpya, nirabhilāpya*) and conceptually unthinkable (*acintya*). Silence is thus so to speak the only adequate way of signifying reality. As said by Candrakīrti (*Prasannapadā* i. 1, p. 57), ultimate reality (*paramārtha*) corresponds to the silence of the Nobles (*āryāṇāṃ tuṣṇībāvaḥ*). And according to the *Tathāgataguhyasūtra*, between the night of his awakening to supreme and perfect Awakening and his Parinirvāṇa, no syllable (*akṣara*) is uttered by the Tathāgata.[477] This principle of inexpressibility and silence is mentioned in a number of texts such as the *Samādhirājasūtra* and Nāgārjuna's *Madhyamakakārikās*.[478]

In the old canon, Noble Silence (*ariyo tuṇhībhāvo*) is praised on the same level as speech relating to Dhamma (*dhammī kathā*);[479] either one preaches the Dhamma, or one enquires of another, or again one does not disdain Noble Silence (*ariyaṃ vā tuṇhībhāvaṃ nâtimaññati*).[480] This Noble Silence – placed on the level of the second Dhyāna and described as resulting from the cessation of reflection and investigation (*vitakkavicārāṇām vūpasamā*) – involves internal quiet (*ajjhattaṃ sampasādanam*), concentration of mind (*cetaso ekodibhāvo*), freedom from reflection (*avitakka*) and investigation (*avicāra*), and origination from *samādhi*.[481] Moreover, the Dharma to which the Buddha awakened is so subtle and profound that it can barely be communicated, as a consequence of which the Buddha at first hesitated to teach it until requested by Brahmā for the sake of people.[482]

Not altogether unconnected with this principle of the conceptual and verbal inexpressibility – that is, the non-discursiveness – of reality may have been the idea that it was by a single sound only that the entire Dharma was communicated. The thesis of the 'univocality' of the Buddha's speech was maintained by all

[477] See the *Tathāgataguhyasūtra* quoted in Candrakīrti's *Prasannapadā* xviii. 7 (p. 366) and xxv. 24 (p. 539). Cf. Prajñākaramati, *Bodhicaryāvatārapañjikā* ix. 36.

[478] *Samādhirājasūtra*, Chap viii and xxxii; Nāgārjuna, *Madhyamakakārikās*, Chap. xviii; cf. *Niraupamyastava* 7 and *Acintyastava* 23. See also *Laṅkāvatārasūtra* iii, p. 142–4; *Vimalakīrtinirdeśasūtra* (ed. Oshika), iii, p. 24 (Lamotte, *L'enseignement de Vimalakīrti*, p. 147); viii, p. 75 (Lamotte, p. 317); x, p. 86 (Lamotte, p. 342); Candrakīrti, *Prasannapadā* i, p. 57; Śāntideva, *Bodhicaryāvatāra* ix. 35–36.

[479] *Udāna*, p. 11. [480] Aṅguttaranikāya IV 153.

[481] Saṃyuttanikāya II 273.

[482] *Mahāvagga* pp. 4–5; Majjhimanikāya I 167–168; Saṃyuttanikāya I 136; Aṅguttaranikāya II 131; *Mahāvastu* III, p. 314. Cf. Nāgārjuna, *Mūlamadhyamakakārikā* xxiv. 12, and *Ratnāvalī* ii. 18.

branches of the Mahāsāṃghika school according to Vasumitra;[483] it was rejected, however, by the Sarvāstivādins,[484] who also (unlike the Mahāsāṃghikas who held the Buddha's speech to be in accordance with reality)[485] did not accept that all the Buddha's Sūtras are definitive in sense (*nītārtha*).[486] In a similar context, the idea of a single sound as 'expressive' of the Buddha's teaching is attested in the *Bhadracaripraṇidhānarāja* (verse 30: *ekasvara*) and in the *Daśabhūmikasūtra* (ix, p. 79: *ekaghoṣodāhāra*). In the *Vimalakīrtinirdeśasūtra* we find *gsuṅ gcig* 'single utterance'.[487]

This notion of 'univocality' probably stands to that of silence, and to that of the inexpressibility or ineffability of absolute reality; as does the notion of the Single or Unique Vehicle (*ekayāna*) – so often alluded to by Mo-ho-yen – to that of the ultimate non-existence of any Vehicle at all (*ayāna*) in the *Laṅkāvatārasūtra*[488] – also emphasized by Mo-ho-yen.[489]

In his preference for Noble Silence and for the Single Vehicle or even the Non-Vehicle, therefore, Mo-ho-yen clearly stands in one major line of Buddhist thought attested in older Sūtras and then stressed by the Mahāyāna.[490] Assessments may differ as to

483 Vasumitra, *Samayabhedoparacanacakra* (Tibetan translation, ed. E. Teramoto and T. Hiramatsu), pp. 4–5. (Cf. A. Bareau, *Journal asiatique* 1954, p. 239; *Les sectes bouddhiques du Petit Véhicule*, p. 58.) Compare Bhavya, *Nikāyabhedavibhaṅga-Vyākhyāna* (Tibetan translation, ed. E. Teramoto and T. Hiramatsu), p. 23.

484 Vasumitra, *op. cit.*, p. 12. Cf. A. Bareau, *Sectes*, p. 145 (no. 55).

485 Vasumitra, *op. cit.*, p. 5: *don ji lta ba bžin ñid du: yathārtha;* see also Bhavya, *op. cit.*, p. 23. Cf. A. Bareau, *Journal asiatique* 1954, p. 239; *Sectes*, p. 58 (no. 5).

486 Vasumitra, *op. cit.*, p. 12; Bhavya, *op. cit.*, p. 27. Moreover, according to Vasumitra's account, *buddhas* are always in absorption (*mñam par bžag pa*), which accounts for their not uttering any name (*miṅ*, p. 5). But Vinītadeva states that according to the Lokottaravādin-Mahāsāṃghikas even one who is *samāhita* speaks; see his **Samayabhedoparacanacakre Nikāyabhedopadarśana-nāma-saṃgraha* (Tibetan translation, ed. E. Teramoto and T. Hiramatsu), p. 41. Compare *Kathāvatthu* xviii. 2 (Vetullavāda), p. 560, on *dhamma* being taught by an 'emanation' (*abhinimmita*) – i.e., so to say, by xenoglossy/xenophony. See also Hōbōgirin s.v. *bonnon*, *butsugo* and *button*.

487 *Vimalakīrtinirdeśasūtra* i, p. 13; cf. Lamotte, *L'enseignement de Vimalakīrti*, p. 109–10. See also on the *pratibhānapratisaṃvit* in the *Ta-chih-tu-lun* (Lamotte, *Traité de la Grande Vertu de Sagesse*, iii, p. 1622).

488 *Laṅkāvatārasūtra* ii. 131; iii. 1; vii. 1; Sagāthaka 188, 245 and 315.

489 Demiéville, *Concile*, pp. 66, 119, 151.

490 Since these doctrines are well known and have been frequently studied, there is no need to insist further on them here. See for example G. M. Nagao, *Studies in Indology and Buddhology* (S. Yamaguchi felicitation volume, Kyōto, 1955), pp. 137–51; Lamotte, *L'enseignement de Vimalakīrti*, pp. 44–46, 317–18; D. Seyfort Ruegg, 'On the knowability and expressibility of Absolute Reality in Buddhism', *Journal of Indian and Buddhist Studies (IBK)*, 20/1 (1971), pp. 1–7; *The literature of the Madhyamaka school*, pp. 34–35.

the extent to which the current of thought which Mo-ho-yen represents adopted an extreme 'ideoclasm' and was essentially logophobic or misologic. Mo-ho-yen would seem in any case to have wished that his silence should on no account be some kind of '*learned* ignorance'.

When Mo-ho-yen cites the eschewing of disputes and learned strife as one motive for adopting silence,[491] he is also standing in a main line of Buddhist thought. Eirenicism is in fact already mentioned in passages of the old canon. Moreover, the Mādhyamika's rejection of any dogmatic assertion (*pratijñā*), in terms of the binary positions of conceptual thinking (*vikalpa*) or of the 'tetralemma' (*catuṣkoṭi*), was connected at least in part with his refusal to engage in vain disputes (*vivāda*) about entities.[492] Nevertheless, whilst the Mādhyamika seeks to eschew assertions of the kind just mentioned together with the related antagonistic positions without necessarily rejecting all philosophic expression,[493] Mo-ho-yen appears to have been inclined to distance himself from all philosophical and religious discourse in favour of a form of quietism (verging sometimes on ataraxia) combined with the pure experience and non-discursive awareness of an ineffable and unanalysable reality (perhaps verging sometimes on pleasure in the empty).[494]

491 *Cheng-li chüeh*, f. 155a (Demiéville, *Concile*, p. 156).

492 See for example Nāgārjuna, *Yuktiṣaṣṭikā* 47, 51; *Ratnāvalī* ii. 4.

493 See D. Seyfort Ruegg, 'On thesis and assertion in the Madhyamaka/dBu ma', in E. Steinkellner and H. Tauscher (eds.), *Contributions on Tibetan and Buddhist religion and philosophy* (Vienna, 1983), p. 205 ff.

494 On *ži ba phyogs gcig pa* and *stoṅ pa bag la ñal* (*ba*), and on the true Dhyāna (*bsam gtan*) of Ma ha yan, see for example *Pelliot tibétain 117* as well as *116* (116 and 190), *121*, *812r*, and *813* (8a–b). (For the allusion to this theme in Bhavya's *Madhyamakaratnapradīpa*, see above, p. 207.) Mo-ho-yen and his followers no doubt intended to steer clear of any desire for mere tranquillity and of nihilistic emptiness. Cf. above, pp. 201–202

INDEX OF KEY TERMS IN SANSKRIT AND PALI

INDEX OF KEY TERMS IN TIBETAN

INDEX OF NAMES